Connecting the Web of Humanity:
A creative Nonfiction Memoir/Journal

John E Zett III

Connecting the Web of Humanity: A creative Nonfiction Memoir/Journal

Copyright © 2013 John E Zett III. Printed and bound, or electronically digitalized, in the United States of America. All rights reserved. No part of this book may be reproduced in any form or by any electronic or mechanical means including information storage and retrieval systems without permission in writing from the publisher, except by a reviewer, who may quote brief passages in a review (be it good or bad) to be printed in a magazine, newspaper, or out on the Internet.

First printing 2023

Visit the website, our Indie way, at:

www.ConnectingtheWebofHumanity.com.

Cover Art provided via Upwork by Nicole Conway

Book Formatting provided via Upwork by Jennifer M. Eaton

Legal protection services provided by Lloyd J. Jassin, co-author of The Copyright Right Permission and Libel Handbook, A STEP-BY-STEP GUIDE FOR WRITERS, EDITORS, AND PUBLISHERS

And Everything Else in this book is just me being me and mine, John E Zett III

Trademark Disclosure

These and other trademarks may or may not appear throughout this book:

Captain Democrat, CBS Late Show, Worldwide PANTS, Ed Sullivan Theater, Top Ten List, Explode-O-Pop Popping Corn, CBS Late Late Show, the book industry's God-Father, OWN, the book industry's God-Mother, CBS News, CBS 60 Minutes, CBS, NBC News, NBC Today Show, NBC, NOVA, PBS, Discovery Channel, TMC, G4TV, Gilligan, Brainiacs, The Science Guy, Weather on the Eights, Gateway, NFL Vikings, NFL Superbowl, NFL Texans, NFL, NFL Packers, Alpha-Keri, Mother Goose, The Wizard of Oz, The Mills Bros., OSHA, ATFM, EPA, Durex Condoms, www.Adam&Eve.com, www.Sclitterbahn.com, Post it, 3M, Pentel Rolling Writer, Bic, Office Max, Panasonic Vacuum, Panasonic, Tic Tacs, Life-Savers, Back to the Future, Marriot Marquis, Writer's Digest, Time Warner, Lagardere, Barnes & Nobel, www.Amazon.com, the late corporate personhood of Borders, Frankenstein, 7-Eleven, Star-

Trademark Disclosure

bucks, McDonalds, Apple, I-Pod, Windows, AOL, MSN, Google, Google Duo, Skype, NORML, MPP, Pop Rocks, and The Cannabis Express. All trademarks appearing in this book or not appearing in this book, listed on this page or not listed on this page, are the exclusive property of their owners. And, furthermore...

Disclaimer

This book is not intended to provide accurate and authoritative information regarding the subject matter. It is also only sold with the understanding that the author and the publisher of the following is not engaged in rendering writing, scientific, religious/spiritual, love making, medical, mystical, political, sexual, or any other professional services. If expert writing, scientific, religious/spiritual, love making, medical, mystical, political, sexual, or professional assistance is required, the services of a competent professional must be obtained. And although the author and the publisher have engaged in exhaustive research to ensure the accuracy and completeness of the information contained in this book; neither the author (nor the publisher) assumes any responsibility for errors, inaccuracies, omissions, or inconsistencies contained in this book. Any slights against people, corporate personhood via Citizens United, or organizations are completely and utterly unintentional.

Disclaimer

This book is not intended as writing, scientific, religious/spiritual, love making, medical, mystical, political, sexual or any other kind of professional advice. Because laws are not static, and every situation is different, neither the author nor the publisher assumes any responsibility for actions taken, or not taken, based on any information contained within this book. All principles expressed in this book are subject to exceptions and qualifications and may vary state to state. And finally, let there be no doubt that everyone understands...

If expert writing, scientific, religious/spiritual, medical, mystical, political, sexual, or other professional advice is required, the services of a competent professional must be sought and obtained. And...

Me speaking for me, me, and me...

We ain't them. At the end of my tiresome, long-ass, and seemingly endless days; I am more of an artist than I am an author. And I kept this nonsense going and got my shit published. And I'm wearing way too many hats all at one time. With that in mind, all I ever wanted was $5 for each/every copy sold, and thank you for yours plus whatever their total turned out to be. Thank you, thank you, thank you and read as much of me as you can tolerate, and throw me out a review wherever you bought a copy of this nonsense.

I: November 2002

Sunday, November 03, 2002

Did you know that authors don't write books? In theory, we write manuscripts, and a publisher turns our work into a book that sells copies.

Let's pretend you want to become a successful author, like me. Let's pretend you want to write yourself into your first manuscript, like I am. Where do you start?

The book industry created lots of rules on how authors are supposed to create the manuscript book publishers want to see. New authors are supposed to creep around and find everything they need to know about following antiquated academic standard formatting. And our self-publishing formats are a different animal. If we are going to become successful authors in our book market, an author has to know (and learn) a whole lot of shit, all at once. And thus far, I've learned...

Everyone has to carve their own path through these perilous woods.

With all the stumbling around in the dark I've done, and unless I hear otherwise, this is the way we are supposed to format our manuscripts. And if I hear otherwise, I'll let you know. I'll change what's in here, until I can't change this anymore.

All of our manuscripts are always double-spaced. Click the Times New Roman 12 Font throughout our entire manuscript and we won't get into any kind of trouble if we use our Courier New 12 font. The point of this is to be consistent from beginning to end. If you use two commas to hook up three conjunctions, keep going there, and do that.

Beginning on Page 2, in the top right corner, list your page number, along with the book's title in all caps, last name, a comma, and your best friend's first name's initial. Ha. Joke. Use your first initial. And...

In place of the page number on the title page, Page 1, type your full name, address, telephone number, fax number, cell-phone number, e-mail address, website, weblog "interweb" site address. In the center, on top of the title page, type the word "Wordage," followed by the total number of words you typed into your manuscript. Everybody prefers to work with approximate word counts, but I have a rebellious nature. On the bottom right corner of the title page, type your agent's and/or publisher's name, address, telephone number, fax number, cell-phone number, e-mail address, website, and weblog "interweb" site address.

Print all manuscripts on bright white 24-pound bonded paper. Or some accept an electronic submission.

Much like anything else we do in life, our manuscripts are fundamentally all about our professional presentation and appearance.

We authors have to grow our own grapes. Then we have to stomp all over our own grapes, mashing them up real good, then (hopefully), a publishing house bottles up our toe jam, turns it into a boatload of books, and that is when it all comes floating back to us. If our books ever get published, the job of actually selling each and every copy of any particular book falls back on the book's author.

A book's success is not the responsibility or obligation of anyone in the book industry, except its author. Authors have to carry their own books. Authors have to tote their own loads. If you are really big, somebody will help you. And...

That's why some well-known authors have publicists and make appearances everywhere. And that's why I'll have mine. Some of us run around like crazy, trying to sell our books. Big trade's marketing department will sometimes fund a new book's marketing or the new book's marketing comes out of the author's pocket. And what do bookworms want? They like to kick it old school. They have forever whole-heartedly believed in the old door-to-door, so...

Today's high-performing authors have to walk their books from bookstore door, to radio station doors, to television station doors, to bookstore doors, to radio station doors, to doors, and to doors, more doors, and more, more, and more.

"Well now..."

Sigh.

Now that I got my first little temper-tantrum out of our way, let's get this rolling back down the right set of tracks, shall we? By the way, our more modern way of emailing or faxing press releases along with personal video is way more effective. So, there's that. And...

Pretend that way back in the day we, together, dreamed up some fascinatingly crazy new mysterious shit for the whole entire (cold) cruel world to think about. Let's pretend our fascinatingly crazy new mysterious shit just one day somehow showed up inside our heads. Let's pretend to drop our fascinatingly crazy new mysterious shit down in longhand. Now, pretend that we reworked everything we wrote, two or three times, and fixed everything we saw, as we went along. Let's pretend to sit down in front of our computer and key in all of our scratches and scribbles. Now let's pretend to rework that whole fucked-up mess, thirty or forty more times, just enough to make it where it ain't reading like it's so broken anymore. Then, let's pretend to endlessly read our shit, and reread our shit, and rewrite our shit, over, and over, and over, all the while, reworking things as we go. Let's pretend we've been spending so much time holding hands in front of our computer, and just being alone together, that when we stepped away to take a break, we'd have to reintroduce ourselves to our families.

It happens every time workaholics step away from all their work. It's like, being rescued from the wild, and being reintroduced to our civilized society.

When we workaholics go out to conquer our conquests, we tend to lose touch with our personal peeps. We can become complete and total strangers to our loved ones. When workaholics come back and spend time with our loved ones, we sometimes have uncomfortable, awkward personal private moments together. And speaking of pretend conquests...

Now let's pretend that you're writing your own manuscript all by yourself. Let's pretend to leave me out of whatever you do with your shit. Knowing what you know about the publishing industry today, what do you think you gotta do to make your fat stack of neatly typed paper turn into a book? When you're done writing your manuscript, what happens next? Well, that totally depends on you. It is what it is.

You can polish your next most-badass manuscript in the whole wide world until your face turns blue, but you ain't ever gonna see no dough until you figure out a way to turn that big beautiful manuscript into a kickass book.

And if you are fortunate enough to get your big bad beautiful manuscript published, your book will still have to fly off the shelves (or at the very least, present some kind of expectation that a few hundred thousand of them will easily fly off the shelves), before you will see any kind of serious money. And long before people ever start talking about the money, they gotta do first things first.

First, we have to choose one of the four following paths:

Path number one is to pay a publishing house to publish your stuff. Vanity publishers want your money. In fact, they probably have an operator waiting to talk to you. If you go with a vanity publisher, you will definitely get your book published, but more than likely, all you'll wind up with is a garage (or spare bedroom) full of books you have to purchase from your "publisher."

If you don't want to drain your savings account and would like to have an actual conversation with a real person in order to get published, we still have three other paths to choose from.

Path number two publishing is a total DIY, publishing your book as an e-book only or in combination with print-on-demand. If you are a DIYer, and you choose this path, e-mail or call a myriad of freelancers offering services to create a professional-quality book anytime. Operators are standing by.

Path number three is to go find a small publishing house. If you don't mind waiting in a long line, a small publishing house might want to publish your manuscript, if they like your work. To make them like your work, you're gonna have to throw everything you've got into your work.

Vanity publishing houses will publish anything we're willing to pay for. And small publishing houses usually don't charge anyone anything to publish a manuscript. But at the same time, they cannot afford the financial risk of giving us hundreds of millions of dollars in one great big advance. I mean, what happens if we flop? If they give us all of their money, and we flop, they flop. You know? If you are headed that way...

Good luck and God's speed.

Our first three paths are different than the one I'm on. I chose the fourth path, the one that leads us to...

If you know you're not going to be a flop, and you want a chance to earn a newsworthy advance on your superbly brilliant and totally average American Joe writing ability, you're gonna wanna play big trade's game.

Welcome to my personal version of big trade's big-time publishing game. My name is John. I've been playing this lousy big-time big trade publishing game for a long-ass time. And I'll be your personal tour guide through the fun and exciting world of big-time big trade publishing. Well actually, and to be more open and honest with you, I'm just barely gonna help you get started. Are there any questions? Good. The line starts way the fuck back there. So, let's all get going that way, shall we?

If we ever end up at the front of this long line, we gotta strap ourselves in and wait for our personal ride to start. Some rides never go anywhere. And some rides take off like rockets. So, let's say that...

You were the first person to work your dog's ass off on your manuscript, and you feel your fascinatingly crazy new mysterious shit, lost time, and expensive energy, deserves a high-minded upfront paycheck.

It's the bottom of the ninth, all of our bases are loaded, there's a full count, but now, we have to drop everything we're doing to consult our little bitty handy dandy SUPER-Secret American Big trade RULE Book.

Super-Secret American Big Trade Rule Number One:

When it comes right down to it, becoming an American big

trade author is a lot like being a small business owner, trying to grab up a fat contract with a big business. So…

Write with passion. Write what you know. Own whatever you know. Write how you know. Express yourself the best damn way you can. Become an artistic expressionist. Show up knowing how to write well. And be sure to bring your credentials. If you don't have any credentials, go out, and get yourself some credentials and/or build yourself a platform. If you write nonfiction, and you ain't got no credentials, and/or you haven't built yourself a big trade author's platform, big trade won't want you. And…

If you write fiction, you'll have to be able to write a whole lot better than me. In fact, you'll have to write real good. And you'll also have to be able to write your ass off. And if you are able to write really well, big trade is gonna want to see a lot of material from you.

Super-Secret American Big Trade Rule Number Two:

What separates any big trade publishing house apart from all our other publishing houses in the entire book publishing industry?

Every big trade author has to have a literary agent.

Every big trade publishing house makes their authors have literary agents. Big trade publishing houses will not work directly with any of our brand-new nobody wannabe authors. Today, a big trade publisher is any publishing house that makes an author show up already being represented by her/or/his literary agent. Go see their websites and look for yourself. All of them have submission guidelines.

And if we brand-new nobody wannabe big trade authors want to find a big trade publishing house to publish our manuscript, we are expected to somehow automatically know that we need to find ourselves a literary agent.

Literary agents sell our manuscripts to big trade. And then, literary agents represent the author/client in big-time big trade publishing deals.

Literary agents are also our go-betweens. Literary agents are like big trade shock absorbers. Literary agents get squeezed between the talent and the talents' industry. Now of course, I don't know that for sure. I mean, I ain't got to try one out yet. Maybe someday, I'll learn more about it all. When I do, I'll let you know.

Some literary agents have huge names and credentials. Some literary agents are huge superstar celebrities within and throughout big trade. Some literary agents have become so big; they will no longer work with brand-new nobody wannabe big trade authors. And...

All their unsolicited mail never gets wherever it was going. But still, no matter what, big trade celebrities are regular people, like you and me.

We may have even sat next to some of these folks, way back when we were in school. And today, much like you and me, they either do what they love, or they are more like those of us who do their boring ass jobs to keep a roof over their heads, and food on their tables, week in, week out, year in, year out. And just like working at any other regular job, some people openly love what they do, and some people secretly don't.

Some people start out doing what they love and end up going to work to just go clickity-clack, clickity-clack, from getting completely burnt out. That and...

Grocers don't upset their apple carts. And speaking of...

Literary agents are only interested in stuff that their big trade publishing houses will publish. Big trade literary agents can't sell our big trade work to big trade if big trade literary agents ain't interested in whatever it is we can't help but write. And if big trade literary agents don't sell profitable manuscripts to big trade, they don't make serious money. The name of the game is...

"Climb to the top of every list as fast as you can."

Every big trade literary agent has to comb through tons of written garbage to find today's publishable treasures. And...

If that ain't just top-of-the-lungs screaming about where America's widespread current below average reading ability is at, what the hell else is it gonna fucking take? Excuse me...

Yikes, I mean...

Currently, hundreds and hundreds of hopeful authors are sending in submissions to the hundreds and hundreds of different literary agents each & every week, hoping to find their big badass big trade literary agent. But hardly any of our authors ever get themselves familiar with all our big trade industry rules. And speaking of my industries rules...

Big trade literary agents are required to reject 99.5 percent of all the new shit they get in. Big trade literary agents have to. It comes with their jobs. And speaking of working hard for their money...

Big trade literary agents shovel 995 "Dear John" letters into every 1000 hopeful authors. Out of every 1000 hopeful authors, only five winds up with a big trade literary agent's autograph on a contract. So, at the end of a really long business day, what do brand-new nobody wannabe big trade authors have to do to wind up on a big trade literary agent's client list?

Beats me. I keep hitting wall after wall, after wall, after wall...

If you are a celebrity, any big trade literary agent will automatically love to see anything you write. In fact, you can probably even format whatever whichever way you want, use any old kind of paper, and scribble the whole thing down using all the colors in your crayon box.

Winners don't have to know how to type.

Celebrities just have to write manuscripts. When they send them in, they win even more. Big trade literary agents love celebrities. Celebrities have, and are themselves, today's author's big trade platforms.

Having an instant audience that will buy a few hundred thousand books carries more weight than actually being able to produce some fascinatingly crazy new mysterious shit or having a really interesting story to tell. And either whatever whichever way...

An easily recognizable name means a whole lot of instant money for everyone involved. A whole lot of money is a whole lot of money. And if you are not already a celebrity, then getting a big trade literary agency to offer you a big trade literary agent contract becomes practically impossible. But should the practically impossible also happen for you, as it will eventually happen for me, carefully look your contract over real good before you sign it. And know that signing a literary agent's contract does nothing more than secure your relationship with a literary agent. It does not mean your literary agent will be able to sell your carefully crafted big bad beautiful manuscript.

Finding yourself a big trade literary agent means nothing more than you now have a legally binding agreement between your big trade literary agent and you. It's kind of like finding a realtor to help us buy and sell real-estate properties. Agents can't guarantee their sales. And we have to stay with one agent until our properties sell or our contract runs out.

After our literary agent's contract is signed, sealed, and delivered, our literary agent will send all of our shit to the big trade publishing houses. And all of the heavy lifting is geared toward pleasing all of the everyday regular people that work in a big trade publishing house.

Most of the big trade publishing houses run like any other big business. I mean, they have a decision-making staff that gets a regular paycheck from some salaried positions.

Being a self-employed tortured starving artist, I really miss all that came with having my steel mill's regular paycheck; like paid vacations, health insurance, and some sort (any sort) of a retirement plan.

Our self-employed health insurance currently runs us $6610.^{00} dollars a year. And compared to the kind of insurance I had when I worked at my steel mill, today, here in 2002, we have shit for benefits. Good health insurance is expensive.

Each and every week, every big trade publishing house receives hundreds and hundreds of submissions from all our big trade literary agents. Each and every week, every big trade publishing house rejects a lot of what they get in the mail too. Yes, that's right.

Only five in every thousand authors are lucky enough to find a literary agent on any given workday. Out of all of them that do, their literary agents face almost the exact same odds when it comes time to find that one special big trade publishing house. A big trade publishing house has to sift through a thousand pitches, which can only come from big trade literary agents, and big trade publishing houses only publish five new books.

If we can get past the five in every thousand big trade agented books getting published by big trade and look at every book on all of our bookstores' bookshelves; every book published faces another round of one-in-ten-thousand (1:10,000) odds when it comes to authors who see any kind of serious money.

Serious money is seldom in any author's equation, unless an author has previously sold, or can effortlessly sell, a few hundred thousand books. This is how our celebrities are able to easily cash in. Our derailed American book industry is so hungry, so starving; it salivates all over itself over any instant audience. Our average celebrity can effortlessly sell a few hundred thousand books. Can you?

Can I? Who knows? But I do know one thing...

Nobody is gonna need a heaping double dose of vitamin college-knowledge to know the odds of making it big in big trade publishing are clearly stacked against any brand-new nobody wannabe big trade author. And with all that negativity going against us, we brand-new nobody wannabe big trade authors have a thousand times better chance of getting rich in our big trade's market, than we got winning our state's big lottery jackpots.

I'm playing the odds. I'm writing my shit. And I went way off deep into my personal shit and got us lost. We are way off track. Let's stop here. Let's back up (beep-beep-beep) and head back to where I was going earlier…

The odds of a brand-new nobody wannabe big trade author making it big rest on the edge of a tiny little crack on big trade's great big door. And now…

Let's pretend you're a brave little big trade author. Let's pretend you climbed your way up to the top of the door and now you're on the edge of that tiny little crack. Some brand-new nobody wannabe big trade authors have slipped through that crack. It's happened. Some brand-new nobody wannabe big trade authors have even been rewarded with some serious money. But more often than not…

The average new big trade author never sees much money. And…

Nobody who spent their time in school slipping through the cracks of our education system will ever be accepted into an industry that was built on the continuation of such a strong institutionally structured foundation. Besides…

If getting rich from writing books was that easy, a lot more people would already be a whole lot richer from just simply being involved in our book industry.

Today, they say, "The vast majority of today's books will never sell more than five thousand copies." And, "Plan on keeping your

Connecting the Web of Humanity:

day job, until you appear on Dave or Oprah." Once you've been on Dave or Oprah, you're home free. Book readers watch Dave and Oprah. Dave and Oprah are turning today's unknown authors into instant big celebrity authors. And...

Big celebrities make big money.

We just have to be ready to hit the road and pop for the cameras and microphones. And if we want to make a whole lot of upfront money with our writing, we're gonna need to know a hell of a lot more than I know right now. Otherwise...

I'd already be wherever it is my soul is trying to go.

The whole entire book industry only welcomes team players. And, that goes double down, down at big trade. So...

Our first job as a team player is to follow all of the rules. Big trade will not tolerate emotionally psychotic rebels and egotists are not allowed to show up demanding goofy outrageous shit.

Sometimes, we all gotta do what we all gotta do. And...

If we brand-new nobody wannabe big trade authors don't play big trade's game by big trade's rules and do everything that big trade's websites say to do, then we won't ever get a chance to sink our hands into a big trade publishing house's monster pile of bookworm money.

Super-Secret American Big Trade Rule Number Three:

Nobody has the time to read everything everyone writes. The people working throughout the entire book industry are buried so ass-deep in their daily business; they don't even have enough time to take a decent shit. When was the last time I had a decent bowel movement? Way too long ago, how about you? And...

To make things halfway sane, the people down at our big trade publishing houses got together in the middle of the night and had a secret meeting. They had to wait until everybody stopped working.

That was when they all decided all of their brand-new nobody wannabe big trade authors needed to come up with a condensed version of every manuscript we create. There was brief nudity, and everyone had such a lovely time that sometime later…

They all got together again at a different place and had a second secret meeting in the middle of another night. And they all decided the condensed versions of our manuscripts needed to be even shorter than a condensed version of a manuscript. And as an industry outsider looking in…

Big-time big trade publishing is more like an endless cocktail party with periodic P&L Statements attached. And speaking of Profit and Loss Statements…

Anything over one page was still way too much for them to have to read. So, they made another new rule. Their newest rule requires us to write a one-page description of each manuscript we write, so that now…

All brand-new nobody wannabe big trade authors have to approach literary agents with a little something the big trade second secret meeting calls, "a query letter."

I don't understand much about them. I'll let you in on everything I know so far, and…

I'll keep you informed as we go along. What is the ideal query letter?

The query letter pitches our manuscript. We, big-time big trade authors, pitch manuscripts to big trade literary agents. Big trade literary agents pitch their talent's work to big trade. Our query letter fits on one page of paper. And query letters are four-paragraph block letters. Now that you know, everything I know…

"Good luck on creating yours."

When we build this little house of cards, we have to be careful. If a big trade agent doesn't like our big trade query letter, they slam their doors shut. Then everything comes crashing down. And then, little pieces break off, and fall all over the place. Then, we have to stop, and pick up all of our broken shards and pieces, and start all over with a brand-new query letter, and a brand-new big trade literary agent. Here, today, in 2002...

We have to totally recreate a different query letter for each literary agent we submit our work out to.

Query letters have to be personalized, without getting too personal, too soon. Query letter guidelines can be found on literary agents' websites and in big trade books about writing our big trade query letters.

If we're lucky, we learn right from wrong as we go along.

Knowing big trade literary agents reject 99.5 percent of the big trade query letters they get in; our job is to figure out a way to make our four paragraphs of black and white stand out from 995 other four paragraphs of black and white. Like finding our life partners, we have to keep going, until we find the big trade literary agent that's right for us. How do you know which literary agent is right for you?

The big trade literary agent that's right for you is the first literary agent that shows you some love. If a literary agent loves your query letter, they won't be shy about letting you know what they love about you.

And if that shit ever happens to you, you are totally on your own, same as me. And the query letter is just the beginning. Because...

Do you remember big trade's first secret meeting?

If you are lucky enough to find your one and only big trade literary agent that loved your query letter, you're expected to already have expanded your big bad beautiful one-page (four-paragraph) block letter into something the first big trade secret meeting calls, a book proposal.

Yes...

That's right.

Screw the part where a big trade author knuckles down and gets after writing their manuscripts. Nobody gives a shit about any author's nonsense. Watch this…

Early on, I mean like years ago, I wasted a solid year researching, formatting, writing, and reworking a thirty-five-page book proposal for the manuscript I was meant to write, the one for this book. Stop reading this and look up at everyone around you right now. And see for yourself.

Seriously…

Pay your attention on whatever is going on around you, and realize nobody cares about us, except those of them that do, and the souls connected to us, of whom, we all care about. And aside from all of that, nobody gives a shit about my lost year of working on a horribly written book proposal. And speaking of…

If we don't write the right query letter and the right book proposal with award-winning writing and jump through all of our other big trade industry's hoops just so, then please don't clog up our big trade's precious time with a non-existent writing career.

Sometimes, we all just end up wasting a lot of valuable time. And sometimes, we all gotta do what we all gotta do. That's just the way things are. And still, somehow…

I know for fact's sake, I can't change the way the world around me works, and yet, I'm still out here writing all this shit. I'm still out here doing my own personal version of pure nonsense. I just can't help but write. Some days, this is all I do.

Today, a full-blown big bad beautiful book proposal contains some, if not all, of the following:

- A fictional manuscript needs to be ready-to-go finished, and then, it still needs your synopsis. And our nonfiction manuscripts will need a serious in-depth

outline of every chapter in our nonfiction book, and then, they want to see three sample chapters.
- A highly polished and creatively written overview detailing our proposed project. In a nutshell, what is our book about?
- A complete and thorough analysis of our book's target market. Who are our customers? Why would all of these people buy our book? What are their names?
- Badass marketing planning. Do something that's never been attempted before. Be creative.
- A comprehensive comparison of our book's competition. What books will be on the shelf next to our book? How much do they cost? How are they selling? And what makes our book stand out?
- Our complete biography. A minute-by-minute account describing birth to present. And everything that ever happened to us in between.
- A credible publishing history. We need publishing credits before we can be published. So, what writing awards have you won? If there are none, where do you work, and what do you do? Are you writing what you know? What speaking engagements have you done? What speaking engagements are you doing right now? And what speaking engagements do you have lined up to do in the future?

And that's pretty much all I know about big trade proposals. It's basically simple. But you'd be surprised by how many wannabes get it wrong.

Some big trade literary agents want our book proposals to spread out across thirty pages. And some big trade literary agents want our book proposals smashed down into four pages or less.

Our big trade book proposal length depends on the literary agents we contact. And long before we can be this far down this set of rails, and by our big trade rules...

A fiction author has to be done writing a fiction manuscript and nonfiction manuscripts are completely different, in that, nonfiction is (and are) generally pitched incomplete. A big trade literary agent uses the incompleteness of a nonfiction manuscript as leverage in negotiating our better big trade book deals. Nonfiction authors are allowed to query our big trade literary agents before we finish writing our big trade manuscripts, as long as they have proof of us having the ability to bring a manuscript to full completion.

But first, right up front, nonfiction authors must be able to provide whatever credentials we need in order to write our nonfictional works to begin with. And we are usually only allowed to write about things that we have the credentials to write about. Our nonfiction publishing world is very restrictive. And for information, look for our big trade literary agent websites, and weblogs, and see even more similar explanations of all our big trade rules, and maybe even a little more, on why we should follow through on us being us, and doing whatever else they say to do. And speaking of...

By the newest rule set forth in the second secret big trade meeting...

A big trade literary agent has to first like our big trade query letter enough to want to see our big trade proposal. And long before any passion stirring big trade query letter can go out of our door, our equally exciting fictional big trade manuscript has to have been collecting dust, waiting to go, before we ever present it to the world. And...

No matter what, with zero tolerance, big trade always starts with our query letter, so...

Connecting the Web of Humanity:

No matter what, with zero tolerance, all of us brand-new nobody wannabe big trade authors have to start out with a query letter. If a big trade literary agent likes our query letter, our big trade book proposal needs to already be done, completed, polished, and ready to go.

Wannabe authors just can't suddenly show up and stomp around all over big trade's institutionally structured rules. And...

If you're following the rules to every letter of big trade's law, three sample chapters of our big trade manuscript is the same as today's 50–60 pages. Some big trade literary agents may want to see less of our manuscripts, and some big trade literary agents may want to see more. Every big trade literary agent has their own special formula of what works in today's 2002 market. We are supposed to anticipate what they want, format our manuscripts the way they want to see all our manuscripts formatted, and have everything ready to be unleashed into today's society.

Kindness and cruelty are parallel rails running in opposite directions. No, not really. Personally, I see a cold cruel cynical world and that's just how things are. Our society needs a lot more humanitarians.

And whenever you take the time to figure out what format each literary agent wants to see, and you think your writing looks exactly the way a literary agent wants to see it written, send your shit in.

You can't win, if you don't play. And then...

Be prepared to wait. And wait. Be prepared to have the patience to wait for as long as whatever takes.

Never send originals. Always send copies. Everything is only one missing link away from being in the middle of nowhere. You never know what might happen. Look at humanity. And speaking of our humanity...

Big trade query letters and big trade book proposals are all about making a brand-new nobody wannabe big trade author's manuscript short, precise, and to the point. And just like that, here we go...

What is this book about? The cover art doesn't even match this shit. And for the love of our humanity, the current reading ability of today's average consumer is creating our desperate need for easy-reading-books we can relate to, process, and understand (Like this...)

I have a hypothetical brand-new soul theory for all of us to mentally chew on. And after saying some shit like that, my soul is finally comfortable enough to share this with you. And...

Yes, Virginia, our souls really do exist. And yes, all of us are constantly engulfed in human spirituality. And somehow, someway, in my next few days of writing this nonsense, I'll have to sit down and figure out a way to prove it to you. Sit back, relax, and get comfy. Just wait. And...

You'll see things with a pair of fresh, fresh eyes. And...

Our brain's unconscious subconscious soul is only restricted by the limited reasoning capability of a conscious cognitive mind.

Our human soul is the innermost part of us. When we reveal ourselves to our friends and family, we are revealing our human souls.

"To be. Or not to be."

If you know, we're done. And thank you for your time. Thanks for quitting this early in. That was easy. The end. Quit reading this and go re-sell your version of this. And if you don't want to quit reading my nonsense this early in, thank you for hanging in there, and here we go...

Connecting the Web of Humanity:

About a hundred years or so ago, Sigmund Freud totally ripped our brains into two smaller pieces. Freud separated all of our brains into a conscious mind and an unconscious mind. And our whole wide world's perception of the way we thought our brains are working was altered forever. And...

Now, let's toss in a little bit of Charles Darwin.

Darwin's undisputable scientific contribution suggests that throughout the course of our human evolution, our brains evolved. Darwin's theory suggests that our pre-human ancestors' primitive, unconscious brain split into Sigmund Freud's modern human's two separate minds. And...

I'm thinking...

Wow!

That's probably how we ended up with a conscious thinking cognitive mind and a soul. And...

All I'm saying is...

Humanity gained total freedom when our brains developed a different mind that gives us our cognitive ability, much like Adam and Eve and the fruit from a tree of knowledge thing.

Our highly developed cognitive ability gives us the freewill that no other creature on Earth has, yet. And until then...

Watch us go, and...

Our souls are giving us our Creator's powerful prehistoric intelligence. And our soul's intelligences are completely detached from our humanity's modern day cognitive intelligences. And speaking of being an intelligent being and being intellectually intelligent...

Our unconscious mind, our soul, gives each of us our own infinite intelligence. Our soul is our unconscious mind's emotional heart. And reaching out toward the end of this limb, I believe all of our souls, and our human unconscious/subconscious mind, and all of our emotional hearts, are all one and the same.

Threesomes…

Eat them up, yum.

I also believe our unconscious/subconscious mind, our emotional heart, and our religious/spiritual soul is deeply involved with everything that has anything to do with us. And it ain't just us. Everyone is all the same, and all of them are exactly just like us. And keeping this choo-choo train rolling on/down this set of rails…

In recent years, bookstore walls have been filling up with books, telling us how we can connect ourselves with our innermost self. Some books teach us how we can discover our hidden real self, our true self, and the old/new person inside us. Some books train us to become aware of our genuine-authentic self, our higher self. Some books find our inner child. Some books tap into our sixth sense. And some books open our subconscious and/or unconscious mind. Tap in and fill up. Advance yourself, and your life, to our higher human level.

If you've been searching in that section of our bookstores, you know that we have lots of books to choose from.

The one common denominator in all those books is they all work to teach us about what our human soul is, but none of them come right out to specifically identify what our human souls are. And nothing points our human soul out the way this is. And when some books almost get there, when one position contradicts every other position, who's to say who's right? And…

Who is to say who is doing everything wrong? And…

To some extent or another, all those books speak the truth and educate us about our humanity's truths. But…

They all also fall short of this new shit. So…

I guess our next newest know-it-all would be…

"Me."

Our modern-day big-thinkers were getting really close in their innovative ideas, but to date, nobody stepped out to the end of this limb, and showed everyone that their human soul is what's giving all of our brains an unconscious/subconscious intelligence, like this is.

"Why?" I don't know.

I think, way down deep inside; they all secretly want me and my peeps to become filthy stinking rich. Can you dig the gist of where I am coming from?

Can you see what I am saying?

My brand-new hypothetical unconscious/subconscious mind soul theory is reaching way out to the end of this hypothetical limb. And our big trade's marketing departments have all the cash to splash.

This manuscript hypothetically shows us how our soul is responsible for all our unconscious mind's unlimited potential intelligence. And...

I got us lost again. Where were we headed? How did we end up way back up in here? And...

I gotta get all my work done before I can open myself up and let my soul play around with all of my personal fun stuff. We need to stop this, turn around, and head back down that way. I gotta get us back to our rather more important task at hand. We've had enough fun for now. So...

All of us wannabe big trade authors have to schtick to big trade's way of formatted manuscripts, and brand-new nobody wannabe big trade authors can't go around breaking any of the super-secret rules in our little bitty handy dandy Super-Secret American Big trade Rule Book. So...

Super-Secret American Big Trade Rule Number Three: (Continued...)

On top of simply writing award-winning text, every brand-new nobody wannabe big trade author is expected to become an expert query letter writer. Then, every brand-new nobody wannabe big trade author is expected to become an expert book proposal creator. Then, every brand-new nobody wannabe big trade author is expected to go out and find a super-sharp agent who falls heads over heel in-love with our award-winning big trade writing. Then, our super-sharp agent is expected to go out and sell our award-winning writing to a big trade-publishing house for a few bazillion dollars. Then, every author is expected to leave home, go out into the world, and juggle "being a door-to-door salesperson and best-selling author of BOOK 1," and "writing BOOK 2," while continuing to work on developing their other career(s).

In my humble opinion, it's a complete and total pain in the ass to already be a successful author. And...

When you're a nobody, and you didn't already build an author's platform, then becoming a published author is a lot of very hard work.

When it comes to finding a literary agent, highly polished formerly published award-winning big trade authors have the exact same odds as brand-new nobody wannabe big trade authors when it is time to snag a super-sharp big trade literary agent. We, brand-new nobody wannabe big trade authors, just have taller mountains to climb. That's all.

And, the sad thing is, when authors do what we must do, and a wonderful new product hits the market, John and Jane Q. Public never gets to rip down the backstage curtains, to take an in-depth look to see all the inner workings of what it takes to get a brand-new nobody wannabe big-time big trade author into a big trade.

...Until now.

Welcome to my personal reality. I'm living this every day. This is my writing life. This is my whole wide writing world. It goes from way the fuck back there, to all the way right here, and I'm living my writing life shit every day, every way. Hey, hey, and...

Literary agents can't sell a manuscript to a publishing house without a badass query letter and an equally badass book proposal. I think somebody should write a big badass book about how to write big badass query letters and big badass book proposals.

Wait a minute...

What the hell am I saying? They got shelves and shelves of them big badass books down in all of our big badass brick and mortar bookstores. Yeah but...

All those books probably contradict each other too.

And my two truths to this matter are, I have not read them all, so I don't know for sure about that and, every single word on every single page of this whole first day of this chapter's manuscript is my book proposal. It's as naked as I can make it. I ain't got nothing to hide. My instinctive nature is to always be rebellious. But I am also always honest and fair and sometimes very wrong. My book(s) will always cover whatever I choose to write about. If I think of something, I'll write it down. Sometimes I don't, and either whichever way, it always seems to end up in here, one way or another. Some of my shit will be brilliant enough to shtick. And some of my shit will look a little bit goofy before it ends up sliding off the wall.

I am a control freak by nature. I just know my soul will end up all torn up over any physical change, plastic coating, airbrushing, resurfacing, and/or other booster enhancement of its raw untrained natural writing ability.

In my own personal overly-heavily-institutionalized structured game of getting a big-time big trade published, I know each and every author's job-one is conformity.

I'm not naïve.

I wasn't just born three days back (the day before yesterday). And...

I'm just feeling like I don't need to put my stinky crap out here in a straight-up, just the facts Ma'am, mighty proper of you, kind of way. "Hey. Hey."

People don't need every nonfiction thing they read to be a cold, hard, professionally written, and grammatically perfect, stack of boring-ass facts. I mean, welcome to our new age.

We have all crossed over into a new millennium.

If our new millennium bookworms think their old millennium ways are still the best way to go, then we need to keep trying to drive our busted old steam train down their old rickety set of Mother Nature's beat up train tracks.

Sometimes we just gotta do something totally new to make a change. And then, if you are the first to make the first thing that's totally different, it stands out and...

"Cha-ching."

And the next thing you know, you're ass-deep in some serious money. Did you know that...?

The vast majority of us prefer to fuck around when we learn new things. We like to have our new shit come at us with some learning fun. Step right up. Don't be shy. And...

My giant vocabulary averages 4.5 characters per word by the word count on my computer. My first book will be exactly 69,000 words, no more, no less. And if I need to, I will chop this off in the middle of my last sentence. My second book begins wherever (and whenever) this book ends up-ending. When we are agreeable, and our lifetime contracts are signed, I'm asking for a few months to finish up this piece of shit.

And to the most wonderful experiences of our lifetime, like my baby sister repeatedly said when we were little kids:

"Cheers, likesa beers." And...

I write all my first drafts in longhand on legal pads we bought at my local Office Max. I love to write with Pentel's Rolling Writers.

I'm hoping to have all this keyed-in, polished my way on my Gateway and, into a few agents' paper-cut hands by the end of the month as a birthday present to the love of my life. Right now...

It's still just November 03, 2002.

I still got a little time.

(Update: It's November 17, 2002. And I'm typing this in.)

I sent some of my earlier shit out. It didn't quite cut the mustard.

Any author can totally waste an entire year creating and grooming a thirty-five-page book proposal. My old book proposal is an adolescent version of my older versions of this shit. I still have it, but I don't use it anymore. I couldn't express myself very well back then.

In the early spring of 2001, my Baby took a 35mm picture of me. I gave my four-by-six print to a friend. He used it to draw an eight-by-ten picture of me. I took the eight-by-ten drawing to my brother-in-law. He made copies and framed the original. And then, after all that, I designed some business cards on my computer and purchased a bunch of two-pocket shiny black folders. I put one hell of a packet together.

After my days and days of researching literary agents, I sent my shit out to a bunch of different super-sharp big trade literary agents.

And...

I quickly found out that you only have to quietly sit on pins and needles for six to eight weeks to get nothing but a solid stream of rejection letters back in the mail. Playing by the rules didn't get me a damn thing. So now I say, "Fuck conformity."

I don't even conform myself to several of the rules I carefully laid out in here. I'm a failure many times over. I mean...

Here it is late 2002...

And I have already collected way more than my fair share of

"Dear Author" letters, way more than anyone's fair share of three-by-five "Dear Writer" postcards, and a couple of semi-personal "Dear John's" along the way.

One day, I hope to frame and hang all my rejection letters on my office walls. One day, I hope to move my overcrowded little bedroom out of my workstation.

One day, I hope to actually build my very own medieval modern-day green fortress around my very own medieval modern-day green palatial real estate, with an oober-modern office that has oober-modern walls. But for now...

Getting us back in the direction we were going earlier...

Big trade literary agents don't have the time to personally address the hundreds and hundreds of authors they turn down each week. And in addition to a serious time deficiency, literary agents can't afford to get personal when they reject anything.

People usually don't automatically open their unconscious mind to everybody that comes their way. Literary agents ain't much different than us, in that...

Getting too personal too soon is a dangerous place to be. The world is full-up with some crazy, messed-up people. And sometimes...

We are all just powder kegs in disguise.

If you are clever enough to send your stuff with a <u>S</u>elf-<u>A</u>ddressed-<u>S</u>tamped-<u>E</u>nvelope (SASE), you will, more often than not, receive crashed-out shattered broken random pieces and parts of your carefully crafted material back from the carefully selected literary agents you cautiously chose to send your stuff to.

So far, in my limited experience, most of my literary agents keep everything I have ever sent, except for the different stages of this manuscript. And whenever anyone sent anything back to me, they always sent a one page, politely worded, one size fits all, phony malarkey, totally bogus, piss-off and go away, go to hell, total bullshit, and extremely non-personal, "Dear John" letter. And that's the part of this writing gig that turns a writing career into just another shitty job. And that's the part that makes this whole damn "in it to win it" thing so damn frustrating. "Fuck me," and...

Since everybody and everything always seems to be in the last place we look, it would probably be easier on the old psyche; if we planned on collecting 995 "Dear John" letters from the get-go. When we get to 996...

...We win. It's just that easy. And speaking of...

Each literary agent wants a different kind of personally personalized non-personal query letter. If authors are really lucky, and know their shit really well, they get a different kind of a personally personalized non-personal "Dear John" letter every single time they get it wrong.

If any of you received a beautifully handwritten rejection letter from every literary agent you submitted your personally personalized non-personal query letter, you're a lot further along (and a whole lot better at this) than me. Buy yourself a stamp and stamp for your SASE, send then both of them in, and see what I mean. And...

I don't mean to brag or anything, but I have been lucky enough to receive actual handwritten feedback from a big trade literary agent, or two. But honestly, and for the most part...

Most literary agents go little past, "It's not for us." Blah, blah, blah... "We encourage you to submit elsewhere." Blah, blah, blah... "Good luck with your writing."

"Dear John" letters usually come in with big stinking piles of rejection smothered under tender little juicy chunks of sugar-coated encouragement. And...

And that's the other thing about this starving artist gig that becomes frustrating at times. Becoming a big trade author is all about being utterly and entirely alone, until we ain't anymore.

Rejection is failure. The endless failure will eventually become frustrating. Those that can't hang, weed themselves out of big trade's annual harvest. Hang in there and...

Failures can eventually be educational. We are all eventually universally adaptive, but only if/when we learn as we go along. If we ain't learning as we go along, we're falling through the cracks of whatever it is we ain't learning. And speaking of...

Let's face it, any rejection hurts us. That's just some plain and simple shit authors have to learn to absorb. But I can offer a little secret that might help ease the pain of rejection from your carefully selected big trade literary agent's totally non-personal "Dear John" letter.

Would you like to know my little secret?

Shh.

Come here.

No, really.

Seriously...

Lean in a little closer, head bob this way and I'll tell you a little secret about all this secret nonsense: everything costs us something. Everything comes with its own price. In order to keep all of this between you, me, and my book's pages; you have to promise me that you won't tell anyone you know, and I'll do the same for you. Okay?

Okay. Here we go...

Are you ready to learn something totally new and exciting? Here we go...

"Business is just business." It's nothing personal.

And there you go, so...

Now you know.

But you still can't tell anyone you know you know. You promised. And...

With big trade's market as tight as it is, every brand-new big trade author is required to build their own stack of rejection letters. There ain't no bones, butts, ifs, or any of our other conjunctions about none of that.

Everyone gets rejected, dejected, and ejected at big trade every day. Everybody. Every day. Big trade's rejection, dejection and ejection are unavoidable.

Some new authors turn their rejection, dejection, and ejection into something personal; and go all politician on their rejecting, dejecting and ejecting literary agents. But deep down inside, authors really shouldn't be doing that. Human beings first and becoming human is…

If we don't have the deep emotional connection with a close personal relationship or some other human being, then things can't get reach the level of very personal between us. We can't personally invest our souls (ourselves, emotionally) until we do. America won't be peaceful until it is. And that just ain't the case right now. And speaking of changing our political policies…

America the beautiful ain't all it could be today.

We could be doing a whole lot better than we are doing today. They should get to work on that. And to make them do what you want…

Register to vote. And…

Vote. And…

When someone emotionally connects with us at work, at the end of the workday, business is just business. Big trade is just a big business, and just like any other big business, in the end, everyone always ends up moving on anyways. And at the end of each and every business day, selling, publishing, and writing good books is a business. And if our carefully selected big trade literary agent personally rejects our carefully crafted material, they will not spend their hard-earned money to call or send a "Dear John" letter.

Literary agents ain't gonna spend no money to tell us we ain't the ones they want. Literary agents have bills just like us. And nobody burns their money like that. If nobody wannabe big trade authors want to experience the honor of being rejected by a big trade literary agent, we have to send all of our work with a SASE to show how much we care about our craft.

Super-Secret American Big Trade Rule Number Four:

Literary agents specialize in literature, like physicians specialize in doctoring. Authors have to find the right literary agent for our writing, like we have to find the right kind of doctor for our body's physical ailments.

Some literary agents specialize in children's books. Some specialize in romance books. Some literary agents will only read manuscripts that make their genitals salivate and get all drippy wet and/or rock-solid erect. Some literary agents will only represent certain religions. And some literary agents only represent professionally seriously scholarly-written nonfiction books that deal with stacks of cold, hard, grammatically perfect, boring-ass facts, charts and graphs and maps. Oh my...

Some big trade literary agents specialize in all of our different genres of books. Some of big trade's literary agents will handle all kinds of different genres. And some agents will only do novels. Some will only do sci-fi. Some will only do nonfiction.

Authors have to match whatever we write to whatever literary agents specialize in. When we send our stuff to the wrong literary agents, we waste a whole lot of everyone's time. So always, always, always...

And if I've said it once, I've said it about a thousand times "out loud"...

"Do your homework. Do your homework. Do your homework." And just like every involved dad always ever said, right now is always a great time to work on your homework.

And just to keep things on the up and up, also do your best to

Connecting the Web of Humanity:

only work with members of the Association of Authors' Representatives, Inc. www.pw.org

The AAR is a reliable place to go to help you make a list of legitimately ethical literary agents. AAR members are guaranteed to be good people.

In order to become their members, a literary agent must agree to adhere to a strict canon of ethics. What is the canon of ethics of a literary agent member? AAR members, themselves, have lots of rules to follow, like the one that keeps them from charging brand-new nobody wannabe big trade authors upfront fees. Did you know that as of today, in my brand-new millennium, it's still completely legal for an unethical literary agent to make a comfy living out of turning desperate uninformed brand-new nobody wannabe big trade authors into chumps?

This (look before you leap) super-secret rule really hits home with me. Because...

About a year ago, I received a letter and contract from a literary agent who wrote to say she loved my work. And...

I was completely overjoyed, to say the least.

My "Dear John" stack was beginning to turn into a small pile. It was such a huge relief to finally find my literary agent and make this monkey business of finding a literary agent be done and over with.

It'd be nice to just concentrate my efforts toward working on this goofy little manuscript and not having to worry about much of anything else.

Man, I'm telling you, when her acceptance letter came in, it was E-N-O-R-M-O-U-S. I felt like I hit all six numbers on a multi-million lottery jackpot. I was overjoyed to say the least. I was well on my way. All my hard work had finally paid off, just like everyone said it would. I made it. Can you imagine? All of our dark clouds went away, and our Sun was finally going to start to shine, so...

I called everyone I knew.

Man-o-live, was that a big mistake. Later, when I was able to settle down, and carefully reread her contract, I found out that she wanted me to send her $1250.^{00} of my hard-earned money. She called it a promotion fee. And here I thought she was on the up and up. I mean...

She didn't charge me a reading fee. But first...

Let me back up enough to explain something else about becoming just some other big-time big trade author. All of us big-time big trade authors don't have to pay for anything more than paper, ink, and postage. If we have to pay for more than paper, ink, and postage, then we are not becoming some other big time big trade author. That's what everyone in my todays say. So, anyway...

Oh well, live and learn. I ain't angry anymore, but if you happen to be the phony big trade literary agent in 2001, who tried to fuck me and mine out of our hard-earned money, and because I now know you weren't going to do a fucking thing to help me out, and whether or not you'll ever read any of this, I finally came up with something to say to you.

I didn't respond to you. I never said anything before because I didn't have anything to say to you, until now. And I know I don't have much of a fucking clue when it comes to our bookworm's way of doing this whacked little writing gig, but at least I did bother to run this shit through the computer's spellcheck before I send it out my front door.

"What the phuck, lady?" Oh my God, you have way too many typos for a one-page typed form-letter. And...

Needless to say...

That whole nightmare ordeal made me step back and reevaluate this whole fucked-up writing gig. And for me, all at once, everything turned rather shitty. So, I took some time to think things through, catch up on my life, and do a bunch of honey-do projects around our house. And...

All that happened in the later part of 2001, and now...

It's the later part of 2002. And I'm back to doing all this shit again. And... Again. And... Again. And...

All and all, I learned two good lessons last year...

It doesn't matter what the fuck happens, I ain't calling nobody for nothing no more. In fact...

From now on, until I get this horrible nasty-ass shit published, I'm keeping a tight lid on what's up and how it's coming along.

Some parts of our personal history embarrass us.

I also learned that if an agent isn't an www.pw.org member, they aren't worth my postage, or my sweet-ass time.

Super-Secret American Big Trade Rule Number Five:

Read your writing about one-hundred-million times before you send it out your front door. If you are writing a book, you need to read your writing over and over to make it right. Each (and every) time you re-read your writing; your mind filters it. Brand-new nobody wannabe big trade authors have to catch all of the "miss takes" that our computer's spell-checker won't catch. And...

If we want to get our manuscript published in big trade, we have to make our writing look professional and clean. We have to appear scholarly trained.

The book industry is steeped in its old-school tradition. The book industry is all about cranking out professionally written clean page-turners that just flow and flow. So...

Carefully read through your writing over and over. Catch, and correct, each and every punctuation, spelling, and grammatical error you happen to find.

Today's brand-new nobody wannabe big trade authors are also supposed to pass their manuscripts around to all of their friends and family, especially if we have a hard time making our writing look bookworm shiny. Let them help you. And then...

After we pass our big bad beautiful manuscripts around to our friends and family, taking all of their input, and making all of the right modifications, we brand-new nobody wannabe big trade authors aren't supposed to let any of big trade's people know what our family and friends thought about our manuscript no matter what, unless...

One of our friends and/or family is someone important, someone of influence, or some kind (any kind) of a huge celebrity. So, what's your claim to fame? Yes, please. Let's play that game. What are we waiting for? And then, let's go here...

Finally, our last rule in the little bitty handy dandy Super-Secret American Big trade Rule Book...

Super-Secret American Big Trade Rule Number Six:

Before we will ever become a big trade author, we either have to really know what we're doing when it comes to writing, or we have to be a really big celebrity, someone important, or someone with influence. And we need to already have a crowd following us, if we're famous enough; someone has probably already talked to us about the wonderful opportunities of having our book(s) published.

If you're very famous, you don't even have to know how to write right. You don't even have to know how to spell any of our little words. If you don't feel the urge, you won't even have to type your name. Have your people contact our big trade people and our big trade people will hook you up with a ghostwriter.

A ghostwriter is someone who "helps" you write your manuscript by writing a manuscript for you. Everywhere else, in every other thing we do, everything is just about us, what we bring, and how we are using whatever we got. Ask any actor phoning it in, but...

Connecting the Web of Humanity:

As far as big trade goes, if you are a big-name celebrity, and you don't know how to write right, that's okay. It's no big deal. Big trade will send you your very own professional author to "help" you write your book(s) and make you look even more "fantabulous" than you already are. And brand-new nobody wannabe big trade authors, and everybody else like me...

We are on our own. We are all alone. So basically...

We're fucked.

Game over. We lose. And...

"Thanks for playing the Big Trade Publishing Game and have a great day. Goodbye." And...

Blue Screen

Presses restart

Rebooting very slowly in 2002. And...

Sunday, November 03, 2002 (Continued...)

Big trade only wants authors who can create enough publicity to get their book on the bestseller lists long before the actual book ever gets released.

"Big trade is all about the pre-sells, Baby." Connecting the Web is...

That's why publishing houses love celebrities. Everyone wants to make a quick profit on every investment they make. Big trade does not dump serious money into completely unknown unproven nobody big trade author wannabes. That shit does not happen to wannabes.

Really big publishing houses and big celebrities make big money together. The fast cash of a celebrity's instant audience keeps the derailed industries wheels-a-rolling.

Businesses operate on capital. Publishing houses aren't interested in taking risks with money. And being frugal isn't just limited to big trade. All businesses are greedy. When it comes to business, it's the nature of the beast.

"Greed's the name of the game."

Big trade isn't the only business looking out for its long-term investments or at the potential for red ink in its profit columns. When it comes to book sales, if a brand-new nobody wannabe big trade author can't show up and also fire off the out-of-the-gate fastball, then we authors stand little chance of ever seeing our footprints inside our big trade's giant ballpark.

If an author wants a ticket to ride on big trade's derailed choo-choo train, they'll need to have something real good going for them in someplace other than our book industry. The days of becoming famous because we wrote a big bad beautiful book are long gone, if they were really even there at all. And if they were really there at all, then all of that somehow stopped happening sometime in the end of the last millennium, pre-2000. Today, it's all about Return on Investment.

Today's authors often have to show big trade their latest self-published blockbuster, or their syndicated television show, or their name and picture plastered all over the news for several weeks, or Facebook "Likes", or #HashTag followers, or oral sex in the Oval Office, or some other juicy claim to fame.

Today's new authors have to already be celebrities. The same as it ever was, and even more so, in today's new millennium...

Today's new authors have to already have an audience

Connecting the Web of Humanity:

following along. Today's new big trade authors have to have what today's big trade calls a "platform." Looking "platform" up in 2002 was not as easy to find as it is in today's world. And...

I'm just saying and...

If you can't show up with the big-time big trade heavy credentials of already being famous, you have to be able to chew your arms off at your elbows in order to ever even get a chance to become a big-time big trade author. Like this...

Talking about my advance before I find my big trade literary agent? Now that's a "fo pa", faux pas.

But so the fuck what? I mean...

Who's writing all of this goofy nonsensical shit anyway? Right? And so the fuck what if today turns into the part of my goofy nonsensical shit that looks more nonsensical before it ends up sliding off the wall. It's been a very long day. And I've been throwing my hypothetical shit on all over these proverbial walls all day long. And does it really matter if the rest of my today's shit turns out to be ridiculous nonsense? And why would I want to hide the fact that I got such a generous amount of money out of some tight-fisted big trade bookworms anyway? I mean...

Business is just business.

Right?

Okay.

Here we go...

I want enough dough to set my family up today. I want $5 on each and every copy sold. On top of that, I want one itty-bitty NFL Super-Bowl commercial and I want another commercial for that same year's Academy Awards, a.k.a. the Oscars. Or...

You can spend that much money on anything in Dave's Pants. Whatever whichever way you want to go is fine with me. And either way we go...

It would be nice if our groundbreaking commercials, #webmercials and/or however else you see fit on splashing your cash around, coincide with this book's big trade's big-time book release. Ballpark...

After my big trade publishing house pays for all of our marketing, and/or whatnot, I'm still thinking my first check is still gonna need to make me an instant multimillionaire.

In the scheme of things, a few million ain't a whole lot of money to big trade. Or at least, it shouldn't be.

And if this business was doing better, it wouldn't be.

When it's all said and done, the book deals my big trade publishing house is gonna have to throw down to cover this big badass beautiful début will be more than enough to launch this rocket into orbit.

It's like getting a multimillion-dollar rocket and some other multimillion-dollars to spend on its fuel. That much money going to a brand-new nobody wannabe big trade author who just said all of this ugly shit is just as disgusting and obscene as it sounds. And...

That's the kind of hype that creates the commotion that's gonna get this whole thing headed in the right direction and rolling down all of our right set of tracks.

But for now...

And...

Here, in the middle of this particular night, as I'm laying here in my bed totally naked, in another one of my totally different Novembers than ever before, I am quietly writing on a legal pad, with my handy-dandy Pentel Rolling Writer, and as the same as the any other times on any other day in every other November I have ever had before, I am just another naked nobody.

I have never done anything newsworthy. I have never been published by big trade. I haven't done anything in front of the general public. I haven't even stood in front of the general public.

In fact, I haven't done anything that would give me a claim to be somehow famous. I ain't got no author's big trade platform. But, I do spend most of my days thinking. And...

I think I better get my ass to sleep. It's way past my bedtime. And...

It's been a really long day. And...

I've been spending my time writing my ass off all day long. Thank goodness for that...

And...

I think I gotta get up early in the morning to go to work. So...Goodnight.

Monday, November 04, 2002

A lot of big thinkers have walked around on this planet. We still have a lot of big thinkers walking around this planet today.

It may be a little foolish of me to think I can hold my own with people like Archimedes, Bach, Newton, Copernicus, Galileo, Nostradamus, da Vinci, Edison, Darwin, Freud, Einstein, Dave, Oprah, that pretty little nameless cave-lady who harnessed the power of fire, or that other pretty little nameless cave-lady who invented the wheel. However, I do happen to believe that all our minds have whatever it takes to produce thoughts in the exact same caliber and as exciting and innovative as our greatest minds were and still are today. For instance...

Being as scientific as my high school education allows me to be, our brains are the little gray melons that are all floating around inside our noggins. And...

Sometime, a long time ago, our minds were ripped into two separate parts. Like separating the white and yellow parts of a chicken egg, the first co-Great-Grandfather of psychoanalysis ripped everybody's mind into two separate parts, and oddly enough, nobody got hurt.

Freud split our brain's minds apart. Freud split Darwin's evolving single brain/mind into our newer single brain with two minds. And from that day forward, just like that, all of us started having a rationally thinking cognitive conscious mind and an emotionally unstable unconscious/subconscious mind. Freud gives each of us human rational cognitive consciousness and an imaginative human soul. Thanks a lot Freud.

We are whatever we want to be.

This ain't brain surgery. It's mind surgery. Everybody stand back. We're gonna have to throw our little gray melons out the window. "The window, the window, the second-story window, high-low, low-high, throw 'em out the window…"

A human brain's two minds operate on two separate channels at the exact same time. One of our brain's minds is active on an awake cognitive/conscious channel. And our other brain's mind constantly runs us on a separate unconscious mind/human soul channel.

When we go to sleep, our conscious mind goes offline. And from time to time, our soul fucks with us via our dreams. Sometimes, we dream, when we sleep. And…

In a prehistoric time, our evolutionary ancestors only had their unconscious mind. Way back when early humans only had one channel running in their brain. Our evolutionary ancestors were cognitively unaware of their own existence. Everyone, way back when, had zero to little conscious brain activity, no cognition, no self-awareness, no cognitive capacity, no awareness of self. At some point, going back down the line in our history of evolving, we were just like all the other animals.

And then at some point, coming back up the line of the history in our evolution, our already superior primitive brain's capabilities expanded, and human cognition began to teach us more about our everything us. And speaking of...

We are in our Cognitive Brain Age. And it's still all Freud's fault. And you are not the last person to this cognitive brain's mind party.

Lots of people still don't know all you now know. And...

Ever since our newer mind (cognitive human consciousness) got switched on, it's been fine-tuning itself. So that now, the first channel (our primitive brain's unconscious mind), blends seamlessly in with the second channel our brain's more modern conscious ability/cognitive knowledge (cognitive mind). And acting and/or being human happens.

So, what sets me apart from all our other modern-day big thinkers? Well, for starters...

I'm opening all my shit up with the completely plain-Jane simple statement of...

Every human being, all the living among us, has a human soul. Every human alive has our shared human spirituality. And that's just the way/how we humans end up becoming human. We are what we think we are. It is what we think it is. I'm doing me. You're doing you. And...

Whatever we do with whatever we have is totally up to us.

We all have our own free will. And...

Every single solitary thing we got going on inside the unconscious part of our mind comes from our soul. And...

We all have our own individual handy-dandy autopilot. But I also have to say that as our lives evolve, we have the responsibility of keeping conscious cognitive control over every single solitary thing we allow our souls to do. And...

I lost control of my soul—a.k.a. "temporary insanity" isn't much of a criminal defense today. We're supposed to learn how to cognitively control the wild and untamed emotions of our soul.

Legally, we aren't allowed to go flying off the handle the way some of us do. And fucked-up soul screams, "what?" And...

Sometimes, we just have to contain the wild kingdom passions of our emotional soul. We all have to do what we all have to do sometimes.

The truth always sets our soul free.

Our soul plays a major role in our everyday life.

When we use our cognitive abilities of reason to recognize what our unconscious mind, our soul, does in our daily life, then life itself becomes even more precious. When we become aware of our unconscious mind, our soul, being the spirituality inside us, we become more consciously aware of some of the possibilities developing in our subconscious mind. And...

We might even become more of a humanitarian to all of the other souls living around us. And then...

We could all live in peas-full American hominy. But...

Being more realistic, and diving back into the fucked-up cold cruel cynical world I feel connected to every day today...

We only care about the souls we feel connected to and nobody gives a shit about anything or anybody else.

And in the end of a very hard day...

We only care about ourselves, except for when we decide to become heroic. And when we can't help ourselves...

Selfless acts turn ordinary everyday people into our ordinary everyday heroes around us. And...

Our soul shows the scientific proof of its existence all the time. Our true friends trust us with their soul's dirty little personal secrets, and we trust our true friends with our soul's dirty little personal secrets.

"Hey, what happened to John?"

"He got sucked-up into some fucked-up webby thing back in his bedroom/workplace."

"Ah, that's too bad."

"Yeah. But whatcha gonna do?

"Yeah... Well, it was nice to see you again."

"You too."

"Yeah. You too. Take care."

Our human soul is not an inactive entity. Our human soul isn't waiting for us to die before it activates and deploys into our afterlife. Our soul ain't waiting for our life to end before it suddenly springs into action. And our soul simply ain't nonexistent, that would just be way too convenient, now wouldn't it?

Our soul leads us through each and every one of our moments, each and every day, and all the days throughout each and every one of our lives. Our unconscious mind is our private imagination generator. When we were all little kids, back before we knew any better, we were all younger and much smaller humans, and our human soul was what was driving us around. Update: Our unconscious mind is still driving us around today.

And I know everything there is to know about you, because I am a mind reader. I see one brain with two minds, and I can see inside most of ours today, and...

If I know my peeps' souls well enough, I can read their thoughts. You can too, if you know the thoughts of the souls in the people around you well enough.

How well do you know the souls of the people around you?

I know the people that know me so well...

We know how each other's unconscious/subconscious minds work.

And we all also know our soul is unconsciously guiding us right now. The private parts of us will always carry more weight than the other parts of us that learned things from reading all sorts of books. Sometimes, our souls rat fucks the cognitive side of our brains. Our souls are the core of our being human and our human being. Our unconscious mind is the most private primal part of our more modern humanity.

We privately hide (and secretly share) our unconscious mind's soul with certain people. Our unconscious mind's souls are as individual as our individual bodies. Our unconscious mind's soul defines who we really are deep inside ourselves. When we go deep down inside ourselves, we start to see our new possibilities.

Human beauty is only skin deep.

Unlock and open an unconscious mind? Sure, no problem. Here we go...

And when we are opening up a bunch of souls at once...

I recommend that we use a super-thick heavy-duty steel cable and a great big heavy-duty electric winch. It's all just a matter of working out our mathematics.

Sometimes, we all play the roles we have to play. We all have to maintain multiple identities and personalities sometimes. One minute, you're on your cellphone talking to your best friend, and the next minute, everything about you changes when you bump into some old acquaintance you didn't like way back when. You close up and hide your real self away.

"Uh, I can't talk right now. I gotta go. I'll call you later. And..."

Human souls are the purest form of our inner selves. Our individual soul is our individual core human identity. Our soul holds all our innermost personal truths and all our best friend's dirty little personal secrets. We can't describe a person without describing their human soul. That's why it's so ding-dang important to stop every once in a while and take a serious hard-core look at ourselves. We have to stop, drop, and figure out things when everything goes wrong.

Tomorrow's salvation starts with our ability to realize the difference between the serious bullshit and the not-so-serious bullshit of our today's current reality, in our today's today.

It sucks when we realize we could have done something different to save some of the fucked-up days we've had.

With or without any of our personal conscious knowledge of our soul's involvement, our life is slowly shaping our soul as we go along. The quicker we consciously/cognitively comprehend the good changes (and the bad changes) our life makes on our soul, the better our life becomes. The quicker we consciously/cognitively see the bad and good changes our souls make on our life, the better our souls become. And trying that same shoe on the other foot...

We shape our clay-like souls as we play this fragile game of life. The goal is to make the innermost part of us happy, worthy of us, and worthy of our afterlife. Or not, it's all based on whatever we happen to believe, or don't happen to believe. And speaking of people having beliefs and people having non-beliefs...

For the scientific proof of our soul's existence in the smack-dab middle of today's scientific world, and to be able to put our souls in the middle of right here and right now, we have this great big stinky mountain of physical evidence to carefully dig up and sift through. So...

I want everybody to roll up their sleeves, grab a pair of safety glasses, work gloves, a hard hat, your very own box of condoms, and please follow me. Shall we?

Is everybody ready?

Good. Here we go...

Science is based on cause and effect. Our conscious mind and unconscious mind can either be our personal cause or our personal effect, affecting us greatly. We have spirituality oozing out of every thought, emotion, action, reaction, and everything else that's happening to make us human. Speaking of humanity...

When we pay close attention to someone or something, our spirituality shows itself to the world around us. When we lose ourselves in the moment, our spirituality shows itself to the people observing us. An open soul attracts an open soul. All we have to do is pay attention. Like right now. Your soul has been pulled into this. And if someone is watching you, they would be able to see your soul reading through this. And when your soul is not deep into this, where does it go? So…

Let's do a mental science project together. But first…

Before we start, we're gonna need to totally untangle our "whole reality" into its two different parts.

Until now, "reality" has always been defined as a single entity, like our (pre-Freud) two minds inside our human brains. And…

Today, when we speak of reality, we refer to it as if it only exists in our scientifically proven physical world. But…

A deeper look into what "reality" truly is reveals two separate streams. Our "whole reality" is currently being created from two separate realities that need to become clearly defined. Nobody has yet. So…

One half of our whole reality is our scientifically proven physical real-world shared reality and the other half of our whole reality is all of our different personal realities. Our abundantly endless number of personal private realities and our shared scientifically proven cold hard cruel (nonfiction) real-world physical reality creates whole reality, both running separately and seamlessly together.

Our dual reality gives us a shared scientific physical world reality and all of our privately shared (or just privately held) personal realities. And we all have the same shared scientific reality. And…

We have an unlimited number of other realities we can share when we escape our shared scientific reality. And now that we have a little better understanding of what our humanity is all about, let's try to nail humanity down a little better while we're here. Shall we?

Anybody got a hammer?

If I had a hammer, I'd swing it all the time. And...

We could say that humanity is the end result of two separate consciousnesses: the unconscious mind's soul and the cognitive conscious, playing out in unison. And the continuum of time is zippering all of us up and down into our dual consciousness together with our right here and now and what all has already happened. And we could stop right there. But that simple definition doesn't explain our collective humanity very well. We're totally missing reality. So, let's back this whole thing up just enough to say...

Humanity is the backdrop of two separate realities, the scientific world's hard nonfiction reality, and our very own personal soft individual fictional realities, and then, our dual consciousness also comes into the mix, and everything blends together in time's zipper. Our dual-reality and our dual-consciousness blend to form "Right Now" and "This Moment."

Collectively, all four are running individually at the same time. All four (dual realities and dual consciousnesses) are working against each other or in simultaneous harmony for our Creator's purpose and our own individual life's higher purpose.

It's like we experience our lives within the four big boundaries that surrounds a human foursquare game. And...

If I accidently lost you, please allow me to demonstrate what I am saying by getting us back to where we can do the little mental science experiment, I talked about two pages (or so) ago. So...

Okay...

Before we begin, I need you to clear your head.

Totally empty your head from everything I said so far.

Great.

"Good job." Looking around in your head, nothing is here. Now all you gotta do is make this great big emptiness turn into a great big square in your mind and cut that in half horizontally and vertically. You should have four somewhat equal boxes. Are you with me?

Okay...

Let's put our cognitive conscious thinking minds in the bottom right square. Put our souls (our creative unconscious minds) in the top left square. Put our shared scientifically proven physical world reality (everything in, on, or around us here on Earth/whatever science knows) in the top right square. Carefully scoop up every private personal moment that you've ever truly experienced in your personal realities and gently place all of that gooey mess of emotions in the bottom left square. Are you still with me? "Great."

"Good job." It is very complicated. But you are doing a great job so far. Now...

Put some sides on your great big square and make it turn into a great big box. Then fill it with water to about 70% full. Next...

Throw in a great big splash of Extra-Virgin Mediterranean Olive Oil, stand back, and observe.

Watch what happens when our lives start pushing our billions of individual boxes around. Our personal and individual functionality, productivity, and participation in the whole wide world around us depends on which one of the four squares our bubble of Extra-Virgin Mediterranean Olive Oil happens to be hovering over the most. If our Extra-Virgin Mediterranean Olive Oil bubble hovers over any one square in particular in any given moment, our moments predominantly end up being made from that quadrant of ourselves.

And somehow or another, all that shit going on inside us hooks up with all that shit going on inside someone else and we become really good friends.

Friends are soul hook-ups. One person's soul plugs into another person's soul, and we become friends. And...

If one speaker wire is hooked up to our cognitive knowledge's scientific reality, and the other speaker wire is hooked up to our personal soul's non-scientific realities, then we are experiencing life from inside our brain's stereo.

Am I making any sense at all? If I'm not, hold on.

Stereo instructions are really hard to translate.

I'm all twisted up and turned around right now. I'm really not trying to confuse anybody. I gotta step back from this great big gooey mess of nonsense.

I need to turn this around and focus exclusively on our souls. I don't want to lose track of where I was going with what I was trying to say earlier.

I apologize for being so distracted. But all of a sudden, I can't seem to pay attention to what I am supposed to be focusing all of my attention on. Can you hear that? I'm all up, inside your head, tiptoeing around, trying to be quiet, and I keep getting distracted because of all the noise I hear around you right now. And just like that...

You hear the different sounds around you. Don't you?

And it's noisy. Isn't it? So much so...

I can't concentrate and focus on my work right now.

Our soul crosses us over into our personal realities when we stop hearing our shared scientific world noises, when our scientific world goes away from our cognitive awareness, when we lose ourselves in our private moments.

The next time you are at the grocery store, and you hear that couple fighting in the next aisle over, you need to know that they are revealing their human souls. We reveal our human souls when we are expressing our inner selves. When we're expressing our inner selves, we expose our soul to the world around us. Sometimes we actually show our private side out in public.

If our soul is not open and honestly expressing our truer selves, we're either just acting or we're hiding our soul away.

Our souls protrude deep into our scientific reality. Take a good hard look around and see what I mean.

Watch your grandkids play.

"See?" Can you see their souls?

Can you see your children's souls?

When we lose ourselves in the moment, our soul shows itself in our scientific reality, and our soul can be seen by anyone in the cold hard scientific reality world that we share. Our soul comes to center stage and our conscious, cognitive mind moves backstage in our brains. Sometimes, our soul can overpower our rational cognition. And when our souls become viewable, our physical world leaves us.

Take our ability to deeply concentrate...

When we are totally focused on our work, or we become absorbed into a very good book, or its movie, our shared scientific reality escapes us. When we escape our shared reality, our automatic physical world noise controller turns on, and we all stop hearing the shared reality noise around us, and time disappears, and our cognitive awareness disappears, and we end up stepping off into a personal private reality. And then...

Our shared scientific reality reappears sometime after we are done making love. If we don't always hear the endless steady stream of noise around us, what happens in the science of sound? Pause and take a moment. Look around. What time is it? What time did you start reading this? What page are we on? This is Page __. "See?"

Go pee, if you suddenly realized you need to go. We'll start right here when you get back. So, take this with you and go pee, already. And I'll be right here with you on Page __ waiting for you to get back to right here. If you are full of pee, and you've been holding it in, and you have a place to go pee, I am making your soul let go of your cognition enough to let you go. So, go, and go, and go . And if you don't need to go and go, don't go. And if you don't need to go and go right now, you will soon. And...

This is page __. (Page numbers vary on our personal digital version.)

And sometimes we are aware of our physical bodies, and sometimes we're not. When we're not aware of our physical world, when we are in the middle of being lost in one of our moments, when we are in the middle of being lost in one of our personal realities, we are exposing our soul to the physical world around us. And occasionally, we do things haphazardly.

If we go to work, and do our job haphazardly, it shows in the quality of our work. When we're at work, mindfulness always needs to be job-one. But that kind of conformity kills our individual individualism. So...

Fuck whatever kind of conformity this is. No don't...

We can't afford to fuck any kind of conformity that keeps us safe and out of harm's way. I mean...

When we go to work, our number one job is safety. And we can't flip our birds, when they go missing. And giving our all requires the full power of our whole brain. When we throw both mind halves of our whole brain into our work, our work shows a shine that's left behind. Good work shines like a bright lighted beacon.

Complicated tasks require the complete involvement of our scholarly thoughtful cognitive mind and a creative soul. Sometimes, we gotta do what we gotta do. Sometimes, we need to be completely attentive and totally focused on whatever it is we do.

Nobody can do their best work when they are distracted, or gravely ill.

Every time we focus our brain's complete attention on something, our soul breaks through the surface of our scientific reality to present itself in a very real scientific way. Whenever our heart and soul are involved in whatever we do, our heart and soul leave our personal marks, our personal sheens, behind. Amen and...

Mental note:

Sometime later, I think I need to write about how focusing our complete attention benefits our sex lives.

"Who's your daddy?" And...

If I tried to present our measly ability to multitask as the only overlooked piece of evidence of our human spirituality, I know I'd fall on my face trying to make my case. I've got tons of shit to say about our souls, and sex, and a bunch of other shit. Obviously...

Otherwise, I would have just written a pamphlet. I wouldn't be busting my ass to do all of the shit I've been trying to do all along.

Our adult souls are in the center of us. And I know I'm right. Our adult soul is in the center of everything we do. And I'm right, because I know that...

The burden of scientific proof is buried within the scientific accumulation of everything separating us from the other creatures here on Earth. And we have a lot of scientific evidence to poke at. Take sex...

The "Sexperts" still can't define sex yet.

Nobody has ever been able to define sex yet. It's today. And the truth is still gonna set you free. So...

Come and get some, or get some and come, or what whichever what way works best for you. And either way, we all rudimentarily know how we all fuck. We think we know why we all fuck. But we ain't got much of a fucking clue beyond all we think we know.

Our genitals are major hubs of sensitive nerves and contracting

Connecting the Web of Humanity:

muscles. When we rhythmically stroke our genitals in pleasurable ways, they swell up, and four out of five women (and virtually all us men) get to experience a very pleasing release. Everything tends to be a little better when we don't have to masturbate, when we find someone who wants to have sex with us. Sex should feel good. So much so, that...

If sex ever bothers you, stop. If you ever become uncomfortable having sex, stop. If you feel pressured, stop. When sex stops feeling good, stop. If sex ever hurts, like in a bad way, immediately stop. And if you're not careful, sex can kill you, so always practice safe sex. And that's pretty much where the science of sex stops. And I'm sure some of the experts out there would disagree with me here but...

Fuck those people. And when we do, know that...

Everything else anyone knows about human sex is either Pseudo-Science or in the realm of the unknown.

And there you have it. And now you know. So...

Goodnight and drive safely.

Not, but speaking of driving safely...

What's up with all our car commercials? Have you noticed how car companies want us to drive their new cars?

"This is a professional driver on a closed course. Please do not drive your new monster all the fun ways we are showing you how you can drive your new monster."

Yeah, right. Here we are...

Just being human, and...

People are killing themselves every way and every day driving into vehicular accidents.

We gotta remember that we're a slowly evolving creature. We are all still just one chromosome away from monkey see, monkey do.

I'd be a little more mindful about where you're pointing that ad thing if I were you. It's just my little friendly cleaning advice from me to you. Take it if you like it. And leave it if you don't. And...

The angry American mob went after big tobacco. The angry American mob is equipped for an easy attack on the next slow-moving target at any given moment's notice. And we currently have a shitload of easy slow-moving targets.

Look at me.

I feel persecuted by the entire book industry for my lack of a distinguished education, my lack of a distinguished writing experience, my lack of a distinguished author's platform, and my lack of my already "celebrityism." But then again...

Nothing is safe from fickle scrutiny. Smoke. Eat eggs. No don't eat eggs. Yes do. Eating eggs is safe, nutritious, and delicious. **Don't smoke**. Always drive attentively.

Putting the cellphones down, safety first, always go hands free behind the wheel. And...

Never let your lover walk away horny.

I think about sex a lot.

Do you?

And now, thanks to my brand spanking new hypothetical soul theory, I'm about to blow everyone's socks off by introducing its spawn, my brand-new hypothetical human sex theory. But first...

A really quick word about women and socks...

Some women can increase the intensity of their orgasms by simply wearing socks during sex. And speaking of while we are having sex...

In order to learn something new about sex, we have to expand our cognitive mind enough to free our soul. So...

Here we go...

This is my, never been seen before, hypothetical human sex theory:

Connecting the Web of Humanity:

All human sex happens within three different ranges on our human (mind, body, and soul) sex spectrum. So...

Let's name the first spectrum range of sex, "Body-sex."

Body-sex is what scientific researchers can observe, test, or measure. Body-sex is bio-sex. Body-sex is what most of the American adult industry is cranking out in VHSs and DVDs. Body-sex is just basic human fucking.

In all fairness to the American porn industry, I have seen a few rare exceptions. We have to comb through a ton of garbage to find our nuggets. I have a few nuggets in my tiny little private collection. And by the way...

I got more porn than I got books.

"Surprise."

And now that I stepped out of my private little personal closet a little bit further, now that I opened my closed off human soul, to reveal myself a little bit wider and deeper, feeling a little bit closer to you, what we are dealing with, and what we are going through, I have let you in on another one of my other dirty little personal secrets, now that I revealed a little bit more of my whole self; I have to completely confess to you, I hope to have a whole lot more of both...

Readable books and excellent porn someday...

Personally, readable books and excellent porn are very rare and hard to find. I think the porn industry doesn't understand sex any better than our bookworms understand the cold cruel world outside of their brick and mortar's windows. But then again, how can they?

When people have to act, they act. That's what we do. When we act like we're acting it out, that's what we do.

And sex is not a very pleasant thing to watch when people try to act like they're enjoying sex. And some people can only do what they've done, until they figure out that they want to achieve more than what they are doing. And I gotta ask...

Where's the technique? Where's the sparks? Where's the magic? Where's the passion? Where's the love? Where's the emotion? Where's the lust? And what the fuck is the hurry?

We can't start a log on fire with a single sulfur match.

The human warmth of a sexual desire's fire thrives on need, anticipation, wanting, and an intense buildup of lustful hunger. In other words, slow the fuck down. When it comes to sex, anticipation brings us a hell of a lot more than playing some fucked-up blame game. And what's up with all these fucked-up soundtracks? Can you hear what I am saying?

When we act and fuck at the same time, we have body-sex. Body-sex is just fucking. Body-sex is physical sex, textbook sex. Body-sex is all about every money shot.

Fuck buddies have lots of body-sex.

"No sweetheart. Don't stare at the camera like that.

Look at him, or just close your eyes, and for Pete's sake...

It's called acting. Can you at least pretend to look like you're having a good time?

I want everyone here to create the illusion that we are enjoying ourselves. So, try to relax. Get into it.

What?

No.

He's the best-looking big dick guy we got.

What?

No.

Don't worry about it.

We'll dub the sound out of this. So...

Keep going."

Body-sex is fucking. Body-sex is our physical sex.

And there ain't nothing wrong with having the physical sex of our just fucking each other, as long as it's not the only thing we do each and every time after time, after time, after time, after time, after time, after time, after time...

If your sex life has ever been stuck in a rut, or if your sex life has ever been on or/and is currently everyday stuck in, the human-biosex merry-go-round, I know you know what I'm talking about.

"I heart quickies." Yum. Yum. And...

Sadly, body-sex is the best range of sex some consenting adults ever experience. Body-sex is missing our soul's and/or cognitive mind's participation.

I'm telling you straight-up, right here and now, I'm loud and proud to say, we're all capable of creating more than just an empty string of body-sex orgasms.

Otherwise, we would not have all evolved as far as we are. And we would still be more like the birds and the bees.

Our life becomes a flat line when we re-experience the same old experiences over, and over, and over, and...

It's never too late to push our boundaries and change our ways. Our life is all about constant change.

We live in a world where too many human souls have lost their way. When we lose our way, when we fall off our tracks, when we're personally derailed, we're lost, and we cannot experience anything more than body-sex. Get this...

"I'm mad as hell, and I can't take this shit anymore."

When we get mad, our soul closes, and we shut down. Our soul goes into shelter mode or we go into battle mode. Well, that and, some lovers' souls never really connected in the first place. That's okay. We can fix all that, and lots, and lots, and lots more.

How well do you know the souls of the people in your house and/or in your life? When our soul is interested in the souls of the people around us, our soul grows closer to their souls. And all of this draws our souls out of our cognition's cognitive shells. Our souls and our cognition are like snails and snail shells.

"Je ne sais pas escargot." (I do not know snail.)

When we're exposing our human vulnerability to the love of our life, our souls open. We become raw. Our emotions come out of the deepest part inside us, the human unconscious parts in our mind, our human soul.

We can't control some of the thoughts happening inside our heads. We have no cognitive control over whatever happens inside our hearts. We have entirely no cognitive control over how we emotionally feel about whatever we feel. We have no control over whom we're attracted to. We can't control who disgusts us. And whenever mutual attraction is combined with love, we have no control over anything. Our soul is uncontrollable in all kinds of different ways.

People can't control how we instantly feel about a person, place, thing, or idea. Some of the bullshit will always find a way of fucking with us. As a people, we are entitled to feel anything humans happen to be feeling. And…

People's feelings are not to be denied.

We just have to cognitively learn how to control what our soul does when we express our emotions.

Emotion radiates from our soul, like skin cancer radiates from our Sun.

We are capable of showing and having emotions. So…

Stepping outside of our scientific boundaries for just a minute or two, depending on reading speed…

I am a horrible reader. My reading speed sucks. And…

Let's name our second spectrum range of sex, "Mind-sex."

Mind-sex blends our physical sensations of sex with the presence of our cognitive mind. Mind-sex is the glue that bonds our partnering souls together.

Body-sex is a physical and biological sexual experience of experiencing human biosex. When we have body-sex, it's just physical and thoughtless sex.

Mind-sex goes way beyond body-sex's physical sexual experience. When we have mind-sex, our cognition kicks in, pulling our human awareness into us sharing a new privately shared reality.

The only difference between body-sex and mind-sex is the mark one person's soul leaves on another person's soul and the DNA left behind.

Mind-sex and body-sex are two completely different ranges on a spectrum of human sex. Body-sex is all about the experience of our physical pleasures and our body's orgasmic responses. Body-sex is all about human biosex. And mind-sex takes human sex up to our next sex spectrum range. Intensified orgasms make our sex lives more intricate and satisfying. Mind-sex happens, when we keep our head in the game. When we are aware of our partner's pleasure consciously, or when we're aware of ourselves having cognitive sex, mind-sex, consciously, mind-sex happens. When we think about what we are doing and focus our attention when we have sex happens in mind-sex range on spectrum. Mind-sex combines our minds and bodies together.

And way beyond all the great sex we may (or not) be already having on our brand-new sex spectrum "range-o-rama", there is our third highest range of human sex that gives us better, stronger, harder, deeper, longer-lasting, more intense, and a wider variety of mind-blowing life-altering orgasms, which leads us into having lots and lots and lots more of consciously thoughtless hot and steamy sexual encounters with the love of our life. So...

Let's name the third spectrum range of sex, "Soul-sex." It's all about our human connections. How deep can human beings connect?

Soul-sex is created out of either pure lust, or entirely out of the pure passion and love from deep in the bottom of a human soul. Soul-sex happens when lovers' souls fully expose themselves at the exact same time to connect and it happens every time our human soul opens-up and makes love.

When you look into your lover's eyes, does everything in the physical world completely disappear and fade away? Do you stay anchored in our shared concrete scientific reality of all the time? Does a crowded room full of noise ever fade away from you when you are with your lover? Or does our scientific reality sometimes go to the back of our personal brain's stage? And if not…

Are you a Vulcan or an Earthling?

Does the need to be firmly anchored into our shared scientific reality ever leave you whenever you have sex with your lover? If it does, it's more than just an illusion. It's magic. It's one of our soul's biggest, brightest, and best magic tricks. In fact, it's the only real magic humans have.

Involving our cognitive mind and/or, leaving it out, our soul intensifies our orgasms. Our soul connects and we receive our spiritual boons.

"Boon" is a very "verbose" word that means something pleasant or beneficial that is presented as a gift or honor. (I had to look it up.) I should have known what that word meant. But I didn't know what it means. So, I had to search my new pocket dictionary for its meaning and…

Everything beautiful bubbles up from deep inside the core of us. When we have soul-sex, our conscious cognitive thinking mind goes away, along with our entire cognitive grasp of our shared scientific reality. We lose ourselves in our moments. And…

We either have physical sex with no presence of mind (body-sex/biosex), the full or partial presence of a human cognitive mind with or without the focused presence of our soul (mind-sex), or we completely lose both of our minds in the moments of having (soul-sex) and our soul glows afterwards, and for days at a time, sometimes.

We all can go into our personal handy dandy autopilot mode, and make love, and when we do, our souls come into our scientific reality, and humanity receives its boon. Soul-sex is our life's greatest miracle of all. Soul-sex is our lovemaking at its absolute finest.

They say our eyes are windows to a human soul.

So, when was the last time you lost yourself in your lover's twinkling eyes? And when was the last time your lover got lost in your twinkling eyes? Or...

Is it more like looking at a doll's eyes, like looking into shark's eyes, all the time for you? If it is, and what happens here, stays here. And...

When we have soul-sex, every ounce of anything that cognitively attaches us to our cognitive knowledge, and the scientific reality itself, goes away. Everything around us fades away. When lovers simultaneously lose themselves in the moment, when we're alone together in our own little private realities, our soul opens and protrudes deep into the shared scientific reality, and soul-sex just happens.

When we have soul-sex, our cognitive brains let our physical bodies unconsciously move to our human soul's groove and we have thoughtless sex. Soul-sex is the kind of sex that washes our soul into our lover's soul and makes this world turn into a better place to live in. Soul-sex gives all of our human orgasms an all-out boost. And if soul-sex ever happened to you, you are fortunate enough to know exactly what I'm talking about. Sometimes, when people fall in-love, they know what that is, and what all it does for them. And...

If you never experienced soul-sex personally, you can't possibly pretend to know what it is. Sometimes, you just don't know, until you know. You know?

We occasionally lose the conscious cognitive control we are supposed to possess in order to maintain our adult status. And speaking of being adult about things...

The next time you get some of the good stuff, relax. Get into it. Don't be shy. Cognitively let go of our cold hard scientific reality. Lose yourself in those twinkling eyes losing themselves in yours. And then...

We need to turn around and backtrack far enough to set our human record straight...

We can no longer use the terms "having sex" and "making love" interchangeably. If we see the difference, there is a difference, and we have a difference. And...

They cannot mean the same thing to anybody anymore. And now, we can see the three separate ranges in a new spectrum of sex. Mind-sex and soul-sex are "the middle" and "the highest" ends of the human sex spectrum. And somewhere in-between "the lowest" and "the middle" is fucking boring. And now...

I'm taking our having sex out one step further, by adding a brand new in-between that fits very nicely in between having sex and making love, mind-sex.

Body-sex is people just having sex. Soul-sex is us making love. And mind-sex is anything in-between us just merely having sex and completely losing ourselves like we do when we make love. Body-sex is purely biological, purely physical, bio-sex. Mind-sex is half biological and half spiritual, like when we're thinking about it during it. And soul-sex happens when we lose ourselves in our spiritual holy fuck. But...

Soul-sex only happens when our private conscious cognitive mind escapes us enough to expose the raw utmost innermost parts of ourselves. Soul-sex only happens when we lose the shared scientific reality.

We have to be able to reveal our whole inner self, unmask our private/inner selves, to our lovers.

Who is the love of our life?

Soul-sex is what lovers experience when they are lovingly lost in their shared soft reality.

The best beautifully soft exclusively private personal realities we experience happen when we are having soul-sex.

Soul-sex experiences are the absolute best that this life has to offer. Ask anyone who knows. Listen to what they have to say. And tell them that...

Soul-sex can't happen, we can't make love, and we can't get lost in each other's twinkling eyes; if our hearts ain't all up in each other's heads in the first place. And then again...

If our souls ain't into each other in the first place, our sex life probably ain't all it can be.

My dad always told me, "Can't never could do nothing." And...

Sometimes, we don't show our private inner selves, we don't open our hearts, our souls, our truer selves. We don't/can't reveal ourselves to some of us. And...

That goes double for people we ain't into. And that's how we work for the most part. And usually...

Our most intimate moments aren't open to the general public. That would just be way too embarrassing to us. Our most intimate moments are usually kept very private. Some of our private moments pull us off this planet, so to speak. We all leave our physical. And...

Scientifically speaking, our ability to have soul-sex (make love) and have body-sex (biosex) should be more than enough "scientific evidence" to prove that our human souls scientifically exist. And...

If we want to understand humans having sex, we gotta understand us having a soul. If we want to understand us having our soul, we gotta understand how people have sex. And...

When we are in the middle of having sex, and we want to experience soul-sex, we have to feel free enough to reveal our souls. At different times in our life, our souls can open themselves so wide, they overwhelm our human bodies, and we become radiant and glow. If not, go fall in love, and experience what I mean.

"OMG... You're glowing. Did you just get laid?"

When we fall in-love, something inside us makes our eyes twinkle. When we fall in-love, we can experience our soul-sex range. When we can see it, soul-sex happens when we stop having sex, and we make love. Soul-sex is extremely intense and totally uncontrollable. And for soul-sex to happen, we have to be in a place that allows us to follow our heart, go with our gut, defy logic, rhyme, reason, and all that jazz.

I hope you are currently at a point in your life that allows you to follow your heart. Because...

Soul-sex is the best possible tool we can use to get things headed in the right direction and rolling back up/down the right direction of any set of human tracks.

Soul-sex is the highest/greatest sex we have on our human sex spectrum. Our greatest sex can go a long way to pull us out of our worst of relationship slumps. But unfortunately, nobody can describe our greatest spectrum of sex, not even me. My description of soul-sex doesn't even come close. Not yet anyway. I'm working on it. Look at me go. And...

That's way too much talk about us and human sex for now. We have to keep this thing moving along. There's always too much to say and never enough time to talk about it all. Talk. Talk. Talk.

I'm starting to feel like a really big windbag here. But...

There's way too much ground to cover. There's way too much more I gotta say. I gotta keep on keeping on going with all of this. So...

In addition to our mind's dual-consciousnesses (our cognitive

Connecting the Web of Humanity:

conscious mind and our unconscious brain's soul's human mind), our two sub-realities (our soul's individually personal multi-realities and our shared reality), and our threesome of sex spectrum ranges (body-sex, mind-sex, and soul-sex)...

We have two different ways to love a lover. And...

In addition to the two different ways to love our lover...

We have one-bazillion different orgasms to explore.

No...

There is way lots more than just that many orgasms.

We have one-bazillion different orgasms for every star in our shared night sky. There, that's a way better explanation of all our different orgasms. So...

What kind of orgasms have you experienced?

If all of your orgasms belong in the half-ass category, you're missing out on all kinds of good stuff.

"Exploring we will go. Exploring we will go. High-ho the dairy-oh, exploring we will go." And getting a little more serious for our next few moments...

And going back into the two ways to love our lovers...

We can either "love" our lover or be "in-love" with our lover. The difference has to do with openness, honesty, and the unconditional acceptance of each other's souls. She accepts me completely for who I am. I accept her (completely unconditionally) for who she is and her just being herself. At the same time, we have to maintain, and fortify, the emotional connection of our deeper inner self, our soul. I mean...

What have you done for your personal deeper inner self lately? And what are you waiting for? Every day is a new day just for you. Being alive says what? And...

How do we rate a love life? Where the fuck is the scientific human scale for that? And on my sex spectrum of one, two, or three (icy cold, lukewarm, or scorching hot); what kind of sex life would you like to be having? How many different orgasms would you like to be creating? What do you want out of your personal love life? What kind of a sexual relationship do you want? What are you willing to give up to get what you want?

Personally speaking, being in love and getting regular scorching hot soul-sex as often as humans possibly can is the only way to go. And...

It is perfectly natural for perfectly normal people to never experience humanity's two different versions of loving or being in love, and/or humanity's three spectrum ranges of sex, and all the other stuff being human has to offer. After all, colorblind people (mostly men) can't see what the rest of us see. And one-fifth of all women will never experience an orgasm. Nobody is being judged here. And nothing is being said here. Other than...

Most of what we know is based on our past experiences. And unfortunately, nobody reads books anymore. So being able to describe the difference between love, and falling/being in-love, is a total waste of everyone's time.

And describing making love, or being in-love, to people who are still sexual virgins to mind-sex and/or soul-sex, is like trying to describe all of the different orgasms we experienced this morning. We can't describe any taste of our different Earthling soda-pops to our Martians.

When our lover is in-love with us, and we are in-love with our lovers, our sex lives, our orgasms, and our everyday life experiences just keep getting better and better as we go along. We simply ain't got no words for that, yet. But I'm determined to do the best I can.

How do you put all this nonsense into words?

What did my psychic call it? Connecting the Web...

It's the bees' knees.

"Bzzz." And...

This is the heart and soul of where I'm coming from...

I believe our soul plays a major role in our everyday life. When it turns out that my hypothetical crazy new bullshit scientific theory about us having a scientifically unconscious mind's religious/spiritual soul is true and factual, our scientific unconscious mind's religious/spiritual soul will become a major player in all of our close personal relationships. When it turns out that my hypothetical crazy new bullshit pseudo-theory is more than just another empty theory, our scientifically defined unconscious mind/soul ends up playing a major role in the spectrum of our sex life. And when all of that starts to actually happen for you, and everyone around you who know you, and when your soul is open, attracted, and attractive to another person's soul, you're gonna need to learn how to take ahold of the reins on all of your fun stuff.

Turn your lover's desire into wild abandonment? Sure...

No problem.

I will totally get that covered. But first...

"Who do you love?" And then...

"Who's your daddy?" And...

The highest versions of love and sex are accessible to anyone who knows how. Having soul-sex and being in-love are within anyone and everyone's reach. And...

Since I am showing everyone how a human soul exists, and how a soul's existence proves we have our human Creator, our ability to differentiate between having sex and making love further proves that we have a human Creator and...

If we truly believe in what we know, we know our human Creator likes to help those of us who help ourselves. And...

Anytime we want to start having better sex in our private sexual relationships, all we gotta do is...

"There's no place like home. There's no place like home. There's no place like home."

"Click. Click. Click."

The hardest part of turning biosex's body-sex into mind-sex is letting go and opening up. The hardest part of turning humanity's biosex's mind-sex into soul-sex is letting go and opening up. The hardest part of revving up human love into our euphoric states of being in-love is letting go and opening up. The hardest part of turning humans having sex into our each other's private individual lovemaking love monsters is letting go and opening up. Right? After all...

Being human and acting like a human...

What exactly are humans supposed to let go of and open up? Well...

When our human brain lets go of our human scientific reality, our unconscious minds open up, and our human souls take over.

And we can't do any better than being lost in a moment with an open soul.

Do you ever daydream?

I daydream all the time. Why just the other day, I was...

Our minds regularly step off this planet. Daydreams are just one of the many ways our soul shows itself.

Have you ever been lost in a daydream?

Our soul yanks our stone-cold cognition out of our hard-cold cruel scientific reality around us and we go off into our daydreams. When we reveal our soul, our cognitive, rational conscious brain goes out the window and totally offline. Knowledge...

Rationality, and with total reason, all humans escape from time to time. We all physically exist in a constant physical world from which we temporarily escape into our soul's realities. Deep inside our heads, we all have our individual human soul's personal realities or not. And whatever...

And we all have our own individual unconscious mind's human soul realities to escape to. When we reveal more of our personal selves, we open more of our soul to other people, and we temporarily escape from the big bad scary, cold, cruel, boring-ass world around us, when our soul temporarily pulls us out of our human physical world's hard reality, things really start to happen.

Books and movies do more than reach inside us and touch our soul. Books and movies draw our souls out into the whole wide cold cruel scientific world around our physical bodies.

Our souls love to be entertained with a good book or one of those really great movies. The book is always better than that movie. And yet somehow, all of our movies ended up generating bazillions more dollars than our movie's books. What's up with that? That's enough of that shit. This is a new day. My badass mind-blowing book is the new way. "Hey. Hey."

Books, books, books, the more we read; the more we know.

The more we read; the more enriched our lives become.

And upgrading a sex life by involving our human soul cannot be easily explained, or scientifically validated, if a human soul does not exist in our shared scientific world. And I think...

Everything is the way it is, until it ain't like the way it is anymore. And that's the peculiar part, isn't it? It's almost as if...

It was time for human souls to be one of the newest pieces of the big old puzzle we need to scientifically define and understand. I also think...

Our soul's time has come.

Oh sure, we can have sexual intercourse for pleasure, general well-being, reproduction purposes, scientific procedures, as a substitution of eating chocolate, and in front of cameras; but for us to truly walk away with our lover's soul's expression firmly stamped around, and all up inside one side, and down all over the over, and all throughout all of a soul for days at a time, or to effectively leave a human soul's impression all up over (inside and out) of our lover's soul for days at a time, partnering souls need to connect our internal supernatural spiritual entities while we're having sex.

We all have our unlimited human imagination.

Our human soul's limitless number of realities begin just on the other side of our scientifically limited world. And, personally speaking for just us and how much me, myself, and I have my imagination...

We are only limited by our conscious cognitive minds. Our imagination is our soul's playground. The next time you step outside, look up. The sky is our soul's limit.

When we want to leave our soul's hot sweaty love marks on our lover's soul, we'll need to get our physical asses to work on having better sex. Do you ever move your ass when you have sex? Or...

Do we just lie there, with eyes closed, or staring off at our focal point and wait for something to start happening to you? Our eyes are windows. When you look in your windows, what do you see? Are we leaving our soul's scorching sweaty hot out-of-breath orgasmic love marks entrenched and entwined in our lover's soul? And...

How much pleasure are we giving sexually? And...

In the other sexual position, we pleasure-receivers have to be relaxed and free enough to open ourselves up to bear our soul if we want to experience better orgasms.

Sex is sex?

My ass.

Do da. Do da. All our livelong do da days. And...

Some sexual experiences are way lots better than other sexual experiences. And some lovers are way lots better than other lovers. And...

Don't get me wrong, every now and then heavily guarded and shielded battle mode souls deliberately having a good old-fashioned hard-reality sweaty hardcore fuck can be very satisfying, and that in itself, can be a bonding experience, if it is well executed. But...

More often than not, people step in and fuck all of that beautiful shit up. Happens over and over. So...

Whenever you reach over to grab hold of your reins, you gotta drive everything to someplace better for you.

"Cheers likesa beers."

Our sex lives are lots better when we avoid repeating body-sex that comes with the same old predictable why bother effort.

Too much body-sex turns people in-love into fuck buddies. Too much body-sex will tarnish any beautiful relationship. Far too often, too many of us end up settling for the quick physical release of body-sex when (no matter what) we all deserve so much more. So...

The next time you have sex with your next/current lover, grad hold of your sex reins and retain enough of your cognitive ability to be consciously aware of the kind of sex you give and the kind of sex you receive. Focus your mind. Concentrate. Or better yet...

Relax, let go, and open your soul up, and...

Let your human soul give and receive some of the good stuff too. Look into those eyes and lose yourselves in your few shared human moments we have and see what happens. And then, afterward...

When you come back to your senses, when we come back to the world's scientific reality, after you regain your wits, when your cognitive thinking mind brings you back into our shared scientific cold cruel reality, and you land back on planet Earth; think about which one of the three different spectrum ranges of sex you just experienced, and be here, and think about all that.

We all started out not knowing anything about anything. We learn as we go along. It's all part of the Grand Design. What experiences have you learned from?

Are you ever deliberate about what you do sexually? Have you learned anything new since you started learning new things? And then again...

We don't gotta learn anything about anything we don't want to learn something about. And I ain't saying nothing about everything except this...

I sure as hell didn't learn much in my English classes. And...

If you didn't notice anything wrong with the beginning of this book, you might not see anything wrong with the rest of this book. And...

I feel your pain. And...

I know you know I'm right about how I had started all my shit. And one match and one log later...

If we are interested in knowing about expanding our sexual capability, or if you and yours ever become temporarily derailed, we can fix all of that too.

I'll teach you how to become a better lover than you already are. I will help you get you back on track. Are you the sort of person who's willing to try new things? Do you want to instantly become a better lover? It's really simple. It's all very easy. Are you ready?

Are you paying attention?

Good.

Great job.

Keep it up.

And that's all we gotta do.

When we pay attention to what we're doing, our soul automatically participates in whatever it is we do. And then, the next thing we know...

Everything always gets better from there.

Paying attention to what you are doing to your lover's body, or to what your lover is doing to your body, raises the first spectrum range of sex, (human biosex) body-sex, to the second spectrum range of sex, mind-sex. And...

Focusing our attention on what we're doing brings our soul, "our unconscious mind", out into our physical scientifically shared world. Our prehistoric modern-day souls have always been an active participant in our modern-day scientific reality. And...

If we're giving our lover our utmost attention, our soul will always leave love marks all over our lover's soul.

Our souls mark each other's souls when we're having sex. And our souls mark each other's souls when we aren't having sex. Our souls can leave beautiful marks all over our soul's physical bodies or our souls can leave the very deep ugly marks in the minds of some people. And...

If our minds don't wander around when we're having sex, if we're not having sex haphazardly, if our thoughts don't stray from us and ours, and what we're doing, we are already sexually better off than most of us. And we got it going on. And we already know what's what. And...

Human is all we do. And...

Tuesday, November 05, 2002

Science ain't threatened by any brand of religion. Religion is simply unfathomable to a scientific person. There ain't no scientific proof of a Creator. Science can see inside our bodies. Science can see way out into space. Science ain't never seen human souls yet. So...

Our human Creator doesn't exist in our scientific world. But I'm here today to try to say something to our entire scientifically leaning community:

The scientific proof of our human Creator is buried somewhere deep inside my brand-new hypothetical humans having a soul theory. And...

Just four hundred years ago, in Galileo's time, strict religious leaders ruled all their day's people.

A long time ago, in the way back day, of when, religious leaders couldn't handle their day's scientific truth. And today, strict scientific leaders rule our world's way of thinking. And today, brilliant researchers (the world over) can't handle our today's truth. The truth about our today is this...

In 2002, over ninety percent of our world's human population is Agnostic and/or somehow religious. And less than ten percent of us are not religious at all.

Over ninety percent of us desperately need our scientific researchers (the scientists out there) to recognize (and legitimize) our (human) souls as what we are primarily made of.

And putting our exact same shoes on our other feet...

Our 2002 scientific researchers, the world over, pretend to be void of all emotion in their pursuit of our purest and cleanest scientific knowledge.

Now honestly, ask yourselves, how will we ever see our soul, if we omit the most crucial piece of solid evidence? This ain't America's "Justice" Department.

It's supposed to be only for Science. And...

Science is only supposed to be the endless search for every possible human answer. And when it comes to answering our scientific fact-finding questions, our fact-founded scientifically proven "human emotions" are being haphazardly discarded scientifically.

Human emotion is just one of many stone-cold pieces of hard evidence that turns our human soul into just another one of our ordinary every day hard-core scientific facts. And...

Intentionally ignoring all of the delicacies, all of the intricacies, all of the complexities, of all the different ways humans express themselves, willfully ignores the human soul's scientific contribution, apparition, and manifestation in/from us. And...

If our scientists recognized and legitimized our souls, we'd have a great big pile of unexplained phenomena becomes scientifically explained rather easily. For instance...

All our lives would be a lot better if we followed our "hearts" a little more often than we do.

My heart tells me to do one thing and then my head tells me to do the opposite thing. And my soul's intellect tells my cognitive intellect to go fuck itself and...

The internal wrestling match between our head and our heart is eternal, or until death, do we part, whatever whichever way comes first. Sometimes our hearts overpower our heads.

The human word for "heart" has another dual meaning.

We all have a gooey mess of an emotional heart in our heads. We all also have a beating blob of muscle in our chests that pumps our blood types throughout our different human bodies. And...

Our head's heart is our emotional heart, our unconscious/subconscious mind, our religious and/or spiritual soul's part of our minds. Or is it the other way around? I'm confused. And either whatever whichever way ...

We have very little conscious cognitive control over our soul's uncontrollable deep emotional stuff. But when we become more educated about the way our world works around us, we start to gain more conscious control over how everything affects us. And when it comes to trying to turn off our soul's emotions, we can't. All we can do is only sort of power them down.

Our emotions come from our emotional heart, our soul.

"I love my Baby - heart and soul. I can't help myself."

Wednesday, November 06, 2002

Emptying my mind with ink on paper allows me to think about different things. Today, I've been thinking...

I would love to also be the first person to ever say our emotional heart has been in each of all of our religious/spiritual human soul's disguises all along. And from this day forward, our heart, our soul, and our unconscious/subconscious mind, all three, mean the exact same thing. In other words...

Heart and soul just became each other's redundant words. Saying heart and soul is saying the exact same word twice. Saying heart and soul is just total redundancy.

We all have redundant thoughts all the time. I just write about whatever it is I've been thinking about that day. And today, it's been...

The battle between our head and heart is actually the battle between our conscious mind and our unconscious mind, our evolving spiritual creative unpredictable emotional imaginative mind and our evolving highly analytical rational-thinking cognitive mind, our soul's intelligence and our learned thinking intelligence, the unreasonable and the reasonable within, outside ourselves. And speaking of all of us having a little something-something inside each of us...

Would I be totally unreasonable if I said, I do not believe the cure for all depressions come from a pill? Pills can somehow correct the abnormalities that occur in the brain of a medically diagnosed depressed person, but they can't offer any relief for any injustice and/or illness that is giving our soul a hard time.

Depression is an extremely loud conversation between our conscious mind and our unconscious mind. Depression is often played out in the deafening silence of depressed people. When a person is depressed, the conversations in their head become extremely loud, and yet, depressed people hardly say a word. Why is that? "I don't know."

Depressed people also sigh a lot. Why is that? Well...

Sighs are another human threesome.

Some sighs are from a lack of oxygen, just people catching their breath. Some sighs are from our relief, as in, a *sigh* of our relief. And frequent sighs are the desperate bloodcurdling screams of a drowning soul. Our souls know another soul as much as we know the people we know. A conversation is just a conversation away. And...

Depressed people avoid having any form of honest and open people conversations. Depressed people's souls hide from other souls. A depressed person's soul even hides itself away from its closest friends. And forget about opening up itself to our closest family. And...

I'm thinking pills can't fix the kind of depression that's caused by loneliness, neglect, abuse, meanness, cruelty, and any other form of our soul's oppression. However, depression pills can correct the physical abnormality that occurs naturally inside our brains.

Pharmaceutical researchers the world over, overcame an incredibly long way, when they invented a medicine that disrupts the physical changes in our brains that happen during our states of depression. They have medicine that makes our depressed brains work better, but in some cases, doesn't the cause of depression still need to be worked on and/or corrected?

I'm not taking anything away from any pharmaceutical pill. Many different pills greatly help many different types of clinically diagnosed depression. And if you think you might be depressed, please go to your doctor to find out. Depression is dangerous. Don't fuck around with that shit. Look...

All I'm saying is...

Taking pills to cure our soul's ailments is like treating a runny nose to cure a cold. And besides that…

All of the medical advances in the world will never be able to heal our wounded souls. It's like that song The Mills Bros sang…

"Money can't buy us happiness when we're growing old. We gotta remember that the world still is the same, and we'll never change it."

It's late. I'm tired. And…

"As long as the stars shine above, we're nobody till somebody loves us. So, go out, and find somebody to love."

I gotta go.

We got houses to clean tomorrow. So…

Goodnight.

Thursday, November 07, 2002

Over the past couple of days, I've been mindlessly cleaning my houses and doing some serious thinking about our big picture. It's time to grab our safety goggles, our thinking caps, and our white lab coats again.

"Safety First."

Is everyone all geared up and ready to proceed? Good. I have a little-tiny itty-bitty question for all you hardcore scientists out there. Beyond our galaxy, beyond every ounce of matter, and every ounce of the dark matter floating around in our rapidly expanding space, and beyond the Big Bang that got this whole thing off and running, where did the great big rapidly expanding empty vacuum of space come from?

Our great rapidly expanding big vacuum of space holds everything our astronomers can see with their big badass heavy-duty multimillion-dollar bionic-satellite telescopes. The rapidly expanding celestial vacuum that's enveloping everything is measurable and came preloaded with our finite scientific rules and boundaries. And if it's measurable and came preloaded with our scientific rules and boundaries, that automatically makes our whole thing become a scientific entity. Right? Is our entire Universe the chicken or the egg? It's either the whole chicken or that chicken's scrambled eggs. Which one is it? And...

A light-year is the distance light travels through space in a year. A light-year is approximately 5.878 trillion miles long. And (so the fuck) what? Right?

Look, I'm starting to get us way off track. So, we need to stop, right now, and back up from here. We need to turn around and head back that way. So here we go...

I'm looking at our biggest picture we have available. And much like Copernicus, Galileo, Bruno, and many other people, were wreaking havoc on our religious community's wave of way back when, I can't help but feel that I'm wreaking havoc on our scientific community's wave of today by thinking that we still haven't figured out all the details of our Cosmos.

In order for us to be here together right now, I believe everything happened for a reason, which makes me ask...

"Why are you reading this instead of doing something else way more important?" Which makes me further ask...

"How did our humanity end up existing here?"

Our great big empty vacuum of space had to have been manufactured into our existence. Something doesn't come from nothing. All the framework must have existed before all this could start where it did. After all...

Which came first... ...our Earthling plants and animals or Earth? ...the Big Bang or our place where our Big Bang happened? ...our How and Whatever happened or our place of where the How and Whatever happened, happened? And my personal thinking is...

Our soul's Creator is our Entity that created the scientific framework inside our rapidly expanding vacuum that we call space, created our human souls, and...

Our soul's Creator also created all the mathematics of all the scientific boundaries and physical limits of everything contained within our physical environment.

And we have barely scratched the surface of what everyone should have already known a long time ago. And everything has to come from something. And long before anybody can go...

"Then, where did our soul's Creator come from?"

Let's just simply take this one step at a time.

Shall we?

We have to crawl before we walk.

We have to walk before we run.

We can only go safely up or down our ladders one-rung at a time.

And if you don't like those rules, then take them up with OSHA. And there you go.

Figuring out what's what is like figuring out our molecules first, and then, figuring out their DNA. It's like figuring out our Solar System first, and then, figuring out our rest of the Universe. It's like figuring out everything we can about our brand-new human soul before we go around trying to figure out everything there is to know about our soul's Creator.

The framework for time and space had to exist before the Big Bang could happen. Or the framework of time and space was Big Banged into Cosmos's threesome together. And any whichever whatever way we want to put it...

Our soul's Creator physically created our universe's physically limited scientific framework. Then our soul's Creator had to have previously created all the necessary ingredients and essential building blocks it took to Big Bang the planets, plants, animals, our bodies, our Freud's two minds, and all of that shit growing in the back of our science labs, into existence. Close the books.

"I win. Where's my money? Who do I gotta talk to?"

If you're a serious hardcore scientific researcher, you're probably still not totally sold on the intrinsic value of our souls. After all...

Scientifically speaking, we are truly nothing more than just some highly evolved species of one of Earth's other animals, which also makes me want to ask...

"Is sex really just the same as eating chocolate?"

"Honestly?"

Lose a few moments of time being lost in the twinkling eyes of the loving human souls around you, be in the moment of having a baby, or fuck your lover like you mean it, and then catch your breath, come back down to Earth, and scientifically tell me what you didn't feel. Tell me what ain't real. Tell me our vibrant emotions of a strong, healthy relationship have no intrinsic human value. And...

If we detach ourselves from all the emotional aspects humanity has to offer, we detach ourselves from our human soul, our real self, our truer self, and we gain the ability to write good nonfiction books well.

Sometimes, our cognitive mind square can reason our heart square right out of our scientific reality.

Ain't human freewill a bitch?

"Sometimes" And...

The latest evolutionary upgrade on our human ancestors ripped their tiny little pre-historic primitive brains into our today's more modern two bigger pieces. Somewhere back down the line in our human history, our human ancestor's primitive brains evolved. And now, today, here in the here and now, our heart says one thing, and our head says another.

My soul loves to smoke. My soul takes advantage of my soul's distractions. I'll reach over, grab a smoke, and light up without ever consciously knowing what I'm doing. When I'm real busy, my soul can smoke a half a pack before I even notice what I'm doing.

My soul harbors my emotions, memories, vices, and habits.

"My soul is hopelessly addicted to its music."

Our soul makes us do the things we do when we don't even know we're doing what we are doing at the time.

Our old habits are hard to break. Why is it we can't help but do some of the things we do?

Have you ever gone from place to place and not know how you got there? Our soul can lead us from place to place without our awareness of consciously knowing how we ended up there. And speaking of going somewhere...

What brings you here to me? What's new with you? What's going on? Do you feel whole? Or are you broken? What breaks when we get a broken heart? Where does our emotional pain hurt?

When our creative soul and our cognitive thinking mind aren't seeing each other eye to eye, we end up with internal conflict. And when we're internally conflicted, we can't see any meaning in anything, and our life is guaranteed to be void of something.

It may just be the great big giant smart-ass in me, but they say love makes our world go around. It's late. I gotta get some sleep. We have to get up early in the morning to clean some more houses.

Why?

That's what we do. We're professional cleaning people. And we're damn good at it too. So, goodnight.

Sunday, November 17, 2002

I'm not debating whether souls exist. In certain parts of my brain, mine does. And everyone has our Creator's gift of cognitively conscious freewill to believe whatever s/he wants to believe or not believe.

In America, we're allowed to talk about anything we choose. As a good solid USA citizen, that's all I'm doing with all of my knee-deep shit. Lots of Americans have fought, and some have even died, to preserve my right to write my shit my way.

Most Americans believe in monotheism. (Meaning, most of us believe in one Creator, and that same majority do not believe in multiple Creators.)

E Pluribus Unum...

"In God We Trust" is stamped on our cold hard American cash. In the middle of our last century, America started stamping God all over our money and into our American lives. It was a very different time back way back when. But that was then. And this is now. And...

Today, and going forward, there will always be people who will never believe in us having a soul or our soul's Creator. And personally, I hope they haven't wasted their time and/or money on my nonsense.

I'm not looking to get into any kind of argument over anything that can be personal as this particular topic is for some people.

All I'm saying is, I define any right and true Religion as any group of people who organize to acknowledge their peaceful monotheism. Anything and everything can always and forever be dealt with passively and peacefully. World peace begins with us, and billions of people like us. Where there's the will, there always is a diplomatic way. And besides all that...

People with wallets, pockets, and purses, packed full of American money, who don't believe we have a Creator, have a currency that is totally worthless. USA money specifically says that if you don't believe in our universal Creator, you are not allowed to use our United States of America's currency for anything ever. And strictly speaking, from my control freak history…

If you're someone who believes our soul has a Creator, then you have the right to do so. If you're someone who doesn't believe our soul has a Creator, that's your right to do so, too. And if you are someone who already believes in our soul's Creator, and you don't want to read any more of my nonsense, you're right. And please quit reading this shit. And if you're a person who believes in our soul's Creator, and you think my past few years of blood, sweat, and tears, ain't a load of crap; please stay tuned. I have tons of other shit I want to write about. I'm sure I will write something you won't like. And then again…

Who knows?

You might end up liking everything I write.

It's good to have opinions.

Opinions give our souls human depth. And…

I do not take my freedom to openly express myself lightly. Obviously. And I think I might have already proven that. And…

It's been a long day. So…

Goodnight.

II: December 2002

Monday, December 16, 2002

Every single solitary day of 2002, every place on Earth, 240-million different people had sex. Durex (the condom maker) is saying each of us will have more than 3000 sexual experiences in our lifetimes, which makes me want to ask...

"How many human orgasms is that?" And...

"What is human sex exactly?" I mean...

With the three different ranges of our human sex spectrum covered, how do we define sex?

"What makes sex, sex?"

In order for us to travel down this set of unexplored tracks, we need to give any sexual experience its own prim and proper definition.

Uh...

Let's see. Uh...

Nothing comes to mind.

Wait a minute. I take that back. I just got an idea.

And then, I looked up "sex" in my thirty-year-old-big-bad-red dictionary. My thirty-year-old-big-bad-red dictionary defines "sex" as gender classification and says to see "intercourse". So...

I had to look up "intercourse". And my thirty-year-old-big-bad-red dictionary defines "intercourse" as communication and says to see "coitus". So, I popped in one of my adult DVDs and...

No, I'm just yanking your chain.

"Coitus" is defined in my thirty-year-old-big-bad-red dictionary as sexual intercourse (gender communication) between two human beings.

Here we are, in the 21st Century, and that's the best we can do? And if it is...

Can a threesome have coitus? And either whichever whatever way...

We still have no scientific definition of sex. I think a proper scientific definition of sex is critical to our development and evolution as a people. So, I'm gonna take a poke at it. Hang on to your wigs and keys. Here we go...

What makes sex, Sex?

Sex is whatever happens when lovers share with each other sexually. And sex is anything that will get you in trouble with your lover. And sex is also anything that will get your lover in trouble with you.

Because running around outside of our relationship's boundaries will end up robbing us and ours from being able to have, and/or continue to hold on to, a righteous relationship. And whether we get caught, we always get robbed of everything we're robbing our lover's soul from experiencing with us.

There. How's that? How'd I do?

It's far better to err on the side of caution, wouldn't you say? It's always a lot better for everyone involved when we all stay within the confines of our sexual relationships. And that creates the need

Connecting the Web of Humanity:

for a discussion about what our sexual boundaries are. Speaking of needing to talk about something important...

Any kind of non-consenting physical contact with any part of another person's body is a criminal act against decent humanity. And having consensual physical contact with another person's body is another matter altogether.

Some of us like to reach out and touch, grab, or strike, other people. Sometimes, we don't like to be touched, grabbed, or struck. Sometimes, we do. By the rules...

We need our written rules, and clearly-written permission, every single time we play with each other's bodies. So...

"How often do you play with your lover's naked body?"

The rules of play depend entirely on each person. Depending on the permission you have (or don't have) in your primary sexual relationship, how much time do you actually spend doing things to each other's bodies?

Do you ever play with each other's bodies? Did your initial constant need of spending time tending to each other fade away? Are we in the middle of our constant need of spending our time focused on each other together? Or are we all alone? If we are...

Our physical human bodies are our very own personal sensory human vehicles. And bodies being sensory vehicles...

Our souls, and our cognitive minds, are working for our brains, individually, and at the same time. It's quite the mental workload. And speaking of a becoming a complete mental load...

I think as a relationship matures, people are more apt to simply go through the familiar motions of their familiar sex. Their familiar sex with their familiar partner becomes more and more familiar. And familiar sex gives room for mindlessness to move in.

Familiar sex always seems to lose its sharpened edge when our soul stops leaving our love marks on our lover's souls.

We all eventually stop honing the edges of our sex life. We all fall out of being in-love and slowly slip and slide into our version of experiencing sex ruts. And if we are ever in a relationship long enough to know what a sex rut is, you know. And if not, hang on, and you'll eventually know what one is. And then again, maybe not, ever hear about the two people who fell head over heels madly in love?

Everything happens by Design. And...

Everything happens for a reason. And...

If everything was beautiful all the time, our lives would be turned into an inescapable flat line. And if everything sucked all the time, we all get a different flat line. Stop. And start trying your next new thing. Some changes can be surprisingly good to us. And...

Without life's peaks and valleys, our life would become an inescapable flat line, and we would have to live our entire existence more like all the other animals live in their existences. Life is and...

We all have a cognitive free will to change the way we live. We get free will from our cognition. And sometimes, we gotta cut straight through the bullshit. So, when you fall into your next sex rut (and you will), you might want a little help getting back to where the two of you were before. And I have to say to that, that some of the sex experts currently out there are totally full of shit on a couple of things they put out there.

First...

Affairs won't help any of our ailing relationships. Every learned relationship ecologist knows that a hot little evening of pure unadulterated lust with a different lover can poke a rather large hole in your primary relationship's ozone layer. Is your primary relationship ozone-free? Are you in an open relationship? Is your sexual relationship ozone-free?

Are you allowed to fuck anyone you want? If you're spinning a tangled web of deceit by fucking your other lovers without your primary lover's participation, written permission, and/or blessing; you're playing with your fire. But you already know that, don't you?

And now, the other thing... (The second thing...)

Some of our sex experts ("sexperts") currently say...

"Whenever people have sex, it is part human nature, and perfectly natural, for us to fantasize about having sex with other people." And I'm just saying...

If we fantasize about having sex with other people while we're in the middle of having sex with our lover, our souls are not exactly in tune with each other (not resonating with each other) in that private moment.

Whenever you and your lover are alone together, and someone ain't there, nobody is home. And then, we each experience our bio-sex/body-sex all alone.

When we do whatever it is we do, we need to focus our attention on whatever it is we're doing. Focusing our attention on something makes our soul show up and pop out of our physical bodies. Look around. What are your eyes searching for? Are you ever lost in your lover's eyes? And if you are not present in the moment with your lover, or lost in the moment of making love, when you're in the middle of just having sex, your lover is...

Tuesday, December 17, 2002

And then...

The next thing we know, we wake up, yesterday is gone, and whatever we missed out on experiencing with our lovers is totally gone, just like last night, and it's tomorrow.

"See?" And the next day is here and...

Sometimes we need our soul and our lover's soul to be lost in the same shared moments together. And whenever our soul and our lover's soul share some precious moments together, our reins drive us to a better place.

And all of this shit makes total sense to me. And I know I'm right because I'm right.

Sometimes, when we learn some of our biggest shit, we start to experience our biggest changes. It's like I was saying earlier. Some of our changes are good and some of our changes ain't no good at all. And sometimes, we just don't know, until we know.

Before yesterday, I didn't write anything for a solid month. It feels good to be back. Are you tracking all my writing dates? Did you notice when I wrote what?

Did you miss me?

A lot of shit happened to me since I started writing this nonsense. It's amazing how much shit changes. It's amazing how many people adapt to change. And speaking of totally changing things on everyone...

It's that time of year. And...

Our customers keep us busy on the weekdays and our family keeps us busy on the weekends. And on top of all that, my mind always goes into vapor lock every time I send my shit out, like I am in vapor lock mode right now.

Ignoring big trade's rules, I skipped the query letter and sent the first few pages of this manuscript to an agency in New York. That was two weeks ago. I'm anxious. I'm bouncing in and out of all my deep-down emotions. I'm at my wits end. I can't relax. And it's only been two weeks. I still got four to six more weeks to wait before I can realistically expect to get a response back.

It's a shitty existence. But I don't have much of a choice. Please take my advice. Don't ever try this from home.

Writing your first manuscript and being a nobody wannabe big trade author ain't worth it. Look at me right now. If you could see me right now, you'd say I look like a train wreck. And what else can I do? When the stakes are too high to walk away from the table, all I can do is keep playing. The wait a nobody wannabe big trade author has to endure is intellectually and emotionally agonizing. But what more can one do?

I just have to be patient and wait.

This shit will happen eventually. And...

Saturday, December 21, 2002

Sometimes the truth comes along and slaps me in the head so hard; it hurts. Most times I can see it coming. And sometimes; I don't. I am a "wize" man. I always felt they cast me wrong when they picked me to be one of the shepherds in my public elementary school's Christmas plays. I wanted to be a "wize" man. I thought I was a "wize" man way back then.

The three "wize" men got to wear the coolest costumes on the stage of my "cafa-gym-atorium".

And I know "wize" is actually spelled wise, but this is something only a book-smart person gives much of a shit about. I'm not a very book-smart kind of person.

There are many different kinds of education. There are many different kinds of Gurus. For instance...

Maturity is the ability to accept the new _____. It's a fill-in-the-blank. (And don't limit yourself.)

I just keep putting my ever-changing stinky crap out here. You may or may not have purchased this work of art, but are you buying into my phony-bologna straight-up truth crap? The book industry people want to see all the facts, Jack. "Wize" people just need to read enough to see our truths. I think I really needed to write this book. For me, right now, it's like that, and...

When was the last time you made your lover's sex organs salivate? I'm not talking being horny like, "It would sure be nice to get laid."

I'm talking horny like drip, drip, drippy wet and/or fully erect. A women's clitoris gets erect like our dicks get fully engorged. And…

When we become super-horny, our sex organs salivate for sex. Our genitals salivate for sex like our mouths salivate for food. Drip. It's our job to make our lover and our lover's genitalia salivate for us. Drip. Drip. It's our lover's job to make us and our genitalia salivate for them. Drip. Drip. Drip.

We get what we give. We give what we get. What comes around goes around. What goes around comes around. If we want to receive some of our lover's good stuff, we have to make our lovers start/continue leaking, like lovers should.

Drippy wet yet? If not, and you have a shitty sex life, fix it.

When it comes to sex, our cures are easy.

If you don't know how to approach your lucky lover, you're both fucking strangers. We're constantly fucking changing. We're slowly evolving all the fucking time. That's the way we were *designed*: to fuck and make do. Life is a constant fucking change. Today is a totally new day. Reintroduce yourself, and who knows? You might get lucky.

I'm one lucky some-bitch. I got a girl who really loves me. We're perfect for each other. And when we're together, we don't pretend to be the people we're not. And when we're alone, we don't make shit up. We don't have the plastic love life. We don't have a shabby sex life either. We fully accept each other in every way imaginable. And we don't keep big dirty personal secrets from each other. As couples go, I think it makes us a little bit better off than most. We're in each other's veins so deep we couldn't think of living without each other. We wouldn't want to. We do life together

Connecting the Web of Humanity:

24/7, $5^1/_2$+ years, counting from today and since 12-31-1997, if you want to count them up for your todays. We rock.

And the two shall become one. It ain't for everyone, but it totally works for the love of my life and me. We are each other's "bestest" friends.

I'm really shy. I say I'm really shy but look at me in here. I'm not about to open my soul to just anyone. When my soul is closed off, I'm usually very standoffish. I don't do chitchat or small talk very well. I feel like I'm awkward to be around, and, that makes me become and feel nervous to be around people. When I get nervous, my imagination shuts down, so...

When I go out and about, I'm quiet. I don't ever say too much of anything. I don't reveal my truer inner self. There are a few exceptions. Those who really knew me know me.

Here in America, we keep our souls closed off in our own unique American ways. There's a lot of safety inside individual isolation. We walk around constantly glancing at one another, never saying much of anything at all because most of us are just stubborn little nervous closed up cranky ass irrevocably damaged irritable souls. And if not...

Why do we spew hatred and run amuck wherever we go? Why are we all monsters on the inside? Why?

Why are peace pipes illegal? Toking on an old wooden peace pipe worked miracles in this land's past.

"Miracles." And speaking of being miraculous...

I think our Americans are ready for a brand-new kind of superhero. David Letterman was an American television superhero. Dave is an "inflectionist" extraordinaire. I want to be an American superhero too. Does a market exist for a new whiney superhero?

Gosh, I hope so.

I don't get how our ancient ancestors survived their climates. I don't get how in the fuck our homeless culture survives out in our currently changing climate.

I can't step out into a Mid-West winter without complaining about the cold. It gets colder than shit in the Mid-West. And the Mid-West only has two seasons, winter and road construction. But seriously...

I was born, and started out living my life, in the Texas panhandle. It's a place that's so flat; you can watch your dog run away, day after day after day, three days straight. But seriously...

I spent my high school days, and most of my young adult life, down in all the small towns between Fort Worth and Waco, where the summer sun gets so hot; it can kill you dead. And that's some serious shit. I complained all the time. It's too hot...

It's too cold...

Peas porridge in the pot nine days old.

I spent most of my life being handed two right ears. I'm usually very polite about taking them. Then I turn around, roll my eyes, and think to myself, it figures.

Monday, December 23, 2002

Shit! They rejected me.

Just in time for this Christmas. Here I go. Perfect timing on their part, with the two days' notice. And...

Shit. Shit. Shit. They rejected this nonsense.

Can you believe this shit? This fucking fucked-up job really fucking sucks sometimes.

"FUCK."

Oh well, going back into my lab, and looking at the upside, this one came back a lot sooner than I expected. Every time I get rejected, I go back and rework all this shit. I figure writing is like being an inventor of the next newest big bad thing. And...

We all gotta start from scratch of the next new thing. And...

I'm just making all this shit up as I go.

And with this shit, there's always gonna be some room for improvement, especially since I'm not a very book-smart kind of guy to begin with. But I think I have great potential. What do you think? How am I doing so far? And can you believe any of this nonsense? And they keep saying no to me, no to this, and no to...

They keep rejecting the sapling of the tree you're reading. Cut this whole fucking thing down and count its growth rings. The shit they rejected back then slowly evolved into the shit I'll eventually get published. Until then, I'm constantly reworking this shit. That's what I do. Artwork is...

Nobody saw this shit coming, nobody except for my psychic, and some up-close personal people in my life I might have told what my psychic said I'd end up doing.

First and foremost, authors have to own their craft. By the current industry standards, I shouldn't even be allowed to touch my keyboard. I'm not writing my shit the way big trade wants author's shit to be written. I am not scholarly. Big trade ain't busy looking for this or me. And yet, here I am.

What the fuck else can I do?

I have to keep going.

I can't just quit and go home. I am home. And I certainly can't quit. The stink I sprinkled all over this shit is way too strong to walk away from or try to disown now. I'm in way too deep.

I own some seriously stinky shit that needs to be said. I own stuff nobody ever said or read before. I gotta keep going. I'll get there someday. I just know I will. I can feel it deep inside my bones. It'll happen when it's supposed to happen. Everything happens for a reason. It is what it is. And we can't rush the forces of nature. Speaking of owning things...

I gotta quit working on my shit right now. We're busybusybusy@playtime(dot)now and...

When the roles of mom and dad go away, my Baby and I come out and play. I gotta go.

Wink, wink... Nod, nod...

Friday, December 27, 2002

Making a person feel special on a deep personal level is a key that unlocks and opens a person's soul. You have to reach out and touch the heart. Does your soul ever protrude into your scientific reality?

My Baby tells me I have beautiful hands. She likes my long square fingers. She said, "They are pretty. Have you ever noticed?" And this may sound like one of those infomercials on our late-night television, but it snot. Digging around a little deeper into the rest of your life...

How's your most personal relationship? How are your other close relationships? Are you tight with the people who really know you and love you anyway? Are you close? Are you distant? Are you angry? Pissed off? Upset? Up a shit creek? Are you having problems or difficulty with someone who matters to you? Do you have relationship issues that make your life maddening? Are you in a relationship where you live your life avoiding your special little certain someone? Do you have a special little certain someone in your life? Do you want a special someone in your life? I understand if you don't. Nobody is being judged here. And...

Do you lie awake, night after night, watching sleeping pill commercials, and wonder whom your soul should and shouldn't avoid? Then call me. What are you waiting for? Pick up the phone and call me. Have your credit card ready. Our operators are reclaiming new spaces and reclining all over the place around here.

"Here I sit all brokenhearted. Thought I'd shit, but I only farted." Don't call me.

I never answer my phones.

When my information comes in, I sometimes get it. And sometimes, I don't.

Take the big "O." We have bazillions and bazillions of different orgasms to discover and explore. Have you ever spent any of your time playing with your orgasms? How far can your orgasms stretch? Orgasms don't stretch. Oh, yeah? Are you sure about that? And...

Have you ever spent any of your time trying to stretch your orgasms out? If you have, you will probably begin to always have stretched-out orgasms. And...

If you are a woman, and you're working on stretching out your orgasms, it can be scary, unless there is someone there who's got you, someone to have you in the moment. The lucky ones of us know what I mean. Sometimes, a woman's orgasms can get so intense; they have to shut them down. Sometimes, the intensity gets so far off the charts; a woman can't take it. But...

If you were to know that a certain special someone has you in that moment of your orgasm's intensity, you wouldn't have to shut any of your orgasms down, and you'd know what is waiting for you on the other side of your stretched-out orgasm(s).

How big, bad, and hard can your orgasms get? Who knows? And if you don't know what your orgasms are capable of, how do you know what your body is capable of? Do you know what your lover's orgasms are capable of? Do you care? I mean...

What the hell has that bitch and/or son-of-a-bitch done for you lately anyway? Same shoe, other foot...

What have you done to earn your own little private piece of

sweet release? We need to think about the role we play in stopping things from happening the way we say we want them to happen. Sometimes we just don't know, until we know. And that's exactly what I'm talking about.

Do you care about your personal sexual satisfaction? Do you care about your lover's personal sexual satisfaction? Do you feel important to your personal lover? Is your personal lover important to you? Then, "Why can't we be friends?"

How does your lover feel about you? Look at yourself. Not through your eyes, step into your lover's eyes and take a good hard look at your soul. Then ask yourself...

"What the fuck is your problem?"

When you step into your lover's eyes, what do you see? When my soul looks around inside different people's heads, I sometimes see beautiful souls living a lovely little peaceful life, one that's full of passion and love, and sometimes I see beautiful souls missing the fucking boat. And I probably could say something to them, but it's not my place, and everything is happening for a reason.

When was the last time your genitals hurt from having too much sex? Have they ever? Are they hurting right now? If they are, "Cheers to you and yours!" And if it's been a long time since your genitals hurt from too much sex, that's totally whacked. And I am here to help you change that. And together, we're gonna reach out around us, and save a whole lot of souls. But then again, that's still totally your call. You have our cognitive knowledge's gift of human freewill. You have a freed spirit. You are on your own. And you have our cognitive ability to think/believe whatever you want to think. And you can do whatever it is you fucking want to do.

The cage around the core of humanity's unconscious mind was opened when our soul received our Creator's gift of our conscious cognitive mind. That...

And our conscious cognitive mind is what's giving us our never-ending thirst for further scientific knowledge thing.

Imagination is our human exclusive. Without the cognitive awareness of an imagination, we would all be more like they are. And speaking of the way they are...

Ants are always gonna act like ants. Tigers are always gonna act like tigers. Yaks are always gonna act like yaks. Polar bears are always gonna act like polar bears. Monkeys are always gonna act like monkeys. And dinosaurs will always just be dinosaurs.

The freewill that comes with our conscious awareness of our Creator's gift of a thinking cognitive was only given to humanity. No other Earthly species has the freedom to choose not to be themselves. Out of all the creatures on Earth, we are the only Earthly creature that can opt out on being and/or acting human.

III: January 2003

Wednesday, January 01, 2003

Happy New Year!

Love brings our souls together and hate pushes our souls apart. Anger and fear are building walls around your soul that turn you into Fort You.

We know the souls our soul bonds with really well. That's the way our souls work. We know the people we know. We see what people's souls all are about, and we know. They know Fort You like you know Fort Them.

As for all the other people on this planet, we don't know, my grandma always said, "You'll always get what you give." Have you heard, "We reap what we sow?" Have you ever put it to the test? Next time you go out and about, see what a few kind words do for you. See what a few unkind words do to you and yours. Our souls reflect human emotion, like our mirrors reflect light. And just like that...

We're done.

Thank you for your time.

"The end."

Doing business as... (Dba...)

Dickheads, bitches, and assholes will usually get back whatever it is they dish out. Peaceful passive people usually get back whatever it is they dish out. Our soul bounces our emotions off each other souls, like light bounces off mirrors. We all live in a dog eat dog world and...

If our top left square is in synch with our bottom right square, if our soul's unconscious mind is in synch with our conscious/cognitive mind, both of our reality squares are probably going through an easy-breezy smooth spot in our lives right now.

Life is the way it is, until things change.

If our soul's unconscious mind and our conscious/cognitive mind aren't seeing each other eye-to-eye, if our conscious cognitive scientific reality is not in synch with our soul's Divine Plan, both of our reality squares are probably in turmoil.

Is your life totally fucked-up right now? Are you easily aggravated by every little thing you see? Are you short-tempered more than usual? Are you frustrated more than usual? Do you need to talk to someone? Do you need to share whatever is in your soul with someone? And speaking of...

Is your soul in synch with your lover's soul? Is your lover's soul in synch with your soul? If your souls are in sync with each other, all should be "righty-tighty" in your relationship.

And when your squares and your lover's squares are fighting, your sex life probably ain't all that it can be. And...

When you and your lover start fighting like dog eat dog, then please stop, and stop doing that kind of shit to each other for a little while. And we all gotta do what we can to get everybody to calm down and talk about our things.

I know I probably can't. And I also know that...

When everything goes good in our shared scientific reality,

things go good in our personal realities. And when everything is going good in our personal realities, things go good in the scientific reality. And when everything goes bad in the scientific reality, things go bad in our personal realities. And when everything is going bad in our personal realities, things go bad in our scientific reality. And speaking of "How are things?" ...

How are things in your sex life? And...

How big of a role does our soul play in the lives of the loved ones around us? And how can we successfully replicate any of this shit in the back of our science labs? And honestly...

If we could figure out a way to replicate all this shit in the back of our science labs, would everyone in every science class believe our results? I don't think so. But...

I do think, 'Our primitive life's force was preprogrammed to love and support our loved ones.'

Was it not?

If our soul and our conscious cognitive mind, aren't synchronized, then we, the person I am and the person you are, Fort Me, Fort You, the whole us, and nothing but us, are probably all fucked-up on the inside. And your Fort You is probably taking a serious pounding by you internally, like mine is with me. And when we're all fucked-up on the inside, we can't do a damn thing to help people out when the inside of them gets all fucked-up too. When everything gets fucked-up for us, we can't do any good for anyone around us. From time to time, we all get stuck in our unpleasant world of negativity. A world of negativity ain't got nothing but negatives.

And either whatever whichever way things are going for you right now, we can't give away whatever we momentarily ain't got. Whenever we are called upon to give away our extra positivity to the close-knit souls around us, we have to have extra positives to give away.

We can't help people inflate themselves when we're all deflated and fucked-up deep inside ourselves. When everything gets fucked-up for us, we get fucked-up, and some of us turn into a serious fucked-up pain in the ass to be around. We can all name names. But, let snot.

And our good news is every human condition being only temporary. Everything and everyone always changes. And...

"So do we." If not, watch and see. And...

Why do people act the way they do? And why do people do the things we do? What makes us constantly change? Why can't everything just stay the same all the time? Why do things have to change? What makes our changes happen in the first place? And speaking of different places...

A relaxed work environment is a million times more productive than a stressed-out work environment. How is your work environment? And how's your home environment? How bad is your daily commute to and from back and forth? And what the fuck do you have to put up with to make ends meet? Is your life's glass full or empty? Do you have to deal with a bunch of dickheads, bitches, and assholes throughout your normal ordinary every day days?

Whenever we are fucked-up on the inside, it's hard to be around people, and it's hard for people to be around us. Whenever we get bogged down deep in our own personal shit, it's impossible for us to help make our loved one's personal shit go away. If they're in good spirits, maybe they can help you make your personal shit go away. You'll never know unless you ask.

In every strong solid relationship, there ain't no such thing as a stupid question.

Before we can use our soul's ability to heal someone else's fucked-up soul, we have to work on getting our fucked-up soul back to a good place.

We need to be in good spirits in order to do great deeds. Whenever your life goes straight to hell, and gets all fucked-up, do you, or someone you know, ever cross the line and stop being human? Aren't we our own personal monsters? Do you have some personal monsters?

How would the person who knows you best, and likes you anyway, describe your soul? How would the person who used to know you, and now hates your guts forever, describe your soul? On that scale, where would you rate yourself on regular days? Where do you rate yourself on fucked-up days? Where do you rate yourself on beautiful days? Wouldn't it be better to have more days that are "beautifuller"? Yeah, I know. How is that possible? Well...

A good start would be falling in love, having better sex, and staying in love. And you can do that by using all you now know about how our human soul works. Because elevating the quality of our love life elevates the quality of our life. And if we don't do it for ourselves, nobody will ever do it for us. So, first of all...

Everybody needs a suitable sex partner. There are millions of different ways to find a lover.

I found my second lover on the Internet, way back in the day, long before our Internet turned in our Interweb. And...

She's a keeper.

And if you already found your life's lover, but you're disconnected to the point you've become familiar strangers, consciously redo all the things you unconsciously did when you first met. "Wait. What?" Exactly.

If you don't remember what you unconsciously did when you first met, sit down, hold hands, and talk about what you and your lover remember about the first time the two of you fell in-love.

Remembering the good old days is a key that opens them big old doors to Fort Us. Open souls are receptive people. How receptive are you toward the love of your life? How receptive is the love of your life toward you? When you talk, does your lover listen? Do you listen to your lover?

Aggravated angry people have guarded souls. Disconnected people are guarded souls. Closed souls are not receptive people. Closed souls can't hear what is being said in our shared scientific reality.

You won't get very far in any relationship if you and yours are being extremely standoffish when you're alone together.

How receptive are you to your friends and family? Me? I could give a rat's ass about so and so. And if it's like that for you, my grandma always said, "If you ain't got nothing nice to say, then don't say nothing at all."

Them grandmas, "Whatcha gonna do?"

Where did we all come from? Sex. And speaking of sex…

How's your sex life? If it's stronger than ever, it's a phase. And you'll lose all you have, one day way too soon.

No. That's wrong.

You don't have to give up having a fantastic sex life and always being horny for each other. Not if you don't want to. Just keep in mind…

The same kind of sex all the time will eventually turn into a flat-line sex life. Just like the same kind of everyday un-evidential life eventually turns our unlimited potentials into our flat-line lives. And…

That's why we gotta mix things up and play. We can all use a little more sexual fun in our lives. We all deserve a little more fun in our sex lives. Don't you agree? And either whichever way…

Our soul doesn't know anything about aging and/or growing older. Our soul does not give a shit about time. Our souls can't even tell time. Here I am letting go of mine. And it's your turn to take the reins of yours.

Connecting the Web of Humanity:

Taking control of our sex life, and yours to do with as you please is...

And if you want to come to your bed with your genitals dripping, drooling, and wanting to fuck the love of your life like crazy night after night until you get so sore; you have to stop, and take a little vacation from having too much sex, and impatiently wait for your genitals to stop hurting; you'd still have to know how the fuck you're supposed to make you and yours super-horny for each other for a few days straight. And that's easy...

Do you ever have the problem where one of you is always horny, and the other isn't much interested in sex much these days, but used to be? That's easy too...

Falling, from the dizzying heights of the just "love-you", all the way down into the depths of "I-am-in-love-with-you", will always help you and yours sync-up with each other sexually.

Falling in-love makes us super-horny for each other.

Were you sexually more in-sync with each other back in the day? Have your genitals ever hurt from too much sex? Are you currently having regular genital hangovers? Did you know that genital hangovers sometimes happen? Do you want to know what you can do to prevent you and yours from getting genital hangovers? Do you really want to know? This is big. This giant nugget of my information is worth all of its weight in gold.

Here's to you and yours...

Are you ready? Okay then, you now know the rules, so...

Sex is genital friction. Frictions cause heat. Our excessive genital heating causes our genital soreness afterward. When we heat our genitals, we're gonna have to cool them down when we're done heating them. If we don't cool them down, all that heat cooks our sexy meat and leaves us feeling our genital hangovers. We gotta cool down our love muscles after a hard workout, like a baseball pitcher cools down their pitching arm after a big game. Otherwise, things get tender.

Unlike the shoulder and other large muscle groups, I'd stay away from using ice. Sometimes, when we get all those nerve clusters titillated, going from one extreme to the other is a bit too much for our love muscles to take. Like any mild burn, a cool wet (but not dripping) washrag laid gently on the outside is often plenty cold enough for any guy and every burning woman. And then again, let's totally get some of, there's something else too…

Lube reduces genital friction. So, go to your favorite sex-toy store and get some jumbo-sized vats of their best water-based lube. That stuff is easily gone in any shower. And if you ain't got no favorite sex-toy store, they ain't that hard to find. Ask around. Check on-line. Or shop at my store… www.AdamAndEve.com

And while you're there, grab some condoms, and buy a vibrator or two, one to keep, and one to give away. They say one-in-five women will never experience an orgasm throughout their entire lifetime. And…

If we are able to reduce the heat caused by our physical exertion—and the causation of genital friction, we are able to stay away from the harm caused by the increased temperature. Do you ever stop to marvel at what makes us human? Well, first thing's first…

Humanity is the end result of our dual consciousnesses, and dual realities, working together. Without our dual minds, we would all be mindless zombies of nature. Yaks do, whatever yaks do. If people had no soul, we wouldn't be able to fall down into the depths of being in-love the way we do.

And contrary to our popular belief, people become distant from other people. And it is far more accurate to say, "We close our soul off from the souls around us."

Our soul is what creates the distance in all of our relationships. We close our soul off from the people we love. We close ourselves off to the people around us, and their souls close off on us, like we do on them, like they do on us, like I am on you.

We build our own personal barriers.

It's Fort Me vs. Fort Us...

Live. Be there. And when we go there...

We react the only way we know how to react. Every possible scenario is nothing more than a simple scientific cause and effect, which further proves our scientific existence of the human soul. And speaking of our human souls' existence...

When you get mad, do you get ugly? If you get ugly, are you ever sorry? If you're really sorry, why can't we just skip those ugly parts?

"Humanity is as humanity does." And...

Maintaining a healthy relationship and keeping humanity's web tightly connected is like a dance. Step. Step. Step. Step here. Watch out. Step here, and here.

"Ta Da."

Step one:

Fascination started everything, including love. What fascinates you? Or better yet, who fascinates you? In terms of connecting our uncontrollable human souls together, a little uncontrollable fascination goes a long way. And putting our same shoes on our other feet, faking uncontrollable fascination can land us somewhere inside the middle of our deepest human shit. I mean...

"When we act, we act."

Step two:

Grace your lover with all of your presence.

Open yourself up and throw all of yourself out there for your lover to love. Be vulnerable. And expose yourself for who you really are.

I'm not the only one who can tell when someone's soul is in hiding. I know when people are being fake and plastic. Being fake and plastic, and hiding your soul away from people you love, will never get you anything of worth and value.

How long have you been looking for a book that keeps you up all night? And when I pretend my soul is open, when it is not open, I'm being artificial and plastic, hiding my soul away. When we act, we pretend. When people are pretending, we ain't being open or honest, and then we end up not being real to ourselves and whomever we happen to be with at the time.

We all have to be fake and plastic every once in a while. We interact with people differently all the time. Our soul automatically opens and closes all the time. Sometimes our soul automatically exposes itself to our friends and family, and sometimes our soul automatically hides itself away.

"See?"

That's what I love about Dave. Dave doesn't fake being Dave. Dave always shows us the real Dave.

When we do the "seek and find" on our lover's beauty, we won't have to try to fake our twitter-pated fascination.

Step three:

Openness & Honesty…

These two go hand in hand.

If you ain't totally open and honest with the people who love you, you are a closed-up liar. Period.

Liar, liar, PANTS on fire…

Step four:

You get what you give. You give what you get. It works that way for everyone we know, every way imaginable. If we ain't willing to give our soul's openness and honesty to our lovers, we can't expect to receive their soul's openness and honesty.

We get whatever we want, like openness and honesty, a better relationship, and even my getting this nonsensical book published,

Connecting the Web of Humanity:

if we're willing to give up or do whatever it takes to make our everything, the way we want things to happen.

Then, after all of that, we gotta go along to get along. We gotta get along to go along. Give a little, get a little. Get it? Want some? Me too.

And what would hiding your soul away and keeping you from your lover getting you? You can't hide your soul from the people who really know you. And when something is wrong with those we know and love, we know what's what, just like our closest souls will always know something is wrong with us. When someone is paying close attention to us, they know how we work. They know how our soul works. They can practically read the thoughts inside our minds. They can read us like we can read a simple easy-reader book.

Don't you want to spend tons and tons of time with your best friend? Are you and your lover each other's best friends? If you aren't fucking your "bestest" friend in your whole wide fucked-up world, then maybe you should switch teams. If you're fucking someone just to be fucking someone, please be careful. AIDS is like a slow-motion heart attack. And who knows what new disease is just waiting to be spread around.

The night John Holmes died, the guys working the graveyard shift in the Melt Shop held a two-minute radio silence tribute. Typically, they'd spend the whole night cackling on the plant radio worse than hens in a morning hen house. One of the guys on my crew made the announcement and gave a hell of an improvised long speech and ended it, with a request for two minutes of radio silence. And the Melt Shop radio went quiet for two solid minutes, out of respect. Then, all of us got back after it until our shift ended. It was a cool tribute.

Why would anyone watch porn? One word...

"Fascination."

Fascination is a key that starts everything new. The new often brings fun and excitement to our soul. Fun and excitement brings receptiveness. Being receptive is being open. Being open, we're talking about your soul being open. Keep up son. Your soul bone's connected to your sex bone. Your sex bone's connected to your orgasm bones. Your orgasm bones are connected to your Buggy Bones.

Why would anyone watch porn? In another word…

"Education."

When we watch people have sex, we can learn some amazing shit. For instance…

Have you ever seen a woman squirt her ejaculate?

"Yummy."

And as it turns out, one-in-four women are able to squirt ejaculate, during an orgasm.

Can you and/or yours?

It's 1:11 a.m. I gotta get some sleep. I gotta go to work in the morning.

Thursday, January 09, 2003

I got my first psychic reading in March 1996. And I kept going back. I've seen her many times. My psychic and I became fast friends. The reason I went in the first place was to confirm everything I already knew. For not knowing anything about me the day I walked in and shook her hand, she sure did tell me a lot of shit she couldn't have already known. It was all a little freaky at first. And now…

I don't hear the spooky music in my head anymore. She was the first one to ever tell me I'd write this book. And look at me now. Thank you…

Thursday, January 30, 2003

My life's greatest conflict is in knowing what people need long before they ever think they need it. When I try to help people out, they always seem to duck and dodge and run and hide.

Is it because they don't want to know, they ain't ready, or they simply can't handle whatever I see?

What makes a person totally freak out?

People can freak out when they're confronted with something they're not comfortable handling. The well-adjusted, the well-educated, and the well-read, tend to be able to remain calmer in these situations. They tend to have a better understanding of most things human. They seem to have a better grasp of the world around them. They seem to have acquired the ability to maintain an unyielding control over their soul when everything emotionally deep-down turns into liquid shit inside their heads.

I know when my guarded souls close themselves off from me, like I know when (and to whom) my soul closes off. I'm aware of the world around me. The love of my life tells me I know too much, too soon. And I know that...

Nothing else says "smooth moves" like slowly building an extremely hot old-fashioned mind-blowing string of orgasms. So...

"Who's your sex guru now?"

IV: February 2003

Saturday, February 01, 2003

I've been working on a lot of personal things lately. Over the past couple of months, I've reinvented my home, and I've reinvented myself. And so far, my family approves.

When everything in your entire universe is fucked-up, and fucking with you, did you ever end up telling the people in your tight relationships that nothing is wrong? Have you ever said something like, "No? Nothing is bothering me. Why do you ask?"? Well...

Me too, and if we have that in common, I bet we have a lot more humanness in common. You might be some sort of special Guru too. And speaking of you...

You aren't the same person you once were. We change. We slowly evolve a little every day. We once preferred to read our facts with proper writing and pleasingly perfect well-educated grammar. We once preferred to read thought completions in sequential order.

We once had a sense of reading propriety. The way books need to be written used to matter.

And if I can pour any more of my shit into this line of thinking, it'd be...

If you can accept that today is just today, and not yesterday or tomorrow, you'll realize that change is happening for a reason. Everything happens by our/the Creator's Grand Design. Every moment is happening for a reason. And the next newest thing is just around the corner. You just don't know what's it gonna be, until you know.

Our holding onto the moment automatically makes our soul appear in our physical reality. And when our soul appears in our physical reality, our brain lets go of our physical reality, and our whole wide scientific world scientifically disappears, when we switch to soul mode.

When we're lost in one of our human moments, our soul takes ourselves into another one of our personal realities, and we temporarily lose our constant cognitive connection to our physical reality. When we're lost in our human moments, everyone around us here on Earth can see our souls emerge. But they won't see anything, until they read all of this, and know that they can see all the shit I'm saying.

We can only let go of our scientific reality in little chunks at a time. We all grew up. If we let go of the scientific reality on a full-time basis, we would need a straitjacket, padded room, and a really good asylum.

"Crazy? I'll show you crazy..."

Our soul shows itself in all the things we do naturally. Our soul is the driving force behind our individual instincts. We get our natural instincts from having a human soul. Our human soul is what gives us our gut reactions.

When we go into an instinct mode, we expose our soul, or

maybe our soul exposes us. I don't know. And it's all way too complicated for me to try to figure out all by myself tonight. But...

Our first answer always carries the most weight. And...

Exposing our soul can be humiliating, embarrassing, harassing, or quite lovely whenever we throw in some googly eyes. And when things go good, things go great. And if things ain't broke, don't fix them. Wink, wink... Nod, nod...

And do you want to know something else?

We love to watch people lose their minds.

People do crazy shit when they go off the deep end.

Look at me with all this shit. It's embarrassing.

We have to be intimately involved with our own soul to really know what's going on with ourselves. It's just something we learn, as we grow older. From the time you were born, up to the day you die, you can't go around half-cocked all the time. Well, I suppose you could if you wanted to, but why would you want to? What would that get you? If we are walking around pissed-off all the time, we are probably getting really tired around bedtime. Being pissed-off all day long is extremely tiring. It has a way of grinding us down and wearing us out.

Besides...

As people go...

If a soul starts beating up people, a mature person is supposed to step in and break it up. We're supposed to stop the dickheads, bitches, and assholes from doing their fucked-up shit.

That's what mature civilized grownups are supposed to do.

Grownups are supposed to step in and stop the fights, even when the deserving dickheads, bitches, and assholes are getting their physical or emotional asses kicked. Grownups are supposed to preserve the peace as best we can. That's what good grownups do. The less-mature, less-read, and less-civilized, are always the first to egg things on. And going all the way back in our individual human histories…

We are all born here with a mini cognitive ability, back when we were all soul. We were all born perfect. Babies have pure unspoiled souls. Babies are pure blank slates. That's what makes babies so precious.

We all started out with no conscious awareness of the world around us. Babies have cognitive baby thoughts. When we were kids, we were more soul than we were cognitive consciousness. Kids are kids. As we got older, we all grew into our "cognitiveness."

"Kids can be cruel. And adults can be vicious."

As we grew, our cognitive conscious mind was supposed to learn how to override our emotional soul. We're expected (by Law) to be able to restrain ourselves, in virtually every physical situation. We all gain our wisdom and maturity at the right times in our life.

Did we overdo it? Did we age beyond our years?

Way down deep inside us, your soul is any age you want you to be. "Are you still young at heart?"

We can be anything we want to be. You can do anything you want to do, as long as you don't break the Law. And that's the Law. If you ain't already doing whatever it is you want to do, do whatever you have to do to make things change to the way you want them to be. We are living in the Information Age. And speaking of information…

Our unconscious square and our thinking mind's cognitive conscious square share our brain's physical body. Our physical body is a mobile vehicle equipped with five senses. Our cognitive conscious mind is our body's conscious pilot. Our soul is our body's unconscious pilot. We use our cognitive conscious mind for thinking and work. And we use our unconscious mind for enhancing our thinking and work, and for our survival, playtime, creativity, passion, love, rage, and anything else that comes from down deep inside us.

When we die, our conscious pilot goes down with the ship. Our unconscious pilot grabs-up all of our important stuff, and jumps over into our ever after, or whatever we choose to believe.

If you don't think you have a soul, you don't. When you die, you die, and you're done. If you want to be worm dirt, you can be worm dirt.

If you ain't got none, you ain't got none. If you cannot recognize your soul's existence, nothing is there. In my personal little private world, my soul is firmly seated in Freud's unconscious mind. And...

If we reduce something to its simplest element, we make all of its counterparts seem big, baggy, and bulky. Seat of the soul? Ha.

Tuesday, February 04, 2003

When we gain maturity, we gain the ability to see things differently. We gained more and more cognitive ability as we grew up. We get to decide if we want to go around being all pissed-off at the souls of people we can't, won't, and don't agree with or understand.

We're expected to control our tempers. Civilized society demands, "Temper-temper."

The Law of our land does what it can to protect the rules of civility. But when there is so much chaos and mayhem in our country's communities, the rules of civility get tossed out the window. And...

The survival of the fittest still rules today.

And that's just one of the many reasons our country needs to legalize and regulate marijuana. We'd see a more peaceful nation emerge. Why are we supporting our current state of chaos and mayhem between our public and our Law enforcers? Legalizing and regulating marijuana makes way more sense than our current keeping on, keeping on, with our all of our current madness. The multi-decade War on Drugs is not slowing down America's supply or demand of marijuana. Many Americans have already "experimented" around with THC. And...

The most effective regulation of our current illegal drug market is done through our employers. Employers can screen people more thoroughly than our American Judicial Branch can screen its citizenry.

American employers are allowed to look around inside our bodies. Our employers do a good job of monitoring their employee's ability to work safe. I've been x-rayed, poked, prodded, lie-detected, piss-tested, hair-tested, blood-tested, and really tested. And I'd be the first to say...

I don't want stoned captains any more than I want drunk pilots. I don't want surgeons smoking dope or knocking back a few alcoholic beverages before they operate on people. I don't want any baked crane operators near anyone. And I don't want our truck drivers, or anybody else on the road, driving around under the influence of anything, illegal or otherwise. Safety should always be job-one. Please...

"Let's all try to stay alive (and keep each other alive) for as long as we can."

And I do not advocate smoking marijuana. If you don't smoke, don't start. Keep your lungs healthy. Live a long healthy life breathing air. Don't fuck your lungs up with smoke. If you do smoke, or do edibles, you ought to have the freedom to peacefully smoke, or eat, in private. We all deserve to be free enough to create a positive environment that melts away our individual differences and facilitates a healthy healing verbal interaction. And...

I ain't disputing that marijuana is a drug. Alcohol, tobacco, sugar, and caffeine are drugs too. It's all about life. And life is all about making our own consumable choices. I mean...

"Why can't we be friends?" Which makes me have to ask...

Why are we at war with each other in the first place? And if we are all at war with each another, why are peace pipes illegal in the first place? Growing up I was taught to believe I lived in a nation of peace. And...

Maturity lies within wisdom's knowledge. I am wise. I'm open to my future. I look forward to my future challenges. I'm open to my financial rewards. I'm open to change. Things have to change for me.

I wanted to pay for my babies' college educations. All the way back to the late 1800's, my bloodline's educations stopped way short or soon after high school.

My family's last college degree was way, way back in the day. I'd like to make our shit change. I want my kids to have the opportunity to receive some kind of education past high school and maybe even become first-generation college graduates. And...

That's a change I would welcome.

I'm ready. And speaking of my kids, they've heard me say it all along...

"Don't start none, and there won't be none."

It's late. I gotta get up early to go clean some more, again tomorrow.

Goodnight.

Friday, February 14, 2003

Happy Valentine's Day!

The oven broke today.
It's been one of those days.

Monday, February 17, 2003

One of our kids broke an arm. That gobbled up a lot of time. We ended up having to go see a bone doctor. That took out most of our day today.

Wednesday, February 19, 2003

My dad had Gamma-knife surgery on his second brain tumor. And we spent the whole day, today, just being there with, and for, my dad.

V: March 2003

Monday, March 03, 2003

Today's x-ray shows the broken arm bone fell. Now the bones are healing wrong. The health insurance's bone doctor recommends surgery.

And here I am at the end of another long day, and it's been so long since I've written anything, I probably forgot how. So...

Let's start today with what I've been thinking about lately. I've thought about lots of different things, like...

Some dickheads, bitches, and assholes are real heart-breaking love stealers.

I wrote so much shit over the past few years, I don't remember what I put in here. One day soon, I'll have to sit down and refresh my memory.

I'm flying by the seat of my PANTS in here. I hope I ain't repeating myself too much. Nobody likes to see or hear the same old boring shit being thrown at them over and over.

Lately, I've been far removed from writing. I've been a very busy boy. Between working, sleeping, eating, and vegging out in front of my television, no.

That's a lie.

I ain't seen much of my television. I think it misses me.

I try to catch Dave. I do the TWC's Local on the Eights. And I work all the time.

During the past few days, I've been working behind the scenes, backstage. I sunk a ton of time reworking this shit. And then, I wrote my first query letter ever. I'm very proud of myself. My Baby helped me shave it down to a couple of pages. That took forever. When we have this much nonsense to sell, it's hard to wrap it all up in just four short paragraphs. I did my best. Yesterday, on March 02, 2003, I sent my brand-new, never seen before, two-page query letter to four different literary agencies.

What the hell?

I can't win, if I don't play. So now...

I just gotta be patient and wait to see what happens. I'm nervous. I guess this nervousness is just part of becoming an author.

To kill some of my anxious time, I wrote some goofy shit to Dave on his Late Show website. I didn't get a response. I don't expect anything.

If Dave had to respond to every swinging-dick that wrote him a "Dear Dave" letter, he wouldn't have any time to work on keeping his secret identity secret.

I wanted to give Dave a fair warning. As of today, March 2003, Dave probably still doesn't know anything about me. Then again, he might. Maybe he is the kind of guy who takes the time to read all of his e-mails. I'm not.

"So, anyway..."

Let's change the subject. I'm turning us around and to go another way.

Over the past few days, I've had one thought that keeps coming up and resurfacing more often than any of the other thoughts that I've been thinking about.

Does that ever happen to you? Does anything personal ever keep coming up over and over inside your head? Do things keep coming up in your head until they eventually get resolved? When something is bothering you, do your repeated thoughts ever keep coming up over and over in your head? Me too, and...

I'm addressing my own personal think-tank shit in here. Bear with me while I set-up my props.

I'm a normal, everyday kind of guy.

I ain't nobody special.

I'm just working on writing my way out of my cleaning business and into a way better life.

That's all.

I am a professional house cleaner. I clean houses for a living, professionally. We clean up to five homes almost every weekday. And we do light janitorial and new construction work nights and weekends.

"It's just good clean work." And...

I'm the Pop, in a "Mom and Pop" home cleaning business, coming up on more than six years now. My Baby and I are each other's business partners. Together, we visit lots of different homes each week. All of our customers are regulars. We have a few customers who have been there from our get-go. And some of our customers are brand new.

We've seen tons of shit over the years. We always keep our heads low. Meaning, we keep to ourselves. I will never compromise the privacy of anyone, other than myself.

I wouldn't ever compromise myself, except I think the world deserves to know how my Baby and I got it going on. My Baby and

Connecting the Web of Humanity:

I ain't got much of a pot to piss in, but we seriously got it going on. And it's more than just as luck would have it.

In our line of work, we've watched children grow up, and leave the nest. We've seen marriages turn to shit and fall apart. We've seen the despair death leaves behind. We've seen the joy brought on by a new love. We've watched the ebb and flow of many different relationships. We've seen relationships crumble apart and somehow completely rebuild. We've seen fortunes flitter away. We've seen people become prosperous out the ass. We've quietly watched families being built. We've seen a ton of private shit go down.

We don't ever talk to anyone about anything important. How's the weather? How's it going? Yeah, our family is doing fine. How's your family? Oh, that's nice. Blah, blah, blah... See you next time.

We won't ever talk about the sex-toys we've seen.

"Oops. Look over there, Baby. They forgot to put that thing away. Man, that looks like fun. We need to try to find ourselves one of those. "

www.AdamAndEve.com

Hell, my Baby and I probably got more sex-toys than all of our customers put together. We wouldn't know for sure. We never go digging around. We ain't that kind of people. If it's out and about, we'll see it when we're cleaning, and we won't ever tell anybody about whatever it is we've seen.

And if everything of yours was always put away, we never saw anything. We only did what we came to do. And that's all we ever do. To tell the truth, I'd rather not know all the stuff I know. I wish I hadn't seen all the shit I saw. And push-come-to-shove, I ain't seen nothing. I will never talk about nobody's private business. And speaking of running a business...

Most of our customers aren't home when we clean. That makes

it nice for us. We get in, do our thing, and get out. We try to put in an honest day's work for an honest day's pay, but sometimes, I just don't know. The not knowing pushes me along the edge above our competition. Being it's just my Baby and me, our small Mom and Pop team creates the edge over our competition. And I'd like to think we always earn our keep, but we're professional cleaners in a microbusiness. And there is always something else to clean. Look around yourself and see. And now that you know where I'm coming from...

Let me pop back out of your head, after seeing what I am seeing around you, and not telling anyone anything about that shit either, and let's get back to what has been screaming at me the hardest, loudest, clearest, and most often, lately...

Sometimes, we need to stop and straighten out the shit that just keeps coming up over and over inside our heads. When you think about something repeatedly, do you ever try to address it? Do you try to ignore it, hope it stops coming up in your head, and hope it eventually goes away? Do you quietly let all those little things grow and start to fester inside your soul? Ain't you got nobody to talk to? Best friends are supposed to trust each other's souls with the deepest and darkest of our dirty little personal secrets and other personal things, like I am doing here with you, with all of my personal shit. And speaking of me...

It has recently come to my attention, (via multiple customers), that some people believe sex is some form of currency, something to barter with. To me, turning sex into currency is totally whacked.

Sex ought to be a separate entity all unto itself.

Keeping our sex life totally separate from our everyday life will help us keep an active sex life in our lives. When we mix our everyday things up into our sex lives, we end up all mixed up.

Mixing sex with work leads to lawsuits. Mixing sex with chores leads to fights. Changing sex into currency turns lovers into banks. And that makes me have to ask...

Connecting the Web of Humanity:

"When was the last time your bank let you fuck them?"

If we're making emotional deposits to withdraw sex, we're missing the boat. Yes, we might be getting half-ass sex every now and again, but we ain't getting the kind of sex that comes with good old-fashioned high-quality soul markings.

Why not?

Anything good is gonna cost us giving away something good. Anything great is gonna cost us giving away something great.

If we want to have high-quality sex, we have to give high-quality sex. And sex is always better when we're sharing our souls with each other. Besides...

Sex for any kind of currency is prostitution. Now, after having to say that, I ain't got nothing against trading sex for money. Suppose we just want to get laid, without all the hassles. People pay for sex every day, every way. I say, if you're gonna pay...

"Pay big."

We get what we pay for. We pay for what we get. Everything cost us something. Shell out lots of your good stuff and reap your rewards.

If you want to experience great sex, you have to give great sex experiences.

Getting high-quality badass mind-altering orgasms will cost you having to be able to give some high-quality badass mind-altering orgasms.

We give what we get. We get what we give.

Are you captivated by your lover's soul? Do you captivate your lover's soul?

"Who wouldn't pencil in a lot of time for a great lover?"

If we want to captivate each other, all we gotta do is have "fantabulous" sex. With a woman, start out slow and easy and soft and gentle, don't make her flinch. If she flinches, go slower, and easier, and softer, and gentler, and take the time to grow everything as big as you can. And then, do what you gotta do. With a man, go nuts, unless he flinches. If he flinches, go slow, and easy, and soft, and gentle, and take the time to grow everything as big as you can. And then, do what you gotta do. And go nuts. How high can we go? How good can we be? How stretched-out can our orgasms get? I don't know. In fact...

Who knows? And, in the meantime...

Our lover gives us whatever we give our lover. Your lover is getting whatever you get. If my sex life lacks luster, my lover's sex life lacks the same amount of luster too, and vice-versa too, and versa-vice-too and whatever whichever way too.

A relationship is a team. And the two becomes one. And if any one lover feels as though the relationship is in the trash, the entire beautiful loving relationship is in the trash, despite whatever the other lover(s) may feel or think. Being in a relationship means you are joined together as one on the same team. And what wouldn't you do for your team?

That's how relationships work. If you scratch my back, I'll scratch yours. If you end up drawing my blood, I'll be drawing some of yours. Our souls are emotional mirrors. And as much as nobody is supposed to admit it...

Our old souls see our world as an eye-for-an-eye world.

People's souls join together. That's how our close personal relationships come into being. Our soul connects. Our soul is what bonds us together. Partners get what they give. Partners give what they get. It doesn't matter if the partners are in a business together or in a bed together. If you want something special from your certain little someone, it's gonna cost you giving your own personal brand of something extra special to your certain little someone. And know that...

Doing your fair share around the house whenever you feel the need to get laid won't cut it for very long. It gets old, predictable, and irritating to the lover who's constantly doing more than their fair share. And then...

The next thing you know, somebody picks up a grudge, and starts to carry it around. Then, the next thing you know...

The foul stench of "human tension" begins to slowly fill the air around us.

And then the next thing you know, when we least expect it, like right in the middle of a fight, when you're having to battle one of life's messy storms, the grudge always slips out like a big fat fucking sword, and somebody's soul ends up getting sliced to pieces. It happens all the time.

No man is an island.

Nobody can single-handedly fix all of mankind's problems. A world without weather is predictably dull. A flat-line life is empty without storms. Flat-line lives make us dull, boring, and uninteresting. And...

Having flat-line (regular, like clockwork) body-sex, three-point-four-times-a-week, gets really old.

Doing the same old predictable boring-ass shit is mind-numbing as hell.

When shit gets repetitive, people become bored. When our shit gets boring, our minds tend to wonder. And then...

We just fall asleep.

And speaking of...

Thursday, March 06, 2003

We went to a different bone doctor to get a second opinion on the broken arm today.

No surgery. Hey...

Things are looking up.

Tuesday, March 11, 2003

We went to our personal doctor to—once again—begin the process of quitting smoking, and someone else's name showed up on my billing record. This is one of my life's messy little storms.

We weren't looking for trouble.

But it sure as hell keeps finding us.

Update: It took a full fucking week to get that shit straightened out.

Nobody should have to deal with this much bureaucracy and red tape. And…

From now on, I can never go back to see my doctor. I have to go and try to find a brand-new HMO.

Friday, March 14, 2003

Today, we went back to see the first bone doctor and took an ass chewing for getting a second opinion. The first doctor was pissed at us.

Update: It's about a week later. Just our luck, we picked two bone doctors who do a regular lunch together. I'm guessing we embarrassed the first bone doctor at one of his lunches. And…

That's probably why his soul barked at us.

Sunday, March 16, 2003

We spent most of today visiting with my dad.

We're back now. And I'm going to write tonight. So…

To keep the wheels greased, and running smoothly, we have to mix it up in the bedroom sometimes. Roll the dice and play around.

Humans can be some serious fun makers. Do you ever make

fun of your lover behind your lover's back? Do you ever put down your lover? What's it getting you? And more important, what's it keeping you from getting?

We create distance in a relationship, or we allow the distance to happen, or our distance comes from...

When I am unbalanced, I am easy prey. Some people take advantage of other people's weaknesses. Some don't. Straight-up, the world isn't as cutthroat as some of us think it is. We just need to keep our eyes on a few crazy individuals out there. A few bad apples spoil the bunch. And there again, maybe I'm just too cynical. Who knows?

Anger bubbles are just bubbles. Love bubbles...

Beautiful or ugly, everything bubbles up from inside.

My relationship is the safest place for me to be. My Baby and I are each other's rock. Our souls are firmly anchored into one another. When our lives are calm, things are peaceful. When things are peaceful, we become whole and balanced. When we're whole and balanced, our soul is resonating in perfect harmonious harmony.

When things go good inside us, things go good in the big bad fucked-up world around us. And speaking of me...

Today, right now, in the middle of all the chaos and mayhem that's going on in my life, today, and today alone, I'm whole and balanced. And right now, I am calm, cool, and collected. I've freed myself from my struggles. I don't know where my feet will land, but I jumped.

I'm throwing everything I've got into writing this messed-up book. I am confident the wind that carried me here, wherever I am today, will carry me to a glorious place tomorrow. I trust in my ability. I have blind faith that I will get where I need to be. I know it will happen. I don't see it any other way. My new life is just a matter of my patience and time.

I am momentarily balanced. You, however, may not be, unless you think you are. If you think you are, you are. Whichever way you think things are going for you is the way they are going. We're gonna start seeing all sorts of new things, when we start to believe in them.

For more information on that, Google: Dr. Wayne W. Dyer.

When we believe things are right and true, they are right and true. When we think things are fucked-up and wrong, we see them as fucked-up and wrong and they are.

And whichever way we perceive everything (and individual things) to be is the way they are. And that's the way all of our individual realities work.

And when people are settled on the inside, we project that out into the world around us. When we ain't settled on the inside, we project all that out into to the world around us.

Everyone rattles their cages. Everyone wakes up on the wrong side of the bed every now and then, and when we do, we tend to lash out at whomever and whatever holds us together and makes us complete. But then again…

I know people who like to rattle their cages just for the hell of it. And speaking of just for the hell of it…

According to NBC News on October 09, 2002, 70 million Americans are obese or overweight. Then the next morning, October 10, 2002, NBC's Today Show said 20 million American parents read too poorly to help their children with their homework. And given what CBS News said about our American children's car seat installation manuals, I'm not shocked.

Sure, they say lots of shit, but what does it all mean?

Who knows? Besides, we ain't going down them train tracks right now anyways. I can't jump tracks and go that way because I'm smack-dab in the middle of a souls and sex thing right now.

An open soul is an open mind. An open mind is an open soul.

A closed mind is a closed soul. When our souls close, our minds close, and nothing gets in. Conversation over.

When people are pissed-off, their souls close. A closed soul is one made-up mind. When our soul is closed, when we are being guarded, nothing reasonable, rational, or truthful, goes in, or comes out, it's almost like rhyme and reason goes offline.

A lot of important stuff gets said and never gets listened to or heard. If a tree falls in your personal forest, and you are too angry to hear it...

A receptive person has an open mind.

And with that said...

Monday, March 17, 2003

I'm beholding to anyone still reading and seriously chewing on my truths thus far. I poured a ton-and-a-half of serious shit-eating truth into my words. I write from my heart, my soul. I have no control over what comes out of me when I write. I'm one of those kinds of authors. That's what good authors are supposed to do. Good authors are supposed to get to a place, where we let go of the world around us, laser focus our attention, and let our soul write a good book well. Speaking of working on writing a good book well...

Great lovers let their brain's soul open up enough to let go of the scientific reality and make soul-sex more than just a hypothetical scientific probability.

When we're having soul-sex, when we're making love, we lose the ability to consciously and cognitively control what we're doing. We don't think about where our hands are, which way our toes are pointed, what our bodies are doing, or what time it is, or anything else at all. When we let go and completely lose ourselves, we let our soul take the reins of our physical bodies.

During body-sex, and fuck buddy sex, our soul is excluded. During mind-sex, our cognitive conscious mind and our soul are driving and riding at the exact same time. And whenever we have sex, we can alternate between being active or passive sex partners.

The good news is we are able to instantly change. So...

One minute we can be having our lowest spectrum range of sex, and then right in the middle of the next minute, our soul opens up and turn that same sexual experience into our holy fuck. Then in the middle of the next minute, right before someone pulls out, and squirts all over another woman's breasts, our soul closes up, and we go back into just having body-sex.

Throughout each individual sexual experience, like blinking, we can instantly bounce around within the three different spectrum ranges of sex, during every sexual experience. The only distinguishing characteristic of each sexual experience is what it does, or doesn't do, for our soul afterwards.

Sometimes, we just gotta try new things. If this doesn't feel good, maybe that does. When we try new things, we change and grow. Sometimes, we have to mix it up. If we don't mix it up, our sex life slowly dissolves into a flat-line body-sex rut. And body-sex ruts suck big-time.

Body-sex doesn't leave marks on our souls because our souls are left out of our body-sex experiences. Are you bored with your current sex life? Are you ready for a change? Can you handle your soul's truth?

Not having a proper sex life can compress us. And then, our stressed-out smashed-down souls' revolt in our individual discreet ways. Oh look...

"It's Fort Us."

That's when our soul picks up grudges and start carrying them around. And then, we isolate ourselves.

When we talk about our grudges, our soul puts them down.

"Ah, makeup sex." And...

When it comes to taking liberties, I am no less guilty than anyone else out there on that. And...

I don't mean to get anybody's dander in a huff, but like any other brand-new big trade author, I'm being forced to write shit that reaches all the way down inside people and grabs them by their soul. And...

That's why I had to make this book the way it is. And...

What's the second reason people buy books in the first place? Soul touching. We buy fiction books for our soul, our unconscious mind. We buy non-fiction books for our cognitive conscious thinking mind. But that's supposed to be kept secret. So, don't be running around telling anyone you know. I had to cross the line and pierce the edge. My shit is like a wetsuit full of gooey information.

Go ahead.

Try it on.

I am not afraid to fuck with big trade's nonfiction tradition. I am not afraid to poke my shtick at a very old institutionally "structured's" only way of writing a great big giant bunch of nonsense. I'm not afraid of writing a great big giant bunch of totally new nonsense. I am not afraid of piercing the edge and living my totally brand-new life. And speaking of me making shit happen...

Are you ready to try something new? Good. Here we go...

From now on, when you see an arrow in front of a paragraph, it means I'm changing the subject. Like...

I probably have A.D.D. And like any family disease...

I have probably had it all my life. But...

So the fuck what?

Who cares? So, ready or not, here we go...

Often, I go to my throne thinking one thought, and then I'll flush, thinking the complete opposite of my earlier thought. I am human. And as a human, I am entitled to change my mind, and my beliefs, as many times as it takes for me to get them right by the newest-old-version of me.

New information can change our beliefs. We change all the time. Our beliefs are based on our most recent information.

I'm just looking for everybody to take on a little more responsibility for themselves and all the chaos and mayhem they allow and create in their lives. I want people to recognize the things that really matter. I want to help people become new and improved for all the beautiful souls around them. It's all about finding world peace in our own backyard, first. And...

I am just a guy whose messed-up little book is pointing to wherever it is your soul is aiming to go. And until your soul gets there, maybe even before it leaves here, I'm working my ass off to turn you into a better lover.

Check it out, "a-ight." (Short a. Long i.)

How many times can we legally fall in love in a lifetime? What is love's legal limit? In your lifetime, how many times have you fallen in love? Well then...

Today is the first day of the rest of your life.

I'd like to keep this brand-new gyratory shit gyrating all night long, but alas...

I need to get some sleep for tomorrow. We have several houses to clean, wrapped around a trip to the dentist to have three cavities filled. It sucks.

My teeth feel fine.

I'm scared shitless, but I gotta go.

Goodnight.

PS.

"To My Favorite Little Leprechaun,

On your way back home from dropping kids off at school, can

you pick me up a pack of smokes? I'd be beholding to you. I'd just love you forever.

It's 3:45 a.m.

Love, Poopy-pants"

Tuesday, March 18, 2003

My dentist was afraid of a drug interaction with the anti-depressant I'm taking to quit smoking (which ain't working, by the way.) I had two cavities filled without an anesthetic.

My third cavity had to be rescheduled.

How the fuck can I eat when my teeth hurt like this?

I got some crazy moneymaking schemes in my head. I ain't scared to share them with you. I trust you with my dreams. If I plant my flag, I plant my flag. If I say I'm gonna do it, I'm gonna do it. That's the kind of guy I am.

It takes lots of money to make lots of money. Everything cost me something. So, this is me, and I'm planting a flag. Here goes...

Someday, I wanna build a waterpark. I have a twenty-something-year-old dream of owning my own waterpark. I love the Schlitterbahn, both in Texas, and on the Interweb. If not, take a break, and think about millions and millions of gallons of water just sloshing around all over the place, and you needing to find some place to go pee. And then...

Go pee. When you're done, blow your nose. And then...

Go see what I'm talking about... www.schlitterbahn.com And...

If they ask...

Tell them that I sent you.

I have dreamed about building my very own waterpark for a long time now. I believe I can visualize it into existence.

I have all the pictures in my head. I'm not going to stop moving this shit forward until I get everything I want. It's March of 2003. And I have already gotten seven years wrapped up in this.

I wish 3M would start making rolls of Post-it Paper Tape from the tops of their Post-it notes. Rolls of Post-it Paper Tape would be a handy-dandy thing to have around. Post-it Paper Tape sticks to anything and comes off clean. (Like me.) That makes it highly profitable. (Like this.)

It's late. I need to get some sleep. Goodnight.

Wednesday, March 19, 2003

I sent four query letters out last Saturday; March 08, 2003. I received three rejections yesterday. I hope I can find the time to send four more query letters by the end of the week. Right now, I just gotta write. I can't help myself. Writers gotta write.

Two days ago, on St. Patrick's Day, President Bush gave Saddam & Sons 48 hours to get out of town. It sounds like a bad spaghetti western, except this shit is for real. I don't have a good feeling about this. I hope whatever the fuck's gonna happen will hurry up, and happen, and end real fast. But then again, how can we make such a serious threat, and not follow through on it? If we say we're gonna do something, we gotta do it. That's the way it is. That's the way we are. And America is beautiful in her way. But...

We live in a scary world. Wars are messy. Some are just. Some aren't. We'll have to wait and see on this one.

We ain't got no choice. Everything's all hush-hush. I've been listening, but they ain't giving very many details.

They say the need for this war is there. We gotta trust that the people in charge of us know what the fuck they're doing. We're all gonna just have to wait and see. And while we're all waiting...

I'll be the one who is looking a little nervous about things. You know?

Yeah, you know.

I talk about a lot of shit all at once. It's a hard thing to try to sell to big trade, until I do.

We know who we are. We think we know what we are. We pretty much know where we are. We know roughly when it all began. We are deeply divided on how and why. Why? Why does the grass grow? Why do the birds sing? Why do only fools fall in-love?

I'm tired and I'm just being goofy.

See how fucked-up I am? I shouldn't write right now. My life has turned into a great big fucking mess. If I ain't got nothing good to write, I shouldn't write nothing at all. I should go to sleep. We have another full day of work tomorrow. And now...

Today's entry is just one more fucked-up thing in a complete and total waste of a perfectly good day. So...

Goodnight.

Saturday, March 22, 2003

At 6:07 p.m. today, we got a call. My dad was on his way to the hospital in an ambulance. At 6:36 p.m., we pulled out of the gas station with an hour and a half drive to get there.

Our kids stayed home. Today was a scary day.

Sunday, March 23, 2003

We went to watch one of our kids do a thing in a church program.

My sisters flew in today. They don't live anywhere near here. We all went to the hospital to spend the day with my dad.

Monday, March 24, 2003

We took our second car to our mechanic for repairs in the morning. Then we took our second car to my sisters in the evening. Three more hours of drive time.

Tuesday, March 25, 2003

The oven got fixed. No charge. Hey, things are looking up.

Wednesday, March 26, 2003

Today, my dad had emergency brain surgery to relieve the increasing pressure on his brain. His brain surgeon carefully removed the charred remains of the Gamma-Knife-Surgery. It's late. We just got back from a very long day with dad.

I gotta get to sleep. It's really late.

Goodnight.

Thursday, March 27, 2003

By the grace of God go I.

Another one of our kids broke three bones in the right hand today.

This has been one hell of a week. We've spent the last few days doing daily trips driving back and forth (three hours on the road) between here and my dad's hospital. He ain't doing so good. It's a long story. But...

I ain't got nothing better to do right now. In fact...

I'm kind of cranked from spending another whole day waiting in a totally different waiting room. And you aren't going anywhere anytime soon, are you? Good.

Connecting the Web of Humanity:

You can be a part of my captive audience. Here I go...

My Dad has brain cancer. He was first diagnosed seventeen months ago. Back then, I was doing my best to catch up on my honey-do list. I was also licking my wounds from that "phucked-up" literary agent's contract.

His first MRI showed a mass about the size of a grape. It was sitting near the top of his brain stem. They couldn't take it out because of where the tumor was located. The first thing they wanted to do was to get a piece of it and examine it back in the lab. They did a biopsy on the mass a few days before Christmas of 2001.

The bullshit word for what my dad has is "Ogolioemyosis." Basically, it means he's got cancerous tumors in his brain.

They gave him radiation, followed by the chemotherapy, followed by the second round of chemo, and the third round. He went through the hair loss thing, the weight loss thing, and all the other fucked-up shit people battling cancer gotta go through.

"Everything costs us something." (My dad.)

Then, after all that, after all this time, they found a second tumor. Five weeks ago, on February 19, the surgeons did a Gamma-Knife-Surgery. We were there. We waited in the waiting room. His Gamma-Knife-Surgery consisted of a series of 200 radiation rays precisely aimed at the second tumor in his head in 2-minute doses. They did a 2-minute dose of 200 rays of radiation a total of twelve times spread out over the whole day.

We were there all day. My dad was even able to join us for lunch.

They had to screw a halo into his skull. It was the second time they had to do that to him. Seeing my dad with a halo screwed into his skull...

Anyway...

Today, and for the past month, he's been dealing with brain swelling. The brain swelling almost took his life five days ago.

Thankfully, the hospital was able to get his swelling to go down with steroids. They also said any improvement would only be temporary.

Yesterday, they gave him days to live without surgery, and months with the surgery. Today, he is recovering from yesterday's emergency brain surgery. They went inside his head and removed the charred remains of his second tumor in order to make more room for the additional brain swelling. At best, after all he's had to endure, they say that he only has a few months left to live.

He won't be alive when all this shit comes out. And that's killing me. And...

The part that's really killing me is our souls haven't been connected for a long time. We're both very busy people. We work. And that is what we do. And I've been working my ass off on this for years. I wanted to set my dad up.

More than anyone else I know; my dad deserves to have the peace of mind that comes with financial freedom. If only I can...

Everything happens for a reason.

Friday, March 28, 2003

The broken hand had to have surgery on it today. The doctor had to put in three pins. We spent our whole day waiting in a different hospital's waiting room.

Saturday, March 29, 2003

It's Spring Break.

We're finally home alone. We had to leave the house at 3:30am to go to the airport and put the last of our kids on a plane. Then we went back to our empty home and took a nap. Then we went to visit dad in ICU.

Gray.

The ICU would only let us stay in his room for fifteen minutes at a time. In between visiting with my dad, my Baby and I visited with my family, and lots and lots of other families, in the waiting cubicles.

VI: April 2003

Saturday, April 05, 2003

Spring Break interrupted. A couple of our kids came home early and unannounced.

"Oh, shit. Quick, Baby, help me grab-up all of our personal stuff and make it disappear."

Sunday, April 06, 2003

Happy Birthday to me...

The rest of our kids finally came home. We had a really nice "all-together" birthday dinner.

Monday, April 07, 2003

We finished gathering and entering our tax data for our accountant.

Tuesday, April 08, 2003

Today, we had an 8:00am appointment to drop off our tax shit with our accountant.

We took both kids with broken bones to the same doctor. One went in the morning and the other went in the afternoon.

Nothing's ever easy. Is it?

In the morning, the arm no longer needs a cast.

In the afternoon, the three pins came out of the hand, but the cast has to stay on the hand a little longer. Recast hand.

Wednesday, April 09, 2003

We went on a field trip with the sixth-grade class at the Milwaukee Museum and had a nice tour.

The museum was near my dad's hospital. We took everybody's brown bag lunches and drove ahead of the school bus. When the bus went back to school, we stayed, and went to see my dad in his hospital. It's been two weeks. They moved my dad out of the ICU and up to the rehab floor today.

Thursday, April 10, 2003

I had a nasty knock-down drag-out brawl on the telephone today. It got ugly and reminded me of the divorcing days. Whatever, and...

Tuesday, April 15, 2003

We picked up our taxes, wrote the checks, and mailed them off.

VII: July 2003

Sunday, July 27, 2003

I apologize for my absence. Let me catch us up.

I spent a lot of time writing, and reworking, a two-page query letter. I sent it out to four agents in March. I just reread it and I am too embarrassed to put that two-page query letter in here and show everyone in the whole wide world. It really is that bad. What? Exactly. And...

I got three rejection letters on the tenth day. The fourth rejection letter came back two and a half weeks later, the day before my birthday. Happy birthday to me.

My life completely fell apart on Valentine's Day, and everything went to shit from there. My Baby wrote down all the little snapshots of our daily life when our shit was happening. And I thought I should share all of them with you. So, I'm typing it all in. And I'm blending in my long-drawn-out handwritten nonsense created after I put in the tiny little snip-it's of our daily personal life. And that's my point.

It's near the end of July, and everything has just now slowed down enough to let me stop and type in this year.

Yes, this year, it's 2003.

My life is totally messed-up. On top of all that, we dumped a ton of cash (and energy) into quitting smoking. We started taking anti-depressants two weeks prior to our quit date. We bought some patches and officially quit smoking on May 5, 2003.

Five days later, on May 10, 2003, I started smoking again. The anti-depressants just made me fat. All my 36's went away, and I had to drag the 38s out for the summer. If you could see me right now, you'd say, "Man, you're fat." And that's enough about my fucked-up life.

How's your life going?

VIII: August 2003

Tuesday, August 12, 2003

Desperation breeds inspiration.
 I gotta do something different. Things have to change.

Wednesday, August 13, 2003

This is my first presentable query letter:

Dear [Mr./Ms. Potential Literary Agent's Last Name],

Soul-sex bathes our soul, which is the innermost part of us, in love. This love-bath leaves a lasting aura of beauty on a person's body. Everything beautiful bubbles up from the inside. The beautiful bubbles stop whenever we become conflicted.

Conflict cannot arise out of a singular entity. Since we have conflict inside us, there's reason to believe we have two separate entities within our brain. Without a soul, we wouldn't have any internal conflict. We wouldn't have any variations in our sexual intensity either.

How can we lose ourselves? Wherever you go, there you are. Right? After all, imagination is our soul at play. When we're having a deep conversation with someone, our souls lock face-to-face and eye-to-eye.

Can the world's reality go away? Where does the scientific reality go when it leaves us? Where do our personal realities go when they leave us? Does the light in your head's refrigerator stay on all the time? Before we start going off into that, let's just keep things simple.

Why do we shut the souls we love out of our life? It's because it is almost the only emotional defense mechanism our souls have. A self-isolating person is a person with a closed soul. An isolated soul can be a lonely place, unless you like it like that.

What makes us push people away? What makes us repel from each other? How does our soul close and push people away? Closed souls have a way of keeping the hurtful and the helpful at bay. Why do we close our soul and prefer to keep "some people" we're shutting out near us?

What does "some people" mean? And how distant are you to the loving souls around you? Are you out of touch, unplugged, or disconnected from the people you love? If we spend lots of time together every day, how can we be distant and disconnected? Isn't that physically impossible?

When our scientists scientifically authenticate our soul, we could clear the board on all kinds of strange phenomenon. But...

Honestly, I am supposed to be on vacation. And it's my first vacation in two years. And it's late. And I need some sleep. Goodnight.

———

I know that this is not the typical query letter. But I am not the typical author. You have just read an entry from a manuscript I started in October 2002.

If you don't want to get tangled up in this, please send my work back to me in my black shiny folder in my SASE. If you feel you might like to be a part of my party, I'd love to send you more of my stuff.

Warmest regards,

Friday, August 15, 2003

Here we go, again. I've been working really hard on this query letter. This is the best query letter I can do right now. It cost me a ton of time and energy. It took a long time to draft it all up and rework it about a million times. My Baby and me shined her up as best we could. I've got the names and addresses of several agents from the go find your literary agent website. I'm desperate. And I'm anxious.

When I send my stuff out, I have to wait for what seems to be fucking forever to get a response back. From the get-go, I have never stopped moving this manuscript forward. I constantly work on it. This shit is consuming my nights and my days. I tell my family I'm going to work, and I disappear to work on this nonsense. I rework my old shit in the evening, and I write my new shit at night. I have completely abandoned my family in my pursuit of getting this published.

And that shit ain't cool.

Friday, August 22, 2003

Getting your manuscript published is a 'paint by numbers' thing. If you stay in the lines and paint your picture with the book industry's assigned paints, you'll be taken seriously. If you don't, you won't.

I don't. But then again...

I don't have to. And...

I am big trade's only exception. I have big trade's only Golden Ticket which says I'm the only one who gets to break all the rules down at big trade. Everybody else has to obey big trade's rules. That's just the way things are. That's just how everything works. I don't make the rules. I'm just calling them as I see them. And...

A general rule out there in big trade literary agent land is authors are only allowed to submit their shit to one agent at a time. We have to personalize a query letter enough to make some sort of connection without becoming too personal.

And the problem is, there ain't a damn thing anyone can do to stop us from doing anything we want to do as long as whatever it is isn't illegal, and that's the Law.

On August 18, 2003, I sent my query letter package to ten different literary agents. And I'm thinking…

'My writing totally sells itself.' And…

I'm so confident that this query letter is going to start this book's word-of-mouth wildfire, I feel sort of bad about sending my query letter package out to ten different agencies at the same time. What happens when they all call me?

What do I say to the slower nine?

Prior to this mass mailing, something inside me would only let me do four agencies at a time. And then, on Monday, I sent my first ten at a time. Ten literary agencies at a time is my new record.

Next Monday, I'm gonna send thirty more query letter packages. I plan on going balls to the wall, until I get a nibble. I can't afford to wait any longer. I gotta get this show on the road. Something needs to happen real fast. My life is starting to go downhill really fast.

IX: September 2003

Friday, September 05, 2003

Once we know what we got and how the damn thing works, we can fix it when it gets broken. So...

How's your emotional heart? How's your soul? Is your heart and soul firmly wedged into the same parts of you like they are wedged in me? How's your sex life?

"Who's your daddy?"

My daddy is dying.

Today, his doctor told us his original tumor is growing bigger and deeper into his brain stem. They're guessing he only has a couple of weeks left to live.

My dad is 59 years old.

The men in my family have some shitty luck when it comes to having any kind of decent longevity. Then again, every last one of them smoked like freight trains. And for that, I hope to quit before it's too late for me.

Sometimes, it really sucks to be me. And if it's sometimes like that for you, too? Go figure.

I was hoping my dad would hold on. I want to set him up and fix everything that's going wrong.

It doesn't look like I'm gonna make it.

"FUCK!"

I have query letter packages out to 37 literary agents right now. Nobody never wants to read my shit. Never...

And I'm hoping my luck is gonna change here real soon.

I received two more rejections today. Both of the agents kept my two-page query letter, my SASE envelope, my shiny black folder, and my business card. I hope they can make some money on e-Bay one day. One agent e-mailed me. The other sent a "Dear Writer" note on a half a sheet of paper in one of her envelopes, and she kept my SASE, and she even paid for her own envelope and postage. So...

Why the hell did I send out all of my SASEs?

I guess prim and proper is a one-way road when it comes to all of this big trade bullshit.

It's late. I gotta get up early to get a jump on a new construction cleaning job. If we don't put in a full twelve-to-sixteen-hour workday tomorrow, all day Saturday, we ain't gonna be able to keep up with our schedule. We have tons and tons of new construction to clean this week. When the money is a little tight, a small business owner has to take all the work that comes our way. So...

Goodnight.

Saturday, September 20, 2003

What happens when we die?

Nobody knows for sure. If you are a hard-core scientist,

Connecting the Web of Humanity:

nothing happens. You die. You're done. And that's the end of you. And then again...

In death, the same is true throughout life; any and every great scientist can only offer their best guess.

Scientifically, we don't know much of anything for sure, except that we will die. Science is based on our best educated guesses. And if you're a religious person, you probably believe something will happen to you when you die. My *only* problem with any particular religion is...

Every ever-after scenario varies from one religion to another. That, and each religion has its own secluded ever-after.

Science disagrees with every religion. Yet, here we are in 2003, and ninety percent of us are religious. So, who's right?

What do you believe? What do I believe? If you are serious about asking me, I gotta go back to...

I believe everything depends on whatever you believe. If you believe something will happen to you, it will. If you believe something will not happen to you, it won't. And I'm not talking about winning the lottery or some kind of sick and twisted fucked-up shit like violence. I'm talking about...

What will happen to you when you die? So...

What will happen to you?

I ain't got no clue.

I only know what will happen to me. So...

What is going to happen to me? Well...

I'm a spiritual person. And...

I believe I have my soul. I believe in my soul's Creator. I believe my soul's Creator created everything around me billions of years ago. I believe my soul's Creator is smarter than I am able to comprehend. I also believe our soul will live forever in our personal ever-after scenario. And I believe that believing in things makes those things so. I believe that if you don't believe in your ever-after, you seal your own fate. As in...

Believing in nothing makes it so.

I believe nouns, like people, places, things, and ideas can immobilize and break my soul. If you don't believe that you have a soul, you ain't got nothing to worry about. If you haven't got one, you won't be needing one. Right?

Which way you believe down deep inside your core being is probably whichever way it will happen to you when you die.

And... My soul feels damaged when I'm abused, neglected, empty, abandoned, arguing, fighting, and bickering.

I'm a very codependent person. How about you?

Where did all of today's fucked-up weird shit come from?

My dad died five days ago. And...

His funeral was on my mom's birthday.

Happy 57th to her.

Wednesday, September 24, 2003

I e-mailed Dave again last night. I know he ain't reading any of my shit. I just know it. I'd like to write to Dave until he tells me to go away.

Yeah right.

Like that shit would ever happen.

Why would anyone purposely choose to have a ho-hum life? All we gotta do is mend our fences. And we gotta do all the "honey-do's" we gotta do in our relationships. Our sex life gets supercharged when we're taking good care of our lover.

Supercharged love. Getting any?

Super-sized sex. Want some?

"Eat'm up, yum."

We have a big day tomorrow, a full schedule. Clean, Clean, Clean... It's late. I'm going to sleep. No...

I take that back.

I need to write tonight. What the hell? I've got shit for sleep for three days. So...

What's one more fucked-up morning?

A little snip-it more of my private life, here we go...

It's 12:19 a.m. I'm laying butt-ass naked in my bed next to the girl of my dreams, skin to skin, and I'm writing this shit down in longhand on a legal pad, so I can type it into my computer sometime later.

My Baby and me have a blended family. We have a total of five kids. As of everyday last month, last week, this week, yesterday, today, tomorrow, next week, and next month...

Two are playing football. One is learning to play the piano. One is taking voice lessons. One is playing basketball. One has a driver's license and two jobs. One is looking for work. One has a job lined up after football. Two are in middle school. Three are in high school. Four are in their school's band. And all of them are in consecutive grades (and hopefully graduating), five years in a row.

We are seven very busy people. Like most families, we get hungry and require stuff to eat on a regular basis. When you're running $2\frac{1}{2}$ to 3 pounds of meat to the table day after day, and follow it up with six gallons of milk, week after week, it's always time to go grocery shopping. We just try like hell to keep up. My Baby and me do our best to be together 24/7. And speaking of being a Mom and Pop...

Our cleaning business has gone way deeper than ass-deep in busy. My Baby and I are completely worn out. My family all went home. Everything is slowly quieting down on the outer banks of the family river. Everyone I know and love is sleep deprived like a big-dog. We are all just barely chugging along.

The homeowner's to-do list is about six pages long. It just grows and grows.

And 2003's winter will be here before we know it.

Sometimes, you gotta do what you gotta do. When you ain't got no choice, and you gotta do it, what else can you do? That's me. Right here. Right now. Here today.

And even though I'm sure I know nobody in big trade gives a shit, I'm begging for big trade's mercy.

Some days, my life can really drain my soul.

Today was not one of those days. But I am tired. In fact, I'm fucking exhausted. So, what you see is what you get. Oops. There I go again. I can't hold back my tears any longer, again, and again, and again.

Change of plans. I'm gonna go write a couple of letters to my sisters.

It's 1:11 a.m.

X: October 2003

Thursday, October 09, 2003

"The Bath"

Ingredients:

Bathtub
Bath Water
One 4oz. Bottle of Alfa-Keri or Epson Salt
Tasty Beverage
Smoke
Atmosphere
Hand Towel (for the smokes)

    Fill the bathtub with water. If you have one of those big bathtubs, dump the entire ($^1/_2$ cup) four-ounce bottle of Alfa-Keri in the water. If you have one of those regular kid-sized tubs, like the kind I'm used to, dump half ($1/4$ cup) of the bottle of Alfa-Keri in your water or follow the Epson Salt instructions.

Share your bath water and share your love.

Adjust your environs. Set up your environment. Use candles, lighting, sound, etc.

Place your tasty beverage, smokes, and hand towel near your tub. The pool rules say to use anything but glass.

Strip down and crawl in. "Chillax". Relax. Take your time. Enjoy the moment. If you smoke, light 'em up.

Tell the whole fucked-up world to go to hell. Tell yourself you ain't gotta do a fucking thing you don't want to do until you're done with your bath.

When you're done, you'll be glad you did.

Eliminate a problem and the cause goes away. Help the cause and a problem goes away. Goodnight.

Sunday, October 26, 2003

I have a little time right now.

I was lost on what to do next. My Baby suggested I write. So here we go...

Everything is in limbo. The search for my agent is on hold. And here's the scoop on what I know so far...

Out of 40 literary agent packets that I sent out with my SASEs, only 26 actually came back. Of those 26, more than half did not bother to send my query letter back to me. And for whatever reason, they decided to keep it, or they destroyed it, or whatever the fuck they're still doing with it, and how the fuck I will ever figure this shit out, I don't know. All I know is...

As of right here and right now, I haven't heard a ding-dang thing from 14 of the 40 agents in my August mass mailing. I've given up checking my mailbox every fucking day. I don't ever

Connecting the Web of Humanity:

expect to hear back from the last 14 literary agents. I wonder what they do with everybody's unused SASEs. What happens to our unused stamps?

If hundreds and hundreds of nobody wannabe big trade authors are sending SASE's with the same $1.^{29} postage I spent on each and every one of my SASE(s), and our stamps don't get used to send all of our SASE(s) back to us, what happens to all of that money? Speaking of...

Why wouldn't they bother to send my shit back to me?

All they gotta do is drop it in the mail. I already paid for it. Kindness don't cost too much of anything. What makes some literary agents be so all-mighty fucking important? Why do some literary agents keep all of our shit? I don't want some agent who's stealing my shit from me. Screw that. There. I'm done. And I feel better for it. So...

Thank you for listening to me vent.

Doing bad things and feeling good about doing them makes people bad people. Nobody can do anything about all the bad people out in our cold cruel world. Doing bad things and feeling bad about doing them makes people good people. Good people can sometimes be mean. Have you ever been remorsefully ashamed about the pain you've caused someone? Me too. I bet we have a lot of shit in common, like you leaving me the fuck alone, and me leaving you the fuck alone. We don't know each other all that well in the first place. This book is just my job. My job does not define me. If it did, I'd just be another starving artist cleaning person. And I'm not just another starving artist cleaning person today...

I am who I am.

And I'm your new daddy.

And, there you go.

So, now you know.

It's late. I'm sleepy. Can you tell?

Goodnight.

Monday, October 27, 2003

Today, I want to bounce back into our human relationships. If we want to put ourselves into a tighter and more loving relationship, we can improve our human sexual experiences. There are lots of really great books on how to have better and longer sex. Go on a shopping spree and see.

If you're open and honest with your 24/7-lover and your 24/7-lover's open and honest with you…

"Cheers, likesa beers." (Become your own "growed-up" little inner kid.)

We can't control who we fall in-love with. We have no control over who turns us on. We can't control who's attractive to us or who we repulse from. We don't have any control over the twitter-pated crushes we have. Our soul is in charge of the love we have and give. Our soul is what gives us our instincts. Our soul is what gives us our unconscious/subconscious urges. When our hearts want one thing, and our heads keep holding us back, we often end up someplace in the middle of being fucked-up on the inside of ourselves. But if we allow our conscious freewill to come into play, if we can engage our freewill, and maintain a constant conscious cognitive control over everything we do, we do. And when we don't, our souls take over, and the whole wide cold cruel world goes away in a hurry. And…

Sometimes that can be beautiful. And sometimes people turn mean, and things get ugly. Always look before you leap. When things get totally out of control, people can go to jail. And that's the Law. Speaking of…

"Bad boy, bad boy, whatcha gonna do?

Whatcha gonna do when they come for you?"

If you're in a relationship, some sort of love and passion is already there for you to work with and build on. If you're in a business relationship, the passion is money. If your relationships are in your home, the passion is love. The passion at home can also come from other things, like money, or selfish personal comforts, and whatnot.

Who takes care of whom when you are home? Who has the comfiest life in your house? Whose body is the most worn out in your house? Who is lazy enough to earn the title of most comfy cozy soul in your house? Whose soul is the most lost in your house? Do you love the people you live with? Do you live with people you don't get along with or like very much? Do you live alone? Do you prefer living alone? If you do, that's perfectly okay with me. I ain't got nothing against nobody.

Everybody is their own individual. Everything is what it is. And we are what we are. People are people. And...

However you choose to live life is okay by me.

I ain't judging nobody for nothing. In fact...

I ain't saying nothing about nothing, except...

Life is some serious forever-changing shit. And if you like what is going on with you, keep on keeping on. And if you don't like what's going on with you, you have to change it for yourself. Why?

If you don't hold onto your personal reins, who does?

The key to a good relationship is communication.

When we have great conversations, when we're being open and honest, and we bond our innermost-selves with the innermost-selves of other people, and then, we have quality time. And speaking of intimacy...

All we have to do is open ourselves up. And we always open ourselves up by talking honestly, and when we talk to each other honestly, our souls connect. For that reason, in order for one to connect to the other, communication has to be a two-way street.

Relationships are two-way streets.

Coincidence? I think not.

And when you talk to your lover, what do you say? How do you say whatever it is you say? When do you talk to each other? Do you ever really listen to what's really being said? Do you always pay attention? Are you really listening? Or...

Are you just waiting to talk?

When you talk, do you ever say anything important? Do you always feel like you are the only one contributing to your relationship? If you do, why are you doing that to your soul? And...

"Don't worry, your little secret's safe with me."

If the other party isn't contributing anymore, what did you do to make the other party lose interest in you? Maybe it's not your fault. Maybe the other party is in the middle of having a personal crisis. Maybe you are disconnected. Maybe the other party isn't bored with you, and it is totally something else altogether.

"Dig in and find out." Talking is talking. And...

If nothing ever changes, everything stays the same. And...

"Wouldn't you just love to snatch some time, sit down, grab someone's ear, and have a heart-to-heart talk?"

Just talking about all the rotten stuff helps all the stinky-ness go away, and then, things get better from there. And then again, truth be told...

If you ignore things long enough, time has a way of working all your problems completely out of your soul.

Time washes our soul back to new, over and over again.

If we can sit down and peacefully chat about whatever's bothering us, things start to move in the right direction.

When we pay attention to what's actually being said in our private conversations, we are keeping our soul open to each other. And being able to keep our souls open to each other can get us going down the right path.

Connecting the Web of Humanity:

When old doors close, new doors open. When new doors open, old doors close. We never know what's waiting around the next corner, until we know. It could be a disaster. It could be beautiful. It could be fantastic sex. It could be a badass new mind-blowing book. It could be spectacular. Or it could be brutal. And...

Outside of a few good psychics, who would honestly know? It might even be a newly re-discovered relationship. Sometimes we just don't know, until we know.

When our soul closes off, we push people away. Our soul can totally block certain people out of our lives. When we get really angry, our ability to reason goes out the door. Our souls turn off our ability to listen to what's being said. Our souls protect ourselves when they must.

Some kids get angry and become real loud. Some kids get real quiet. That's just how some kids are.

We give as good as we get. We get as good as we give. And then again...

Humanity has an exception to every rule. That's just the way humanity is.

I'm deliberate about having a nice tight relationship with all of the good people around me. When they have something to say to me, and they say things in a nasty or painful way, I turn into a giant sponge and quietly listen. I do what I can to keep my inner being open enough to cognitively understand what's really being said underneath all that frustration and anger. And sometimes...

I don't. Sometimes, I go off like the popcorn kernels in a microwavable bag of Explode-O-Pop Popping Corn...

"America's only atomic popping corn."

It's Dave's popcorn. Ask for it by name.

We process new information and make our personal adjustments according to how the information is delivered (inflection) and who delivers it.

Our soul is an emotional mirror. If criticism is delivered in a hurtful way, people usually won't take it in at face value, unless they're building grudges. Then, they need those brand-new support beams to make their grudges bigger and roomier.

Angry is as anger does.

Constructive criticism delivered passively and peacefully carries a ton of weight. If we can figure out a way to keep our inner beings open when we're working on our inner beings, our cold cruel fucked-up world would become a more beautiful place.

And I know my peeps ain't out to maliciously hurt me. And my peeps know that I ain't out to maliciously hurt them.

I block malicious people out of my life, for life.

It's like I always said, I believe in decency, unless I don't like you. I dislike the people who disrespect me, unless I like you. And I am a very forgiving person, but I do have my limits. And I'm at one right now. And I'm really tired. So, goodnight.

XI: November 2003

Friday, November 14, 2003

It's 3:30 p.m., in the afternoon. My Baby and I are naked in bed together. She's napping. I'm writing to you.

When we're really worked-up, all hot and horny for our lover, when we are in a desperate need of a good fuck, we are a good fuck. When our lover is really worked up, all hot and horny for us, when they're in a desperate need of a good fuck, we get a good fucking in.

When we ain't all that worked-up or interested in fucking our lover, we ain't gonna experience our best sexual experiences. If our lover ain't worked-up or all that interested in fucking, we ain't gonna get fucked very good.

When people ain't horny, they ain't in the mood for sex. If our lover isn't horny, sex ain't worth the effort, no matter how good of a lover we are. So, what gets you sexually excited? And what sexually excites your lover? Foreplay ain't just another dirty word on the old chalkboards in our sex education classrooms.

In my opinion, as far as sex goes, if you ain't gorging, you ain't living. And what does it take to feast on a fantastic sex life? You gotta put tons of hard work and lots of physical energy into it all.

It's all about our foreplay.

Good hardcore high-energy new relationship sex gobbles up a tremendous amount of physical energy. Good hardcore high-energy new relationship sex produces the most amazing orgasms. Good hardcore high-energy new relationship sex makes us need, and helps us get, lots of good rest. Good hardcore high-energy new relationship sex gobbles up tremendous amounts of togetherness time. And the same goes for the beautiful sexual experiences of a renewed relationship. And the same goes for those who maintain good hardcore high-energy new relationship sex throughout an entire relationship

On the other end of this pleasure spectrum, piss-poor sex consumes a small amount of oxygen, tiny amounts of effort and time, and occasionally, we might even end up enjoying a wimpy orgasm, or two. But why bother to have lazy sex so "bothersomely," if we can just eat some chocolate, masturbate, and make everything feel better?

Are you having wimpy orgasms? If you are, next time...

Just say, "No."

The love you make is equal to the love you make. And if you're gonna make it, make it count. Make it big. Make it hard. Make it hot. Make it passionate. Make it sing. Make it ring. Make it beautiful. Make it rock. Why?

The reactions of our actions can either be our souls' rewards or our souls' consequences. And if you get the consequences, you also get to make all of your own cognitive decisions. Cognition, and...

Our sex lives are ours to make.

Easier said than done?

Gnaw. Grab your lover by the hands, and really look at whoever is looking at you, and see what I mean.

It's 4:30 p.m. I can still catch a nap.

We're still in the same day, except now, it is nine hours, and one minute, later. My Baby is sleeping. She works the morning shift. I work the night shift. She does breakfast. I do last call. We're perfect for each other. We're each other's natural counterparts. My Baby and I like being together 24/7. Together, we form a seamless parental entity. We're each other's nearest, dearest, and "bestest" friends. And...

I work better when I know my momma hen and all our little chicks are down (and out) for the night. Some nights...

No.

Scratch that. I'm gonna start over.

Almost every night, I get shit for sleep. I'm up really late. I either work on this shit or I do something else altogether. When I get sleep deprived, I am either a little goofy, or I turn into a real grouchy bear. When my life is rolling along really nice, my sleep deprivation makes me goofy and fun. When my life is running through broken glass and briar patches, when I'm white knuckling my way through my life, my sleep deprivation makes me grumpy, and grouchy, and I growl all day long.

If you know me, you know. In many ways, I am a carbon copy of my dad. If you knew him, and you know me, you know.

They say...

"Time heals all of our soul's wounds."

Our relationships are a lot like our bodies. It's like pumping iron. If we want to get a lot of big strong muscles, we gotta put in some serious time and energy. If we want to be limber when we're old, we gotta continuously stretch and move our body. Sometimes, we just gotta be better lovers for our lovers. Use it or lose it. No...

Not really, not when it comes to sex. But...

Everything does cost us something.

Whatever we give is usually whatever we get back. So...

Investing some quality time and tons of energy into our relationships helps us have better relationships.

Are you and yours really tight? "Dino-mite."

I realize that some of us are so busy; we ain't got no time. And to you I say, "I don't know what to say." And speaking of never having enough time...

It's 1:59 a.m. I need some sleep. I'm dead-dog tired. I'm cooked. I'm deep-fried sleepy.

Somebody stick a fork in me, I think I'm done.

Goodnight.

Now it's 3:05 a.m. I can't sleep. I want to sleep, but my brain won't let me. My brain is running a million miles an hour right now. I may as well work on this. So, here we go...

When we drop all of our soul's grudges, and talk with each other as friends, peace will rule the day. And...

That's not very likely to happen anywhere in America, anytime soon.

We're at war with big tobacco. We're at war with America's illegal drugs, three decades and counting. We're at war in Afghanistan. We're at war in Iraq. And our book industry is having a cold war with anyone who doesn't regularly buy books. And I'm in a rather heated war with the book industry over that. Then, we got the Democrats filibustering the Republicans. And whenever they ain't doing that, we got the Republicans filibustering the Democrats. Then, we got this whole undigested regurgitating Roe versus Wade issue looming over everyone's heads. Then, we got brilliant scientific minds and brilliant religious minds beating the hell out of each other over our souls. And then, we got Mars vs. Venus, race vs. race, country vs. country, sexual preference vs.

sexual preference, and the Minnesota Vikings vs. everyone else in the NFL.

My Baby loves the Minnesota Vikings. She's a diehard fan. She goes way back. She got hooked-in when the Vikings had their Purple People Eaters. She was in high school.

If everything happens for a reason, then everything had to have happened for a reason. Right? If we didn't do everything we did in our yesterdays, we wouldn't be where we are today.

One thing leads to another. It's like one moment leading to the next.

Like right now, it's 3:30 a.m. Goodnight, for real.

It's 3:44 a.m. We also got American freedoms vs. censorship, every other book in our favorite 2003 bookstores vs. my brand-new personal form of artistic expression.

I am my Baby's Baby. As one of my readers, you ought to know that I wouldn't have been able to do any of this nonsense without her constant love and support.

In today's big-bad scary world, I'm really glad we found each other. I love you Baby.

Goodnight.

Wednesday, November 19, 2003

Thanksgiving is coming. I hope to put my pen and pad down for a little while. I want to spend some time with my family. Between cleaning, chauffeuring, rehearsals, practices, performances, games, shows, cooking, homework helping, grocery shopping, cleaning, writing, and reworking all of my writing, I haven't seen much of my kids since school started.

We are all way too overbooked. We are all way too over extended. My family and I need to spend some time reconnecting with each other. Something has to go. So, "Buh-bye." See you in December.

Wednesday, November 26, 2003

My Baby thought it would be a good idea to set this work down for a while. After a week of me bouncing off the walls, she told me to go back to work on this. So...

Authors do what we can't help but do. We bounce off the walls until we can't stand it. And then we...

If we built a time machine and went back in time, we wouldn't be able to convince the people, way back when, to believe in things we know to be true today.

If we went back to Galileo's time and ran around telling everyone what we know about time and space, everyone would call us crazy, and try to kill us dead. Go ask Bruno. Oh...

That's right. We can't. So...

Where would we be way back then? And...

Look at where humanity is today. Humanity has made lots of progress on some parts and not so much on others.

Thursday, November 27, 2003

Happy Thanksgiving.

Let's say I said, "In my heart of hearts, I know _____ to be true." What exactly am I talking about?

What exactly is in the heart of humanity's hearts? Ain't whatever's in our heart of hearts really just whatever's deep inside our souls?

Beauty is relative. Beauty is in the eye of the beholder. Love is dependent upon beauty. That makes love relative. Yet as relative as love is to life, love hasn't been relative in the science lab, unless two (or three) of each other's lab partners have been fucking each other's brains out like some lovers sometimes do.

Love is one of our life's constants. The beauty of someone can whip-up our soul's constant love up into a sexual frenzy. Then the next thing we know, people start fucking-each-other's-brains-out like some lovers sometimes do.

In a way, love is a lot like the continuum of time. Angry people screw-up their love life like our soul screws up our ability to always be cognitively aware of the time. And…

Always remember, what comes around goes around.

Negativity and positivity are boomerangs. They always come back at us no matter what.

The really cool part about negativity and positivity is they don't always come back at us the exact same time (or way) we give them.

Most times they do.

Sometimes they don't. But no matter what…

Negativity and positivity will come back around. And…

Find us.

Design, karma, kismet, or call it what you will…

More often than not, everything comes back around at us. In my heart of hearts, I know it's real. And I know this is true.

And if we know in our heart of hearts that we've done wrong, somehow, someway, we'll always end up paying for it. When we know we did someone wrong; grief, guilt, and/or remorse will automatically punish us through our soul, and that kind of stuff will always end-up keeping us from achieving the good stuff. See?

When we do good deeds, our soul's rewards are righteous. And when we project goodness out into the world, more often than not, we receive goodness back. And if we project bad karma out into the world, more often than not, bad karma comes around back at us. And…

We can't hide from it. Because…

Wherever we go, there we are.

When you shake the shit out of your rugs outside, you get covered in the rug's dirt, and it don't matter whichever way the wind is blowing.

Give a little, get a little. Get it? Got it? Good. Goodnight.

Sunday, November 30, 2003

I keep a legal pad and several Pentel Rolling Writers beside my bed. I never know when the next good thought might happen. I miss way too many.

We are catching a break from all our new construction work and what did I do? I worked. Over the past three days, I built some temporary walls in our basement to give three of our "youngers" a more private space to illegally live in. They are supposed to have an egress window and they don't.

I worked my ass off this whole Thanksgiving weekend, until today. Today, I didn't even get dressed until 3:30 p.m. An hour later, I changed back in my lounging clothes. Today, I rested.

Right now, I'm writing, "My entire body hurts." And…

It's 6:45 p.m.

My Baby is watching the tube, the TMC channel. We love the old "black and white" movies. I'm soaking in my Baby's used alfa-kerized bathwater, in my tiny, way too small for me, 35-year-old light blue bathtub, and I'm writing this for you. Share the bathwater and share the love. And when I'm done, I'll be glad I did.

Now it's 2:45 a.m.

I got out of my tub around 7:30 p.m., went online, and found some really cool shit. And right now, I'm watching a segment from CBS's 60 Minutes that I recorded on my VCR, which originally aired (seven days ago) on Sunday, November 23, 2003. The segment's name is "Porn in the USA." Trevor Nelson and James Kroft produced it.

I'm pushing the play button. And...

Here we go...

The adult entertainment industry generated ten billion dollars last year. In 2002, we rented 800 million VHS and DVD adult movies, and the porn industry made 11,000 new movies.

The social stigma around pornography creates its high-profit margin. What's porn's impact on society? What does the Justice Department hope to do about it?

Right back after these commercials...

Update: My Writer's Digest tells me 195,000 new book titles were published in 2003. And now...

Back to the "Porn in the USA" show...

How did it all begin? The VCR.

In 2003, there are 180 million hits on a Google search for "sex." America has computers in 70 to 80 percent of our households. Attorney General John Ashcroft bought expensive blue drapes and used them to cover up the United States of America's statues of our Spirit of Justice and our Majesty of Law.

A government spokeswoman said the government is not out to stop the porn industry. The Feds are watching everything, but they're only on the lookout for violent, gruesome sex. They are only looking for the largest quantity and distribution of the wrong kind of material.

And that's all the room I had on my VHS tape. So...

It's rewinding right now. So...

Apparently, pornography is like marijuana, except pornography's not illegal. Porn is covered by our First Amendment. But just like the illegal drug trade, our USA government is only concerned with the largest quantity of material, the largest area of distribution, and any of the other really big trophies it can find.

The main reason we, as a nation, can't put serious issues on our national kitchen table is because we can't let our private shit be known unless you're out. But even then…

You gotta play the "don't ask, don't tell" game, unless you're totally out of that closet, and you just don't give a shit about playing those fucked-up games anymore.

Closeted people are only tight with the people they let into their personal closets. And I just gotta say…

"Knock knock. It's me, John. Let me in."

Some of us are just tremendous troublemakers. And with over six billion people on this planet, everybody has plenty of people to disagree with. And that's our humanity.

We all know some dickheads, bitches, and assholes. We all can be dickheads, bitches, and assholes. And either way, we get the consequences, so we get to decide.

My need to have this book published with my individual artistic expression has been very disturbing to all the people I've contacted thus far.

But just like Elvis was to rock-n-roll, I can become a total contender with all the revolutionary shit I packed in here. I just need to find somebody looking for something that is almost ahead of its time. And so far…

It ain't been easy.

It's late. I can't see the clock. But I know its way past my bedtime. I'm falling asleep trying to write tonight. Goodnight.

XII: December 2003

Monday, December 01, 2003

I was digging around on the Interweb today. And I have great news. I just found out I'm in the middle of writing creative nonfiction. This shit is creative nonfiction. Oh man...

"YEAH!!! This is almost as good as a Holy Fuck!"

I can't tell you how good it feels to finally fit in some place. I've felt like a square peg in a world full of round writing holes. How in the hell am I supposed to describe all this? It does not fit into any of the writing establishment's current classifications. This is not fiction, and it's not our standard nonfiction either.

Sometimes, life is like driving through a long-ass dark tunnel. Even with our headlights on, the only thing we can see is what's right in front of us. Sometimes, we can't even see that.

I don't know where the hell I'm going. I'm totally lost. It's completely dark. Then, from out of nowhere...

Along comes a sign. And...

It says, "Creative Nonfiction that way." And...

I think to myself, 'Hey, I'm going that way. How fucking handy is that?'

I've been writing, and rewriting, and writing, and pouring my soul out on paper, and punching it all into my computer, sending it out, and never getting anywhere. And after all this time, I just found out what this shit is supposed to be called. Today, after all this time, I just now found out this nonsense is called creative nonfiction.

This is so fucking exciting. Now that I know where I'm going, and what I'm doing, maybe things will finally change. Now that I know what to call this, maybe I can finally sell it to someone in big trade.

We get to have the whole day off tomorrow. It's 3:30 a.m. I need to go to sleep. Goodnight.

"See?"

All through the past however the hell long I've been writing my ass off, I always thought big trade was holding me back. It was like I was being pushed around by the whole entire book industry. Turns out…

I've just been gearing myself up for this new creative nonfiction genre to open up. Turns out…

All the ranting and raving I did about big trade belongs in my failure column too. Turns out…

I know jack shit about the book industry. And…

Oh well, they sometimes say…

We learn something new every day.

I'll tell you what…

I'll keep writing my straight-up truth. Look at me go. I am getting it done.

I'm getting all of my nonsense down on paper as fast as I can. I'm memoir/journaling in creative nonfiction. It's an art form.

The whole wide world never saw this shit coming.

I gotta go.

Tuesday, December 02, 2003

About a year ago, I wrote, "Everything I think and write can't be absolutely brilliant all the time." Now I'd like to add...

It's okay if I made mistakes along the way. If I fucked-up here and there, on this and that, it's okay. This is my first time to do all this. We are all supposed to learn as we go along. Everything is always gonna be an education. And being so, everyone's gotta cut me some slack. That's just the way things are. No one else can write all my shit, except me. Who am I?

"I am an artist's artist."

And I can't tell you how happy I am to finally find a home to call my own. This genre is Creative Nonfiction. Well actually, I'll probably have to call my shit Extreme Creative Nonfiction. And I'm excited to finally have an answer when someone asks me what my book is about.

"Uh... It's art."

Sunday, December 07, 2003

Our minds are a lot like computers. In that...

We have a limited amount of processing capability in our minds. We can only process so much shit at a time. Too much shit, all at once, overwhelms us. The information from both halves of our whole reality enters our brain at the exact same time. And...

Everybody has their own perspective. Everybody lives in their own realities; everyone lives in a totally separate reality from our shared scientific reality. Everybody tells a different story of what happened. And I ain't got no, except for...

Everything is blending together to form our good shit, our bad shit, and all of our ordinary everyday shit.

Monday, December 08, 2003

Humans are all the same biological creature on the inside. People are all made up from our same parts and pieces. And...

There are always two sides to every coin.

Your side. My side. And speaking of freely choosing...

Battling the beliefs of Religion, and the science of Science, is like trying to win the war on terrorism, or the war on America's marijuana. We cannot win wars waged against beliefs or organic plant appetites.

Things aren't always gonna be like they are. But...

Things are the way they are, until they ain't no more.

Some battles against some people's beliefs, or organic plant appetites, or smokescreens, are not winnable. When we wage a war against marijuana smoke, the peace pipe smoke will win every time. Smoke a peace pipe. And speaking of...

I want somebody to tell me...

If we're supposed to be such a peaceful nation, why in the hell did we have to preemptively strike Iraq?

Somebody please tell me...

Why did we have to invade another sovereign country preemptively?

Why are we in another Iraq War? They did not provoke us into this war. We attacked them first. We bombed them first. And...

Throughout the history of The United States of America, we have never invaded another foreign sovereign country preemptively, until we invaded Iraq. Since the birth of our nation, as a world player on the global stage, we have attacked counties in the defense of democracy, but never have we ever invaded out of spite. This seems petty and beneath us. And then again...

America is a peaceful nation?

My ass. If we ever were, we are not anymore.

Americans ain't peaceful people.

But one day, things will change, and our smokescreen will drop away, and our American government will end one of its battles in the war that's been waged against its own citizenry. The American "War on Drugs" is not a war on drugs. It's a war against American drug users. It's a war that's being waged against ordinary everyday American citizens. And it is what it is.

Did you know that we arrest one million American marijuana users every year, after year, after year, after year? And truth be told, we escalate the number of marijuana arrests every year. In fact, we're building prisons so hard, and so fast, they're starting to turn up on the 2003 New York Stock Exchange.

America is battling a humungous war with Americans. And...

Either side you're on...

You're losing.

If we can lock up marijuana in our liquor cabinets, why are we spending our tax-dollars on locking up peaceful American marijuana users? Why can't we all just be fat and happy, instead of just fat? Why can't we turn our ATF into the ATFM, or the MATF?

Here in 2003, the United States has one hundred million households. And our entire USA population is less than five percent of the world's population. And ninety-five percent of the people on Earth don't call themselves citizens of the United States of America. We are the baddest of the bad, the strongest of the strong, the richest of the rich, and one of the fewest of the few. And...

When we mathematically turn each country's population into percentages, we maintain the highest prison populations in the world. Jail cells are becoming another thriving big business in the good old U. S. of A.

Big oil.

Big tobacco.

Big pharmaceutical.

Big insurance.

Big lobbyist.

Big government.

Big bank.

Big money.

Big trade. And...

Big prison. Big pen. Some-great-big-old...

Big ink...

And...

I ain't talking about Pentel's quality craftsmanship. And...

Speaking of an insinuation of rolling ourselves a big fat one...

If we, the strongest of the strong, the leader of our free world, ain't willing to start the search for world peace, the rest of the world will never find it. Where the hell are all of our politicians on our peace pipe issues? Why are our politicians hypocritical about marijuana use?

Who has and who hasn't been naked and baked? Step forward and state your name and claim your name to fame. And speaking of stepping up, and speaking of being a good solid American citizen...

And speaking of my First Amendment Rights...

It would be true to our country's roots for everybody to do something totally revolutionary. And speaking of me...

Right now, today, here in 2003, I'm more in-line with the Green party. If we were all looking at the whole American political spectrum, from right to left, I'd go hard left. I'm an oober-liberal-ist. But I think I will become a rock-solid Democratic Party member going forward. I just need a lot of other rock-solid Democrats to come out of their closets in favor of legalizing and regulating marijuana. And speaking of stepping out of our closets and speaking up...

Did you know that that ever since, here in 2003, we have had a bit of controversy over the speech Abraham Lincoln gave to the Illinois House of Representatives on December 18, 1840?

The speech went...

"Prohibition will work great injury to the cause of temperance. It is a species of intemperance within itself, for it goes beyond the bounds of reason in that it attempts to control a man's appetite by legislation and makes a crime out of things that are not crimes. A Prohibition Law strikes a blow at the very principles upon which our government was founded."

Our 2003 controversy is in whether or not President Lincoln actually gave this speech or someone else made it up and said he said it. And then again, and either whatever way...

Marijuana has definitely become today's Volstead Act.

Marijuana is not a crime against humanity any more than alcohol, nicotine, sugar, and caffeine are crimes against humanity. I don't think our government needs to arrest its peaceful citizens over their appetite for peace pipes.

"Let freedom ring." And speaking of "freedom"...

Isn't "that" what our Revolution was all about? Besides...

Our government already gave our employers the right to control their employee's moralities. Employers can fire people for what they do when their employee is not at work. And people have done their best to see that their rights get thoroughly enforced in our exhausted court system, with our employer winning more than not.

And with the regularization, legalization, and taxation of marijuana, we would have a hell of a lot more money to spend on our country's safety-net, and a hell of a lot less drug crime in our communities, than we currently have in the horrendous war we are waging against our American cannabis users. And that's all I'm saying about that. Besides this…

My American government ran a commercial, paid for by our Drug Counsel, about somebody, that bought some marijuana from somebody, that got that marijuana from somebody, that got the marijuana from somebody, that shot somebody. Did you see it? Do you know what I'm talking about? And either whichever way…

If marijuana were legal in the first place, nobody would have gotten shot. And speaking of people shooting people…

I recently heard that some of our South American countries are refusing to provide assistance to us in our war on drugs.

They say our appetite for illegal drugs is too great.

So basically, they are also saying that our current American policy "…goes beyond the bounds of reason to control a man's appetite by legislation…"

Just take a minute and look at our more recent Presidents and their alleged illegal drug use. I think that it is "high-time" we untied the knot that the 1912 American government tied into our Constitution, four-score-and-eleven-years-ago from today's December 08, 2003.

I just heard Cheech say that he and Chong are going to get together to make a new movie. It can't happen for a little while from today. Right now, today, Tommy is a trophy/victim/prisoner of our war on drugs. Tommy is in jail for something to do with bongs. And…

Tuesday, December 09, 2003

When we're learning how to water-ski, the first lesson we have to get is to let go of the ski rope. You would think it would be how to get up out of the water. But it's not.

Connecting the Web of Humanity:

Whenever wannabe skiers don't let go of their ski ropes, the boat drags them through the water. Some of us get dragged through the water for long distances before we learn to simply let go of the rope.

All we gotta do is let go of the rope. It seems really simple and easy, but it snot.

Life has a way of caging our free-spirited souls.

Rattle your cage and see where that gets you.

If you are having troubles with something, someone, or each other, all that horrible shit clings onto you like whatever chains are wrapped around your soul. And...

Life has small chains like...

"Good grief." *Sigh* "Not again."

And life has big chains like...

"Get all of your nasty-ass shit "outta" here! You free-loading, lazy, good-for-nothing, cheating son-of-a-bitch!"

When our soul grabs hold of its chains, like wannabe water-skier holding on to our ski ropes, the boat of life can drag us around for days, months, years. How long?

All we gotta do is let go of our life's troubles, let go of the chains wrapping around our soul, let go of the chains our souls are holding on to. Mentally visualize yourself releasing your soul's chains. Or just talk about your shit with someone close to you and let go of whatever is bothering you. Let go of whatever is clinging to you. Let go of the negative whatever keeps coming up in your head over and over. We gotta stop carrying all of the shit we are carrying around with us all the time.

You and your soul will both be happier, gentler, and more receptive when it stops getting dragged around behind your life's boat of time. So, seriously...

Take some time, sit down, and have an open and honest talk

with someone you love about whatever's bothering you. Motorboat, motorboat, go so fast. And...

Guilt is a built-up ball on a love chain. And speaking of family diseases...

"Pass them on."

It's 1:57 a.m. We are off tomorrow. I plan on working on this on my computer. I need to key in my handwriting and do some editing. My Baby wants to decorate the house for the holidays. I don't know how far I'll get with this. She always comes first.

I gotta blow out my writing candle and go to sleep now.

Wednesday, December 10, 2003

I just finished 12 hours of working on this on my computer. I reworked some of the shit upfront and keyed in some of these past few months.

Whenever you get to the end of today's nonsense, you gotta go back and reread some of my new nonsense upfront. It's awesome.

It's 4:45a.m.

I'm very tired. I gotta get up and go clean homes in the morning... Oh, wait...

Whatever...

Thursday, December 11, 2003

I just finished keying in the rest of my handwriting that I didn't get keyed in yesterday. I still need to go back and rework my whole fucked-up mess. I ain't nowhere close to getting started on all of this. And...

We're way over halfway to the end.

There's always way more I gotta cover. There's so much more I still gotta say. There's always too much to talk about. And...

That's pretty much why I'm writing my ass off, but not anymore today.

I'm really tired. I'm headed that way.

It's 1:45 a.m.

Thursday, December 25, 2003

It's 4:03a.m. Merry, merry...

Happy, happy...

Before we can help people turn back into humans, we have to turn ourselves back into human beings.

Being human is...

XIII: January 2004

Thursday, January 08, 2004

I think I've been selling this shit all wrong. I just got a rejection telling me, "I can't write any old way I want. I can't just say anything I want to say." And another one of my recent e-mail rejections said, "If you don't follow the rules, nobody will think you're serious about your craft." And honestly…

I don't know how much more serious I can be. Even if she couldn't, you have to see how serious I am about this. Can you see that I'm committed to seeing this project through all the way to the end?

I've already tried and failed miserably. But…

I'm not done. I'm still here. And I ain't going nowhere.

If I did something that made you distance yourself from me, I'd like to know about it. The last thing I ever meant to do was to make your soul want to pull away from my soul like this. I absolutely hate that we have nothing to say to each other. Why are we so quiet when we're alone together? Why do we no longer have anything to say to each other? What's our problem? Why do we just keep going on like this? What went wrong with us? When did it get like this? How did it get like this? Why don't we look deeply into each other's eyes anymore? I don't understand. Oh, wait...

Maybe I do. Maybe I shouldn't have told you how I felt.

I always paid my attention to you every time we were alone together, and if you ever wanted to find out how much I already know about you, play my game...

"Who's the daddy of them all?"

XIV: March 2004

Wednesday, March 17, 2004

This is my best query letter yet:

You are the strongest of the strong, the biggest of the big, and the baddest of the bad. I am an unpublished wannabe big trade author, a meager and simple artist of words. Everybody needs somebody. And I need you.

I'm not getting anywhere with my first manuscript.

I hope to find a large publishing house offering an elephant's weight in gold, but you know how things are. Most people would rather watch television, or be on the Interweb, than buy any particular book.

I've been working on my book for several years now. It took me a hell of a long time to figure things out about the book-publishing business. Sometimes, progress takes a long time, and sometimes, not so much.

My dad always said, "Nothing in this world is ever free. Something will always cost you something."

So, I'm letting you see the first part of my manuscript for free, three pages a day, beginning today. I hope you like it enough to pass it around.

I'm ready to be unleashed to the world. The good news is you made the list. Who's on my list? I ain't saying. I know I'm taking a huge risk in doing this. It's like my first big gig. You know what I'm talking about. I'm nervous as hell. But sometimes, you just gotta do what you gotta do.

I do what I can to protect myself with the poor-man's copyright. I mailed myself a duplicate copy via USPS just to keep things on the up and up. Other than that, what can I say? When your ride pulls up, you gotta go. Oh, look. Here comes my ride. Ready or not, here we go...

I have a brand-new concept that unites our soul and our unconscious mind as one and the same. My book makes us become aware of our soul and the other souls around us.

The more we are cognitively aware of what's really going on in our world, the more beautiful we can make our life, our lover's life, and any other relationship we choose to enhance. Beautiful relationships have a way of making life deeper and more meaningful. A beautiful life has a way of making our relationships deeper and more meaningful. Speaking of...

How's your lover's love life? Do you want to help your lover have a better love life? If your lover's love life dramatically improved, what would happen to your love life?

This ain't just any other book. I ain't that kind of author. My first book is in Extreme Creative Nonfiction. It links our unconscious mind to our soul. It also presents lots of other crazy "new shit" to think about.

I need help digging around in the yellow-lily-livered book-publishing industry. I'm hoping to find some guts. If you know somebody I need to know, please tell them about me. Tell them I'm

John E Zett III

here. Tell them I'll be here for the next thirty some-odd days, unless you want me to send more, or ask me to stop spamming my unprotected artwork to this e-mail address.

XV: April 2004

Monday, April 12, 2004

Happy 57th.

When you and your lover are real comfortable being with each other, alone as a couple, you tend to have tons and tons of Earth-rumbling sex. When you and your lover are uncomfortable being alone together, as a couple, you tend to have less and less Earth-rumbling sex.

Yummy sheet-soaking sex helps us become better people. Yummy sheet-soaking sex makes everything change for the better. That's the way our humanity works.

So...

I picked ten of the greatest people in America, ten out of 240,000,000 Americans. It wasn't easy.

If I'm going to change the world, I thought I'd by-pass all the barriers, and go straight to the top.

I've been working my ass off day-and-night getting all of this ready.

Yesterday, around the time the Late Show would be on if it was broadcast on Easter Sunday, I was sitting there with ten e-mails loaded up for the ten greatest people in America with my strongest query letter yet, and it was all ready to go. Then, I froze up. I got stuck in the moment.

Then, my Baby started softly snoring, and I snapped out of it.

And I launched this shit out there.

We can't win, if we don't play. So…

"CHARGE!"

"Look out world."

"Here I come to save the day."

XVI: May 2004

Wednesday, May 12, 2004

One month ago, on Dave's birthday, I e-sent Chapter XIV to ten people. Chapter XIV was my first three-page letter. Then I kept e-sending three pages of my manuscript.

And I've been e-sending daily three-page e-mails ever since. Everything got off to a rough start, but I was able to straighten it all out early on. Lately, things have been running pretty smoothly. Now, it only takes me 30 minutes per day. I've been cutting and pasting three pages of my manuscript, and e-sending it out to the ten most wonderful people in the United States of America, every day for a solid month. I only have one more week to go.

I e-sent Chapter XIV on the first day. Page 1, Page 2, and Page 3 on the second day. Pages 4, 5, and 6 went out on the third day. Pages 7, 8, and 9 on the fourth... Pages 10, 11, and 12 on the fifth... (And on, and on, up to today.)

Today, I e-sent Page 79, Page 80, and Page 81. I'm stopping at

Page 96. Today, May 12, 2004, Page 96, is the first page of 2003, the first page of Chapter III. And...

I'm really hooked into an e-groove.

I already know I'll miss it when I'm done. It's been fun. It keeps me busy. It gives me something to do. I would like to keep going, but I gotta quit. The anti-spam e-mail Interweb Laws are about to kick in and start up. I don't want to become an e-criminal. Sometimes, you just gotta do what you gotta do.

Big trade left me no choice. I'm sick and tired of beating on doors that ain't getting me nowhere. This thing needs to get going. The last literary agent I contacted told me, "I needed to have a national platform before she would even consider me." Who needs that nonsense? I'm not running for the President of the United States. I'm just writing this goofy little book. Fuck that shit.

I wasn't getting anywhere by following big trade's rules, so I quit following them. Instead of doing this crap their way, I'm e-sending my shit to ten highly successful people. And none of them work in our structured bookworm's industry.

I handpicked ten high-profile people who have enough of what it takes to do any damn thing they want to do to big trade. My ten people are mighty powerful people.

Who are my ten powerful people? I will never compromise the privacy of anyone, other than myself. I wouldn't ever compromise my privacy; except I think the whole wide world needs to know just how I got it going on. And it's more than just as luck would have it.

Pete and Repeat were sitting quietly in a boat. Then all at once, Pete stood up, screamed at the absurdity of the nothingness that was going on, and jumped out of the boat. Who was still in the boat?

Okay.

Pete and Re:Pete (one chill dude) were sitting quietly in a boat. Then all at once, Pete stood up and...

Because my viewpoint may differ from everyone else's viewpoint...

I'm never ever gonna tell you who my ten powerful people are. In return, I hope like hell I never find out who makes one simple telephone call that saves me and mine. I don't want to know who my secret Santa is. No...

That's bullshit. I do want to know.

It's really late.

I gotta get to sleep. I'm headed that way. Goodnight.

Tuesday, May 18, 2004

Well...

I did it. And now I'm done. About fifteen minutes ago, I e-sent my last e-mail. Page 94, Page 95, and Page 96 just went out to ten of the most wonderful citizens in my United States of America.

I've done my part. I just finished working my ass off. Now I just have to sit back and patiently wait to see what happens. Fuck...

This is a whole lot of very hard work.

Wednesday, May 19, 2004

My concept is simple. It's basically simplistic. How extraordinary is it to say; our souls are already playing a huge part inside us? To say; we all have dual intelligent minds? It's so simple. Its simplicity makes it universal. Its universality makes it highly profitable.

My "purely hypothetical" little sex and soul theories are easy to understand, easy to grasp, and yet as deeply profound as we are. Like the color white is basically simplistic, and on the other hand, extremely profound, when you consider it takes all the colors of our rainbows to make white happen in the first place. Diving in deeper...

We don't see all the colors when we see white just like we don't always see our souls when they are revealing themselves. And other than all that...

How much more real of a human do I need to become in order to make this shit happen for me and mine? I'm ready to get this show on the road, so to speak.

Monday, May 31, 2004

Our local Memorial Day parade was canceled. From what I've heard, it's the first time they have ever had to cancel this particular parade, and that turns it into a pretty big deal. Then again, we did have 175 verified tornadoes rotating across our country this past weekend. And it looks stormy today. I guess it is better to err on the side of caution, wouldn't you say? So anyhoo...

This unexpected cancellation gives me some unexpected time to work on making up more new shit. So, here we go...

Thirteen agonizing days ago, back on May 18, I e-sent my last e-mail to my ten people. All total, at a rate of three pages per day, it took me five weeks to e-send the entire first one-third of this manuscript. Outside of a couple of my closest souls, and a few literary agents, my ten people are the first to get the chance to actually read some of this shit. And...

It's been days and days of nothing but a whole lot of painful silence. I ain't heard nothing back from nobody. I never do. I should be fucking used to it by now, but I'm not. And I'm still all alone.

It would be nice to hear some positive feedback. It's time to get this thing headed that way. I ain't getting any younger.

The house cleaning business has been real. It's been fun. But it ain't been real fun, except for a time or two, and every now and again. But then again...

It was just like that back in the steel mill too. And...

Everyone occasionally needs rock solid advocates. And...

No one can deny my people's compassion toward humanity, just like nobody can deny me of mine. Whatever comes around in the advocacy department will go around in the advocacy department.

What the hell am I doing?

Do I want this? Am I ready?

What choice do I have?

I don't have any fucking choice and I didn't ask for any of this shit. It just is what it is.

XVII: June 2004

Thursday, June 03, 2004

Nothing yet...
    What else can I do?

Monday, June 07, 2004

I'm wallowing in my self-pity. We all wallow in our self-pity from time to time. We were all designed to have tough times every now and then.

And since we can't save each other's souls, when we're all fucked-up on the inside, don't be expecting much out of mine today. I haven't been able to do shit for nobody, not even myself. I'm down in the dumps.

My spirit is thoroughly tangled-up and completely broken. And therefore...

So am I. My soul is my inner me, like your soul is your inner you.

When you ain't got nothing good to say, you're supposed to not say nothing at all. So, I shouldn't be writing right now. But what the fuck, you know?

I've sent my shit out to many, many people over the years. Nobody has ever had a good thing to say about me or this.

What the fuck? What the hell does a guy gotta do? I don't get it.

Why the fuck am I still out here all fucking alone?

Okay.

So be it.

Fuck it all.

Something has to change, or everything is gonna be just like it is right now. I'm tired of the way my life is right now. So here goes...

Tomorrow, I'll resume the hunt for a literary agent. I'll try to play big trade's game again. It's 1:00 in the fucking morning. It's late. I gotta get some fucking sleep. We got a big fucking day tomorrow. Lately, they've all been big fucking days. Our fucked-up schedule is just fucking full, all the fucking time. Between work, and another school year winding down on our kids, we ain't got no fucking kind of time for nothing, not even fucking.

And that's enough of my fucking fucked-up shit.

Goodnight.

They say that sex is a misdemeanor.

"Duh more we 'miss, duh meaner' we get."

Saturday, June 12, 2004

Looking for a big trade literary agent with a messed-up attitude is going to get me what? Which leads me to...

If car-seat manufacturers have to start drawing picture books to help us properly install our children's car seats, it seems as though some of us really screwed ourselves out of our personal educations. And speaking of our personal educations...

Big trade doesn't have a very strong customer base. Why?

Super-book-smart authors follow all the rules. Super-book-smart authors are writing all the books on our 2004 bookstore's shelves. And most of our books won't ever sell more than 5000 copies. Doesn't that say something about the current state of the book industry?

Bookworms only want to sell books that bookworms would love to read. Look around in our bookstores and see for yourself.

If you can finish any three random nonfiction books in a row, without having to pull out your brand-new 2004 pocket dictionary, which don't do a damn bit of good, because our pocket dictionaries ain't got none of the words you're looking for, you might be a like-minded bookworm too.

Why do we make things more complicated than they need to be? What do we do with books we can't read? What do we do with product we can't use? And then again...

"Whatever makes any good book great is subjective."

Everyone in the book-publishing industry wants their products to be neat, clean, trim, and fit. In order for their products to be neat, clean, trim, and fit, when we create the new product, we gotta know a lot of shit about writing right. We have to be well educated. We gotta become really book-smart. We gotta know these rules and those rules, these guidelines and those guidelines, these by-lines, and those by-lines, etc.

When we spend the amount of time it takes to learn all of the shit we have to know about to make our writing shiny enough to make all of the bookworms of the world want to publish our writing, we become super-book-smart people too.

Then whenever we actually find enough fucking time, and finally sit down to write all of our shit out, and rework it once or

Connecting the Web of Humanity:

twice, and then, type it up and send it in, we end up with the exact same limited audience that every other bookworm author currently has.

Nothing personal... I'm just an outsider looking inside...

And business is just business... And money is just money.

And our linguistics coach changes from each generation to the next.

"Golly-gee. Swell. Neat-o. Groovy. Cool. Dude. Gnarly. Rents. LOL. . . ;)."

We can't do anything to slow evolution's progression of our living language.

The sacred preservation of our perfectly written word is great for our timeless classics and for anyone of you among us who aspire toward achieving the pinnacle of the beautifully written word, but our perfectly written words ain't got shit to do with making money today. And...

The majority of us did not reach for the brass ring in our English classes. And...

Today is a new day. And...

Times, they are a changing. And...

We're all in desperate need of a new way.

More and more, I think the book industry would rather just keep on keeping on, clinging to its old millennium ways. But...

I'm not going to let them.

If the book industry wants to have more customers, if the book industry wants to see more profits, if the book industry wants to become a larger entity, it has to step up to where I'm coming from. Straight-up...

We all gotta stand up like adults and face our cold hard scientific facts like the grownups we are supposed to be.

What are you able to sell to me? Well...

I'm glad you asked. I can't read for shit. And I know I'm not alone. Do you have any books for me, and the rest of our regular non-book buyers like me? If you don't want us, we'll go spend our time and money elsewhere. BTW... "What's playing down at the movie picture shows?" Big trade's snootiness about the way everything has to be is the only thing that is holding them back from cashing in. And besides that...

Big trade is kicking its own ass...

Live. Be there.

(We already are.)

Every nobody wannabe big trade author has to write a really good query letter for the manuscript. Every nobody wannabe big trade author has to write a really good book proposal. Big trade literary agents don't read any wannabe's manuscript, unless an agent happens to like the query letter and the book proposal.

I don't know how to write the right query letter or the right book proposal.

"Strike One."

I know jack-shit about writing this book the correct way.

"Strike Two."

Who the fuck am I?

"Foul Ball."

Who the fuck am I?

"Strike Three."

And just like that, I'm out. And...

I'm all alone, again. And...

I'm all by myself. And I'm totally isolated away from everyone, everywhere. It's just that plain and simple. But...

I ain't giving up. I came to play. So, ready or not...

Fuck me. I'm "outta" here.

Goodnight.

Tuesday, June 22, 2004

Compared to today, scientists of the 17th Century didn't know shit. Everybody got lots of stuff wrong back then. Every kid in school today learns a hell of a lot more about today's version of Science than any of Science's founding forefathers knew about their day's version of Science. Our understanding of the world around us evolves every day.

Our scientific forefathers made a name for themselves by going against the grain. Each forefather made his own unique mark in the world of Science and faced the whole world all alone.

I can totally relate.

I can totally feel their pain.

Each scientific forefather stood up and endured whatever it was that made him worldwide famous.

Me too. Me too...

I wanna be a worldwide famous scientific forefather too.

Do you think Science will accept a whiney forefather?

Science's primary focus is on the glass of life.

Try to picture life as a window in your head. Look at it inside your mind. Do you see it? Anything can be smeared on windows. Every window can be studied in a laboratory. And...

Thinking outside of the boundaries of the best Science our money can buy...

Our eyes are our soul's windows. When you look your peeps in the eye, do you see just their eyeballs? Or do you look through their eyeballs and see into their soul? How much time do you lose in your lover's eyes? Do you only see the biology of your lover? Or do you see past all of the biological stuff? Do you see the soul's endless possibilities on the other side of our glass?

Do you have my glassy view of life? If you do, can you see our religious reflection in our scientific reality?

We cleaned all the windows on a brand-new house today. It took us all day. Half of the windows were in the hot summer sun. Half of them weren't. And in this moment, I am sun burnt. And all of my sunburn hurts right now. But…

All the windows are done. So tomorrow…

We get to go back to what we do best, the interior. A cleaning person's job is never done. It's late. And I really need sleep. So…

Goodnight.

Monday, June 28, 2004

We are going to take a long overdue and much needed vacation in four days. My Baby and I are traveling and taking our family away for a week of some badly needed family time.

When I get back, I'll go through all of this one more time. I'm ready to get this show on the road. I need to get this kite off the ground. It's time to make my shit happen.

People like me have to start at the bottom. Though most literary agents deserve a whole lot more than they'll ever get, they're the first rung on big trade's ladder. It looks like I have to start there. Two months ago, I tried to work it from the top down. It didn't get me anywhere.

I e-sent the first part of this shit to ten of the greatest people in the United States of America. You were there. You read that part. And nothing happened. Speaking of…

Nobody did nothing. And…

Nobody ever does nothing. And…

You left me all alone. So…

I'll be leaving you all alone.

"My personal grudges are huge." Please…

Don't be calling me when this shit kicks.

Rules is rules. And…

Fuck you too.

When my soul closes, I don't say important shit to anyone outside of my little itty-bitty inner circle. With the world the way it is, I'll isolate and barricade myself in the cozy confines of my smaller, and more comfortable, inner ring of my closest souls. My peeps.

We'll have to wait and see what happens.

Who knows what I'm going to do next? Sometimes I don't even know, until I know.

It's late. It's 12:30 a.m. I gotta ton of shit to do before we can make my family getaway.

Goodnight.

XVIII: July 2004

Sunday, July 11, 2004

We're back from vacation. And I'm more worn out than I was before we left. How does that work? Here lately...

There seems to be too much stuff that needs to be taken care of. Like right now...

I gotta get to work on this in my computer. I got lots of changes. I need to add some things, things to cut, and other shit to do. I've had some time to think about everything and I gotta go.

Thursday, July 15, 2004

I've been busy working my ass off at my cleaning job day after day. And late in the night, I've been working my ass off on this book. I'm working on getting all of this ready to go. Like right now...

It's 3:25 a.m.

"Shit."

I gotta go to bed.

I gotta get some sleep. Goodnight.

Saturday, July 17, 2004

I'm still hard at it. I've been killing day after day, night after night, this whole week. I'm tired as hell. I'm completely worn out. This is my sixth straight night of 3:30ish a.m. I gotta go to bed, like right now. Goodnight.

Monday, July 19, 2004

Nothing new. Same shit. Different day.

I've been going hard and heavy at this, eight straight 3-something AMs in a row, plus my cleaning day gig. I'm throwing everything I've got into polishing this. And the deeper I get, the further behind I feel. Tonight, it's 3:15 a.m. I'm done. I'm outta here. Goodnight.

Tuesday, July 20, 2004

Writing don't come easy for me. But then again, I always have had to work my ass off to get whatever it was I wanted, and especially when it really counts. That's life.

We gotta work both days of this up-coming weekend. We gotta clean all the windows on two new houses. It sucks to be me. Oh well, at least I get to have most of this afternoon off. I'll be able to work on this today. It's 1:24 p.m.

Now, it's 12:34 a.m. I'm keying this part in. And...

"This" concludes the first run through of my adding and polishing series. It only took me nine straight days and nights. I'm going to print all this and read through it again. Why? That's what separates the wannabe authors from those of us who do. If you know, you know. You know?

I just work, and work, and work, and then it's...

Saturday, July 24, 2004

I just pulled my second all-nighter to complete the second run through of this polishing series. Edit and Re:Edit were sitting quietly in a boat. And...

The third time is the charm. After that, I'm back on my way to literary agent land. I don't know when I'll get around to my recent third read through. All of a sudden, we're very busy in our cleaning business. In fact, I gotta go get ready for work. It's 9:30 a.m.

I gotta go.

And I gotta quit doing this to myself.

Monday, July 26, 2004

Whatever it is we decide to do, whatever our goal, with all the shit that goes with whatever it is, it ain't ever gonna be easy. Everything has its price. Worthwhile goals have worthwhile prices. Multimillion-dollar shit demands multimillion-dollar work.

I ain't afraid of my hard work. Sign me up.

"Throw me in, Coach" I came to play. And...

Humanity is a "dualopoly", like monopoly, only dual. It's real simple. All we gotta do is think about our ability to focus our attention, and when we do, our souls materialize and present themselves (ourselves). "Dualopoly" is...

When you were back in school, did a teacher ever fuck with you about spacing out on them? Yeah, me too. And speaking of me spacing out on you right now...

If my shit happens the way I want it to happen, it will be a fucking miracle. But I've watched a lot of movies and they all taught me a thing or two. Sometimes...

Miracles do come true. You just never know, until you know. You know?

I carry a ton of my dad with me everywhere I go. In many ways, I am his carbon copy. And it's as if, I'm the next rung up on my old family ladder.

We gotta work on those parts of us that cause us to not want to bond with our parents. More importantly, we gotta figure out why our parents didn't (and probably still don't) get along with us in the first place. Otherwise, we pass all that shit up onto the next rung on our old family ladders. If nothing changes, everything stays the same.

Apples don't fall far from their trees.

Maybe you're having nice tight relationships with your kids. Maybe you were close to your parents when you were a kid. Maybe you and your parents are having a nice tight relationship right now. Are you close? We are our parent's kids. Our kids are our parents' grandkids. We are our grandparents' grandkids.

It's late. I need some sleep. We got so much cleaning work right now, it's scary. We're freaking out about getting all of our work done on time. On top of all that, we're just seven days away from being home alone, again. And...

Somehow, someway, and someday...

Americans will have a legal way to instantly decompress from a fucked-up day and reconnect their disconnected souls.

Wednesday, July 28, 2004

We are busier right now than we have ever been in the entire history of our little cleaning business. We ended up cleaning our weekend away again. It's becoming a regular thing. On Monday night, we came home from work at 11:30 p.m., dead-dog tired. Last night, Tuesday, we got home from work at midnight. Tonight, it was 9:00 p.m. We could have kept going. The work is still out there waiting for us. But enough is enough. You know? I'd like to see my kids for a little while before they leave again. And tomorrow, we can't come home until we're done cleaning another great big brand-new house.

Tomorrow is gonna be another long hot summer day of grueling work. We do everything we can to make our deadlines. And I'd like to make a little announcement…

My little old cleaning gig really SUCKS sometimes. And then again…

Every job I've ever had sucked at one time or another. When I'd rather be doing something else, work can become as grueling as school was for me.

Work is a grueling job, unless you love what you do.

Right now, it's 1:57 a.m. I gotta get to sleep. We're just a few days away from our "working vacation". We get to have a couple of weeks of nobody home, just my Baby and me.

It's just gonna be just the two of us and a few long days of cleaning houses.

When you have to work extra days, and extra-long hours, whom do you really want to spend your time with? My baby and I like spending time together. How else can we really connect with anyone we know? What's up inside us that makes us hookup, connect, bond, and stay together?

There's never enough time in each day. Then one day, I'll be able to quit my cleaning job, and things will change. I'd have more time to spend with you, in here, doing this nonsense. But that day has yet to happen. And…

Today is just today. And…

It is what it is. And I ams what I ams.

But when I make things happen the way I want them to happen, and that shit happens, big trade's whiney excuse of the electronic market reaching over and digging holes in big trade's profits becomes a great big stinking pile of double-scoop poop. I think they are kicking their own ass. On top of all that, and besides all that, and besides all of this...

I'm the only big badass in the whole wide cold cruel world who can spell out all of these necessary big trade changes. Ready...

On my mark...

Get ready...

Get set...

Go!

IXX: August 2004

Tuesday, August 10, 2004

It's late. We got another heavy-duty day of cleaning tomorrow. I ain't got no time for nothing more than jotting this little thing down on a yellow legal writing pad with my Pentel Rolling Writer. It's 12:15 a.m. So…

Wednesday, August 11, 2004

This is gonna to rescue us. I just know it will. It's just got to. Our small business exit strategy is and has always been "this". "This" is our parachute into a new life. "Its" like twinkling eyes falling in-love. "Its" like fuck all the fucked-up bullshit in the world. "Its" like all that, and more.

It's like really late. And I'm like really tired. So…

Saturday, August 14, 2004

My Baby went shopping at BARNES & NOBLE yesterday. I just counted and she bought me my twelfth (what a weird word to have to spell correctly) book for my personal collection, The 2002 Guide to Literary Agents. The barcode on the back of the book says the US price is $22.^{99}, but today it only cost $4.^{00}. I'm sure the 2005 book is out by now. If they ain't got the 2005 book out yet, they're late. We're in the middle of August 2004.

The front cover of my brand-new 2002 guidebook says there are over 600 agents listed inside. Using the handy reference in the back, I only found nine that match all of the different genres I am covering in "this" book.

A year ago, I sent my first presentable query letter to two of these nine.

One sent me her standard rejection letter and kept my stuff. And the other e-mailed her "Dear John" and kept my stuff.

Looking through my new book, I found several literary agents I have already queried. And I now realize why most of them rejected me. The AAR website doesn't give out the specifics on what genre literary agents specialize in. We gotta pay somebody for that information, or we gotta search the Interweb, or we gotta spend all day at the public library. Sometimes you just don't know what people want, until you know. You know? And what we don't know can stop us in our tracks. Did you know? If not, and either whatever way...

I'm gonna send a query letter to all of the rest of these big trade literary agents. But...

I'm only gonna hand out one copy of my manuscript at a time. It will be on a first-come/first-served basis.

No more fucking around. It's time to get this show on the road. And speaking of just fucking around, for the time being...

I feel like all I've been doing, from my get-go in the early-on of all-this-shit, is just me fucking around. And...

To anyone who says, anxious wannabe authors ain't supposed to appear desperate, I don't know any other fucking way to be. Walking a few miles in my shoes is what all of this shit is about. This is really just all about me and the gigantic load of whatever I'm toting.

We cleaned houses all day today. We got home two hours ago. It's 11:29 p.m. I'll try to get as far as I can tonight, but I can't stay up too late. Tomorrow, Sunday, we have to work all day. And then...

Another perfectly good weekend will be shot all to hell again.

Someday, I'll hang-up my handy-dandy trusty Panasonic Power Wave vacuums, my Canadian lamb's wool dusters, my USA eighteen-inch dust mop, my seasonal goofy looking Gilligan cleaning suit, and all of this shit will be over. Then...

I'll just have my family, my crib, and this. That's all I want. I can't wait. I am an anxious nobody wannabe big trade author, I'm desperate, and that's just how things are.

Right now, I gotta go to sleep. So...

Goodnight.

Sunday, August 29, 2004

Today is our first day off from cleaning since the last day we had off when we were home alone. I wrote about it.

We left our home and went to work, day after day, weekend after weekend, every day between August 03, and today, August 29. The fact that we quit cleaning long enough for me to work on this some more is huge progress for me. I hope to have everything ready to go in about a week. And speaking of more good news...

School starts in four days.

"YEAH!"

XX: October 2004

Sunday, October 10, 2004

It's 3:39 p.m. I just finished the last rework on my fourth printing. I still have one more printing to do. I know I said, "Three's the charm." But before I can send any more of my shit out to anymore big trade literary agents, I got a lot of broken shit that still needs to be fixed. I'm going to go back to work on this some more. So...

It's 3:48 p.m. The Vikings just beat Houston in overtime. My Baby is very happy. I gotta go. Later.

Tuesday, October 12, 2004

It's 1:45 a.m. My dad would have loved Wintergreen Tic-tac's. When I was a little kid, he would steal both of the Wintergreen Lifesaver rolls out of box he always bought for me to open every Christmas morning. And I did the same thing to my kids when I became a dad.

As dads go, he had a certain special way about him that I really miss. He was a real good dad. I miss him, bad.

We checkout. We go away. We go into our own private reality. Then, someone said...

"Earth to John..."

And I snapped out of my personal private world. And our soul leads us where?

We got lots of new construction cleaning to do this week. And tonight, I'm not making as much progress on this as I'd hoped I would. It's 2:30 a.m. I'm cooked. Goodnight.

Wednesday, October 13, 2004

It's 12:13 a.m.

My Baby and me are still burning our candles at both ends. Our cleaning workload is still very heavy. And our personal To-do lists are very long. And our physical bodies are completely worn out. I don't know how much more of this nonsense we can take. Everything is even bleaker than it was before.

I'm way too over committed to do this writing job and my cleaning job right now. I ain't got no down time. I ain't got no time for me to play with my family.

Right now, my life is so fucking serious all of the fucking time. I just want to experience the peace of mind that comes with finding the right big trade literary agent. Our play time vs. serious time and...

I just gotta keep going.

It's only gonna take one match to start this word-of-mouth wildfire. I've been stacking-up all this kindling for years and years. And...

Just knowing our lives are about to change for the better makes all of today's shit seem less shitty. I just have to keep going.

If your life doesn't ever happen differently, nothing ever changes. And everything will stay just like it currently is. Then you'd be just like me, and this...

Everything looks bleak. All hope is lost.

It's 12:52 a.m. Goodnight

It's 1:26 a.m. I can't just turn off my fucking head and go to sleep. So here we go, some more...

During the past few years, I've been throwing darts in the dark to find a literary agent. Thanks to my brand-new 2002 guidebook, my agent search has been narrowed down.

And the pressure is on.

One literary agent turned out to be a dud. He is all over the Interweb, on the 'avoid at all cost' lists. So, I sent my SASE to another literary agent. And she was one of two literary agents I contacted last year with my first presentable query letter. She paid for postage and mailed me another exact same "Dear John" and kept all my stuff again.

I can't send any of this to the other lady I queried last year. That one kept all my shit and simply e-mailed me her drop dead and go to hell shtick. Someday...

And to that day... "Cheers, likesa beers."

And that goes double for all the rest of them.

Wednesday, October 27, 2004

This whole book-writing thing has been one big disaster after another for me. Like right now, my current literary agent search is gearing-up, and at the same time, winding-down. I started out with a list of nine literary agents. And now, I'm down to my last three. And...

In batches of three, everybody eventually always turns me down.

Connecting the Web of Humanity:

With the process of finding a big trade literary agent, with all of the required research and experimentation, writing query letters, some going around big trade sideways to be ignored some more, and developing book proposals, with this manuscript sitting in my closet collecting dust, and me always left holding the bag and sitting around wondering what to do next, and slowly growing disenchanted by the whole thing deep in the dark-damp-corner of my personal closet's shit, and me being the writer saying becoming an author has to be the most frustrating job on Earth. And...

Getting published has to be the worst part about this whole fucked-up writing gig. If you know, you know. You know? But...

I gotta keep going. And...

I'm in way too deep into this shit to quit now.

I got three agencies left. I'm hard at work, going at it full speed, with all I've got. And this is enough for today. It's 2:11 a.m. And I'm really sleepy right now. So, goodnight.

XXI: November 2004

Sunday, November 07, 2004

We had a United States record turnout this past election. Somewhere...

About 120 million people voted. And that means millions of the citizens of my United States of America were eligible to vote in our United States of America's 2004 election and millions of eligible voters didn't even bother. Our voter turnout was fucking pathetic. And...

President Bush won his second term and marijuana is still illegal (by a margin of a 2004 60/40) in Alaska.

"Thank God."

You know?

I've been working my ass off. I'm trying to get things ready. I sent a three-paragraph query letter to three agencies last week. I'm anxiously waiting to hear back from somebody. In the meantime, I need to print all this and go over everything one more time, just to be sure. I feel like I'm just wasting a bunch of trees, and speaking of...

I'm gonna go. It's 11:54 p.m. And it takes 90 minutes for my old worn-out family friendly printer to print all of these pages.

Whatcha gonna do?

Thursday, November 11, 2004

My life just seems to be getting worse and worse.

It looks like we might have to buy some windows. We cleaned all of the windows on another brand-new house last weekend. The manufacturing representative says the cleaners' rags scratched the windows when they cleaned them.

We are the cleaners. It's just my Baby and me. We do all of our own backbreaking work. So more than likely, the rags, in question, were probably our rags. And we got the call today.

"SHIT."

Our cleaning business insurance doesn't cover shit like this. As of today, we only have to replace two of the windows. We'll have to wait and see. We were told we might end up having to replace all of the windows. And we cleaned them all, lots, and lots. We cleaned seventy-something windows in that brand-new house. Halfway through, I lost count.

Every business has risks. Risk is what the business beasts are all about. If all those brand-new windows need to be replaced, we're gonna end up losing our little cleaning business. Like most small business owners, we are only one small catastrophe away from going under. If we have to eat a giant house full of windows, we're done. We're riding along the edge of our finances as it is.

For now, we just gotta be patient and wait to see what happens. Do we get to keep our little cleaning business? Or are we about to lose our way of life, for the past $7^1/_2$ years? How much more fucking intense can things get? And speaking of things getting intense...

It's hard to get back to a place where we can make love with our lovers when we are white-knuckling our life, the bills, our job, the road, an experience, and the rest is just a simple fill in the blank. (And don't limit yourself.)

I sent my last three queries out to my last three literary agents from my brand-new 2002 guidebook, one week ago today. Two days ago, one of my query letters came back un-opened. So, I went on-line, did a quick copy/paste, and e-mailed it. She e-mailed her "Dear John" the next day.

I still got two queries out to the last two big trade literary agents from my brand-new 2002 guidebook.

And sometimes, no news is good news.

I wish I could write all night but, I gotta go. It's 2:30 a.m.

Saturday, November 13, 2004

It's been one week, and we still haven't heard whether or not on the windows. And I still ain't heard nothing back from the last two agencies. Work and wait and see. That's all I do anymore. I don't know much else. Except, today is Saturday, and we had to put in eight solid hours of cleaning. Work, work, work, and...

To make things work out right, we gotta put in at least six solid hours of cleaning tomorrow. And then...

We gotta get home so my Baby can catch the game between the Vikings and Packers. And I'll get a chance to go to work on some more of all this.

Next up will be my fifth time to print all of this since we had our family vacation back in July, four months ago. I'm chewing this stuff up. Look at me go.

When I get done going through all of this nonsense this time, I hope to step away from all of this for a little while.

I'm very happy with the way it is progressing. I'm starting to think it might be close to being ready.

Not that this time will be any different than any other times I thought this shit was close enough to being ready to go. And then again…

What else can I say?

You wouldn't believe how much time I invested into this project. And quite frankly…

I'm getting sick of working on all this. Some people have an easy road. And some people don't. Speaking of…

It's 2:06 a.m. I gotta go to sleep.

We gotta be out the door and down the road by 9 a.m.

Monday, November 15, 2004

We left late yesterday, and my Baby ended up missing the first quarter of her game.

"My bad."

Life can really beat the shit out of us sometimes.

Two weeks and we still haven't heard anything on those windows.

We're still waiting. And…

We still ain't heard nothing from the last two literary agents.

Ever since our little vacation back in July, I've just been working, and working, and working on this. This shit's gotta kick. It's just gotta.

It's 2:41a.m. I'm out of here.

Thursday, November 18, 2004

I mailed three (three-paragraph) query letters 15 days ago. My second query letter came back today. It also say's...

"Return to Sender."

It's been two miserable fucking weeks of pins and needles, and after all that excruciating pain and agony, and all my miserably wasted pins and needles time, and all my miserably wasted pins and needles energy, and...

Nobody saw it.

It didn't even get opened.

Fuck this shit. I quit. I give up. I don't want to become a published author anymore. I'm done with all this fucked-up nonsense.

I'm done. I am going to sleep now.

Friday, November 19, 2004

Once this nonsense finds its big trade literary agent, I'll quit writing about finding my big trade literary agent, and I'll write about something else. Till then...

Everyone who knows anything about big trade knows the book business is crazy. And I show up saying stupid shit like...

All the King's horses, and all the King's men, couldn't put big trade back together again. And...

"Here I come to save the day."

"CHARGE!" And...

What makes me think big trade will let me get away with writing stupid crazy fucked-up shit like this anyways?

Saturday, November 20, 2004

When you got all your marbles riding on one thing, and that one thing blows up in your face, what happens to all of your marbles?

That's me. I'm totally fucked. I'm totally screwed.

Sometimes, it really does suck to be me.

I got my third rejection back yesterday.

And another one of my dad's favorite sayings was either...

"Son, you gotta be smarter than what you're working with." Or...

"Son, you gotta be smarter than what you're working on."

He'd drop one of those on me at the utmost perfect time when he could see me struggling on whatever. The wisdom in my dad's catchy little "dad-isms" has always worked miracles for me. I just don't get how I'm supposed to apply my dad's wisdom to my fucked-up writing gig. I'm sure I'll figure everything out with enough time. But I ain't got no time. I need this shit to get going. I am very confused, and either whichever way...

I just don't know how much more desperate I could be. We are so screwed.

Financially, I'm scared shitless. It's only a matter of time before everything could come crashing down around us. And then again...

Deep down inside my soul, I know this fucked-up thing will catch us before we fall all the way down. It's just gotta. And I don't know what more to say right now.

It's 3:29 a.m.

Friday, November 26, 2004

Good news...

I contacted a literary agent from several years back. He wants me to e-mail him some of my stuff.

"YEAH!"

Here we go.

I'm sending him my first 116 pages. It's the same shit I sent to the "Ten Greatest People in America", except today, its twenty pages longer, because I reworked it a few times. It had no flow before.

I gotta go get my 116 pages ready to send to a literary agent. My Baby tells me the butterflies in my belly are natural. She said, "You just need to get them to fly in formation, toward your goal."

We still ain't heard no word on the windows. We'll have to continue to wait and see what happens.

Saturday, November 27, 2004

Today, I e-mailed my first 116 Pages to a literary agent. This is the first literary agent to ask to see any of this shit. This big trade literary agent could be the one. In the meantime...

I'm totally lost on what to do next. I'm vapor locked. This is my first real casting call. I'm scared shitless and extremely excited at the exact same time. My hands are all sweaty. This is just the pins and needles part of this big trade bullshit.

It's 2:29 a.m. I can't sleep. I need to share what I'm lying here wide-assed awake thinking about.

Am I'm totally fucking up? What the hell am I doing? Am I ready for this? Do I have any other fucking choice? I've been digging on this hole for a long fucking time. I know things will change when they do. I know some things won't always be the way they are, and some things will. And if certain things ain't that scary...

Then they ain't that real.

Fuck. Becoming an author comes with a lot of pressure on some of us.

What the fuck? Well...

It's been fun chatting. It helps. And I feel better.

Thank you for listening. Maybe I can get some sleep now. It's 2:38 a.m. Goodnight.

Sunday, November 28, 2004

Whenever whatever happens happened, everything happens for a reason. Everything happens by design. If things don't work out with this literary agent, I'll keep going. I just have to. I've come this far so far and...

It's just one foot in front of the other. I gotta fight my way all the way into the humungous big trade beast. I gotta save me, my Baby, and the whole wide fucked-up cold cruel world to boot. Why? That's just what I gotta do. I just can't help myself. And...

Everything is flowing along pretty good. Our cleaning gig is beginning to slow down. Today is Sunday. We're in the middle of having four days off in a row. It's been a long time coming. My Baby made me take Thanksgiving and half of Black Friday off. It was really strange to not be doing my regular routine cleaning thing.

I've been working from the time I crawl out of bed till I fall asleep. When we're not cleaning, I'm spending all my free time working my ass off on this. I'm farther along now, than I've ever been before. And then...

Somebody finally asked me to send them some of this shit. And then...

When things finally started going my way, I get totally and completely freaked out. And I get panicky. And now I'm asking...

How fucked-up is that?

Why can't I write my own ticket? Why can't all of this happen the way I laid it out in here? Am I asking for too much? How much is too much to ask for? What's too much?

Why can't I be a nobody wannabe big trade author who gets big trade's biggest baddest book deal ever done before? Why can't I spend the rest of my life in my Baby's palatial estate? Why can't I have my own privately owned waterpark? And...

Why can't I chase after my American dream? And speaking of dreaming my American dreams...

I gotta get to sleep. Because tomorrow...

We gotta go back to work. A cleaner's job is never done. It never ends. There's always something else that needs to be cleaned.

Small business owners never know when the phone is gonna ring, with the good news, or bad news, or when more work will come. Speaking of...

From now on, every time the phone rings, it might just be my agent on the other end. Will I be ready? You bet your ass I'm ready.

I think. It's 2:34 a.m. And for some strange reason, it seems later than that.

Thank goodness it's not.

Goodnight.

Tuesday November 30, 2004

At this point, I don't know what to do with myself anymore. And I ain't got nothing better to do, at this minute, other than write more of my nonsense. So, here goes...

Would you like another little-bitty taste of my personal life? Okay. Here goes...

It's been three days since I e-mailed my first 116 pages. After three days of being on pins and needles from one moment to the next, going on-line to check my e-mail twenty times a day, same as it ever was, wishing and hoping, some itching and some scratching, and I just found out my e-mail submission can't be opened by the last literary agent I contacted. Then...

On top of that...

He said I formatted it wrong or something. So...

I did what I could with my limited technological knowledge and "re-e-sent" it to him again. Then...

One agonizing hour later...

He said my second try didn't work either. Before I go to work tomorrow, I'll try again. I would like to try again tonight, but my Baby is sleeping next to me, keeping my naked body warm on this extremely cold quiet winter night, and I can't log onto my kid's Gateway without her. I don't know how. She does. Everybody has their own password.

I'm a copy/paste guy. I have never attached a Word Document to an e-mail before. This whole e-mail shit is all brand-new to me. But my kids do it all the time. So, I'm gonna try to get this shit to go through my kid's new Gateway computer, off my old Gateway computer and on to a floppy disc, doing it the way one of my kids showed me on theirs. And how whacked is all that nonsense?

This writing a book thing ain't easy. And then again...

If it's not one thing, it's always gonna be something else. For me...

This has been one big giant fucking failure after another big giant fucking failure every fucking step of my way.

I don't feel any pressure to jump back into my souls and sex stuff right now. I fully realize that we're getting deep into the back of this book, but I thoroughly, completely, and totally know that I can't save anyone when I'm totally fucked-up on the inside of me. So...

It's 2:00 a.m. Goodnight.

Now it's 3:41 a.m. I blew out my writing candle. And...

In the very extremely way too cold quietness of tonight...

I worked out a backdoor way to get into my kid's Gateway, in my head, so I can e-mail my shit out tonight. And...

I did it. And I think it worked and I was successful. But right now, I am frozen to the bone.

And sometimes we just don't know, until we know. You know? Maybe this third time is the charm.

Maybe this literary agent is the super-sharp big trade literary agent I've been searching for all my long-lost time. Maybe he ain't. If he isn't, I wrote another query letter on my Baby's birthday. I spent a shitload of time polishing it up. It's ready to go. I also have been working on another list of literary agents. It's almost ready to go. I spent some serious time drilling down into that. And all that is on hold.

I'm not gonna make a move, until I hear back from this literary agent.

It's 3:55 a.m.

"Brr."

XXII: December 2004

Wednesday, December 01, 2004

Turns out, my latest literary agent couldn't open my e-mails because he is in Paris. He says he'll read my stuff when he gets back to his New York office on Friday. I gotta leave on Friday to do a traveling weekend family thing.

We got another big day of cleaning tomorrow and lots to take care of before we can leave. There never seems to be enough time. No rest for the weary, unless you're really fucking tired, like me. I'm gonna get sleep some now. It's 11:51 p.m. Goodnight.

It's 1:32 a.m. I can't fucking sleep. Fuck me.

You remember in that Back to the Future movie, when the train was pushing the car down the train tracks toward the canyon, the canyon with the bridge that wasn't there? Well…

That's our financials.

All we gotta do is hang on. This shit will kick. And…

"Poof."

Things will instantly change. And then…

We won't be in this fucked-up reality no more. We'll be the remake stars of our own private picture movie. Except...

We ain't got no stunt-doubles, and our shit's always done live, because we are actually living in this in real-time. This is my life. And it won't ever become a movie because it is dull, boring, and uninteresting. So much so...

All of this barely even fits in this book. This is my personal reality, my world, my life, my story, my personal memoir/journal, my words, and it goes all the way over there to all the way over here. It's all about me and mine. And speaking of us...

I know we ain't the only ones who are barely hanging on financially from week to week. A lot of people ride along the edge of their financials.

I also know that nobody gives a shit about nobody else's pain and suffering, unless they're sympathetic to the same mutual causes. Why?

Causes connect our human souls. Connected souls are people with connected souls. Connected souls care about what we like, and what we don't like. That's just how we are. That's just how our humanity works. And...

Authors are supposed to suffer in complete silence. We're supposed to drop our individually personalized SASE query letters in the mail, sit back down on our pins and needles, and keep our mouths shut, like we like doing things this way.

And if a big trade literary agent likes our big trade query letter, they'll ask us to send more stuff. Then, they expect us to send them whatever they want, and we go back to quietly sitting back down on our pins and needles. If we get a "Dear John" letter, or if we don't hear back from a big trade agent, either we can be totally cool about it, or we can contact that agent and totally chew that ass. But either whichever way, in the end, we still gotta pick ourselves up off the floor, and move on. We gotta quietly pull all the stickers out of our soul's ass and start our same old shit all over again. We gotta pick up all of the shards of our broken pieces and move on. And...

All of the dickheads, bitches, and assholes are gonna get back whatever it is they gave out. Karma is karma. And...

It's always gonna be easier on you if you just pick up and move on. Speaking of moving on...

I gotta go.

But before I go...

I can't walk out of tonight and leave you with some dickheads, bitches, and assholes to deal with. So...

Remember when I said it is your job to make your lover super-horny before you ever start to have any kind of sexual intercourse with your lover, and it is your lover's job to make you super-horny before your lover ever starts to have any kind of sexual intercourse with you? Then, take the time to make it all it can be. And...

It's 2:20 a.m. So...

Goodnight.

Friday, December 03, 2004

The big trade literary agent who was in Paris says he read my stuff. He also said he "didn't feel a pulse" and wished me luck.

It's 4:30 p.m.

"FUCK."

I gotta go pack our minivan and do some things around the house before I get to drive for the next few hours to do another "fantabulous" traveling family weekend thing.

I have to go pack up all my family vacation stuff right now. And...

I'm moving on.

"I gotta do what I gotta do."

XXIII: January 2005

Tuesday, January 04, 2005

After only nine weeks, we found out we only have to buy two windows. We are looking at a total of only $287.^{00}. Its money we ain't got, but it won't bankrupt us. Hopefully, all that horrible shit is over.

It feels good to finally have that big fat monkey off our backs. I was starting to pull my hair out.

And this "nucking" shit of a book was driving me "futs." But then I realized…

It still is. So, I went away for a little while. And now…

I'm back.

And I'm even more frustrated than I was before I left. I went back and reread the shit I e-mailed to that New York agent who was in Paris. As it turned out, I overworked this shit.

I didn't even know that overworking your own writing was possible. But I'm here today to say, "As an author, it is super-easy to overwork your shit."

Connecting the Web of Humanity:

I had a hard time reading my own writing. And…

It was all typed out.

Now I see why he said he couldn't find a pulse. It doesn't have one yet. I'm gonna have to go back and work on figuring out a way to give this piece of shit a fucking pulse. But right now…

I'm gonna create some new shit with my pen and paper that probably ain't got no pulse neither. What else can I do? So, here we go…

Just like everything else, hot and horny sex has a short shelf life. Hot and horny sex doesn't stick with us for a very long time. I mean…

How many times can you go to your waterpark before your waterpark turns into the agony and drudgery of going to work? The same old, same old, gets predictable. That's what makes some work really boring. So, let's up the ante…

"Shall we?"

How many different orgasms have you ever had? How many different orgasms have you given to the love of your life?

We won't start getting something new and improved, until we start giving something new and improved.

Thursday, January 06, 2005

I have to update you on all of my life's 4-1-1 later. Right now, I gotta interrupt all that for a late breaking update…

I am being a little redundant in this book. But…

In all fairness, who is the one writing all of this nonsense? And…

If you feel a little redundancy is too much to take, take some comfort in knowing that you only gotta put up with the bits and pieces of my shitty existence of this miserably redundant cleaning way of life. Like right now…

It's already January of 2005. And…

Living check to check, I'm constantly running out of money. And…

I'm way past being out of time. The straw that breaks our only camel's back could come slamming into us any minute. My current life is so fucking stressful. And…

Fuck all this miserable shit.

I can't fucking get away from this fucking book long enough to make this shit flow any better than it's fucking flowing. I can't breathe life, or force a heartbeat, into this piece of shit right now. I need to put all of this down, and let it all go, for a long time. But I can't. I ain't got no time. And…

My body is really beginning to fall apart.

It's 3:30 a.m. And…

I have said way too much tonight. Goodnight.

Saturday, January 15, 2005

Ding-dang it.

"How can I be groundbreaking, if you won't let me break new ground?" And…

"You know who you are."

And sometimes, I really hate this writing gig. And sometimes, some of our literary agents say the damndest things. If you know, you know. You know?

Wednesday, January 26, 2005

Today, first thing this morning, we lost our biggest customer. Wait a minute, hold on. I'm starting over…

Give me a chance to set all this new shit up…

Construction companies build brand-new big badass homes.

Some homebuilders sub-contract house cleaners to clean out the new construction protection, trash, dust, grime, stickers, and whatnot. That's us. We turn our construction company's jobsites into their customers' brand-new homes. We have been extremely busy making new homes move-in ready.

This morning, we lost our largest construction company. Last year, we cleaned twenty-two new homes for them. We cleaned our last one last November. This year, someone underbid us. They pulled the rug out from underneath us. It wasn't from a lack of satisfaction on our construction company's part. The decision came down from the construction company's customer. Money is just money. Business is just business. And I don't care what business you're in...

Shit always rolls downhill. And...

The shit just keeps rolling downhill. And...

It just keeps coming, and coming, and coming, and can you guess who's at the bottom of our fucked-up hill?

We do nothing less than a professional job every time we show up to do our professional job. I don't get it. It doesn't make sense to me. Then again, what does?

XXV: March 2005
Yup. I skipped 24. 'Cause I can.

Saturday, March 05, 2005

I'm hopelessly optimistic about being on the rebound from getting all fucked-up over my personal financials and not getting anywhere with all this fucked-up shit. I'm flying blind. And everything is very gloomy. And even more so now, everything is completely and totally out of anyone's control.

Look at it go.

And I just this second, right now, figured out I'm supposed to just keep driving this choo-choo train forward.

I won't get to wherever it is I'm going if I stop trying to get there.

I need to strip-off everything that's keeping me from achieving what I want to achieve. I have to keep moving this thing forward. So here I am...

I'm ready to trade in my old cleaning life without any money at all for my new life with all the money in the world and nobody cares. Big trade don't care. You don't care. No one cares. Please, take a moment. and pause long enough to look up and...

"See?"

Fuck the shit. I'm going to sleep.

It's 12:49 a.m. And...

I know lots of people have to deal with a whole lot tougher stuff than anything I have ever had to deal with in my life. I see the world around us, both of us. I live in that reality. I know what's what. And...

XXVI: April 2005

Friday, April 01, 2005

"April fools."

"This" was the 64,741st word. With my first book's 69,000-word limit, we only have 4,259 more words to go. So…

How is it going so far? What do you think?

Am I doing a good job? Did I slowly become one of your newest favorite authors?

Do I get the job? Would you be willing to buy my next book? Big trade is all up in a book's pre-sell capabilities.

XXVII: June 2005

Thursday, June 16, 2005

It's 11:57 p.m.

It's been three months since I've written anything new.

On Tuesday, May 31, my Baby and I flew to New York City. That was my first time to ever visit the city that never sleeps.

I felt right at home.

On Wednesday, June 01, we went to an all-day writer's conference for nobody wannabe big trade authors. And I got to check out some of my competition.

On Thursday, June 02, we flew back to Chicago and drove three hours home.

On Saturday, June 04, our oldest graduated from high school. The past three months have been totally crazy.

My first trip to New York City went well, considering everybody out there had me pegged from the get-go.

Somehow or another, I must have tourist written all over me. And...

We stayed at the Marriott Marquis on Times Square. Our room faced south. We had nice weather during the day. And the evenings were surprisingly chilly. Who knew?

I took my first cab ride. Really. And that was a trip. I had my first limo ride too. The limo went under a tunnel to take us to our hotel and the cab went through Central Park and over a bridge to get us back to our airport.

The Marriott Marquis is so tall; the elevators have rush hours. That was a trip. The hotel lobby is on the eighth floor. That was a trip. And…

I ain't never seen so many Starbucks in all my life.

They put a Starbucks anywhere and everywhere.

We walked north to the Ed Sullivan Theater. When we made our reservations to go to New York, I tried to get tickets to the Late Show, but Dave was on vacation.

"It figures. Two right ears. That's just my luck."

Every nobody wannabe big trade author should go to (and attend) at least one writing conference. If nothing else, just to be able to say you did. So anyway…

I officially went to my first and last conference. Bite me once, shame on you. Bite me twice, shame on me.

Everyone had lots of advice for us nobody wannabe big trade authors. The speakers I heard said the complete opposite of what the other speakers I heard said. "What?"

"Exactly."

One of our morning speakers said we shouldn't follow any trend. He said everything in big trade is a least a year out. The big trade book deals of 2005 are the new releases of a year from now. He said, when we hop on a bandwagon, and start following the developing trend, a million people show up with our exact same book, and everybody always gets lost in the first bestseller's backwash. And then…

An afternoon speaker came out and told us nobody wannabe big trade nonfiction authors that we should all be writing books about keys, steps, and ways. He said the key, step, and way books are the hottest thing in nonfiction. He said we should follow the trends and only tap into what's hot, current, and happening. And then...

One guy got up during lunch, and almost had a nervous breakdown trying to describe big trade's derailment, except he didn't know that was what he was trying to describe to us. But...

I know exactly what he was nervously talking about. And...

"I feel you, dog." And...

"I heard you, bro." And...

"I'm doing everything I can." And...

None of the attendees at the conference, except that dude who almost had a nervous breakdown, and me, believed anything is wrong with the way things are in the book industry. It was so crazy; it made me start to feel like I was crazy.

One of the afternoon presenters, and a different published author at the conference, both said we needed to be published in magazines before the industry will publish our first book.

And when we're in Rome, we're supposed to do as the Romans do. So...

I guess I will totally give-up on doing this and go to work on writing magazine articles.

But you know something?

"Fuck all of them and a whole bunch of that." And...

"Fuck all of them who want me to do all of this nonsense any other way than the way I gotta do my own thing."

"I gotta be me."

I'm doing my own personal branding thing up, in here. And, at any rate...

My first book conference was a complete bust. And...

John E Zett III

My first visit to New York City was a complete trip.

And I can't wait to make that trip again, and again, and again. If you know, you know. You know?

Dear Dave,

"Call me,"

John

XXVIII: August 2005

Saturday, August 13, 2005

Happy anniversary Baby!

Today, our oldest also moved away to go to college. And then...

There were four. Today was a good day. We have way more room around here. And...

More often than not, and every now and again, I think I make a pretty good dad. And speaking of me and mine...

I figure I gotta keep walking this dog to get it noticed.

I combed through everything in here, from the very beginning all the way to here, about five or six times in my past few weeks. It has evolved. It reads much better than it was. I think my piece of shit might even start to "have a pulse". It's way cleaner and way clearer now. So...

We create the distances between each other. Our souls pull

away from the souls around us. We detach. We unplug. We disconnect. And we lose being in touch with our peeps.

Like a lot of other big-money troublemakers, I'm completely detached from my family right now. I'm detached from everybody I know, except my Baby. I'm detached from everything I love to do, except for working on this fucked-up shit for you, and the only reason I am doing any of this fucked-up shit in the first place is to be able to spend all of my time with the ones I love, and that is my God's Honest Truth...

I've become an addict of this fucked-up writing gig. I'm totally addicted. And...

I gotta go back to work on my tired-old worn out Gateway. So...

Monday, August 15, 2005

I just got back home from sending this entire unsolicited manuscript to the one and only literary agent I ever called.

What can I say? Creepy guys are everywhere. I am what I am. Look at me.

The people at my local UPS store told me my little heavy white box would be in her office on Thursday. Remember when I said that authors have to wait on pins and needles? That was nothing. This is the real pins and needles of becoming an author.

Everything I've ever done before this was just me monkeying around. This shit is for real. I just sent my whole manuscript to another literary agent. And no, she didn't ask if she could see it. And no, she doesn't even know it is coming. And yes, I am being the only me I can be today. And yes, I'm breaking all of the industry's big bad scary rules. And yes, I am a big trade bad boy. And yes, I think my shit don't stink. But...

Only with you. And...

Only in here. And...

Only when I write. Out in our shared scientific real world I am just a frail old professional cleaner in disguise. And I have a little more soul-revealing deeper-view into my isolated cynical, cold, cruel, harsh world reality than most and...

I ain't like this when I go out and about in our big bad scary real world.

"Passivism" says what?

We are all different people to different people. We're all different people to the same people. Our souls make and leave our impressions. Our souls are what is making our humanity happen.

We all collectively cast and create our individual basic human expressions. And...

All of our human souls are saying what?

Monday, August 22, 2005

My first and last literary agent I ever called on the phone, wrote me a rather long personal letter to tell me how much she genuinely hated the most recent version of the manuscript I sent to her. That's rare. Most big trade literary agents grab their "Dear John" off their pre-printed stack. So anyway...

My television just told me, the Associated Press is saying, Connecticut is saying, "No Child Left Behind" illegally requires expensive programs and testing, which the "No Child Left Behind" doesn't have to pay for.

Long story short, Connecticut wants an idiotic Federal Law repealed. And...

"I feel their pain." Volstead Act and Marijuana...

It's 12:00 a.m.

I just got done watching a Discovery Channel show called "Our Earliest Ancestors" that ended with the narrator saying, "It seems we are apes who simply got lucky."

"Ain't that some shit?"

That's the best that our Science can do today? And I thought that getting lucky had something to do with sex. Our life is way too fucking delicate to be hinged on surviving via luck. Fuck that shit. Even Einstein said as much with his other math equation...

"Knowledge < Imagination"

Our souls are screaming to be loudly heard. And it's like our scientist aren't even listening. And it's like all of our religions are completely blind and/or haven't ever even started looking for their souls. And it's like all of the book industry people I've contacted don't care one way or another about anything more than just keeping on with everything they keep doing year after year. And this might just be me thumping my chest by saying this, but...

But seriously...

I hope not. And...

When we do, do you ever think about shit that ain't got nothing to do with nothing? Me too. Like this...

A game of chance ain't got nothing to do with the life our soul experiences. We are who we are. And...

"Money can't buy happiness when we're growing old...As long as the stars shine above; we're nobody till somebody loves us, so go find yourself somebody to love."

Einstein probably got to hear The Mills Bros sing their songs on his radio. I'm not completely clear on their histories or their timelines. I don't know if Einstein was around when The Mills Bros were around and vice-versa. I don't even know if Einstein had a radio, or if The Mills Bros were ever even on the radio. I mean...

We don't know officially what is what until we personally experience it. And...

I, personally, did not officially experience any of that. I wasn't even born yet.

XXIX: September 2005

Friday, September 23, 2005

My psychic named this book on March 05, 1996.

For the past 3489 days, I've called it by the name she gave it. Today, I fucking changed this thing's title.

From: Connecting The Web...

To: Something Else...

ComPETELY DIFFERENT...

It may not sound like a big deal, but it was for me.

XXX: November 2005

Tuesday, November 29, 2005

It's 1:01 a.m. I'm tired of fighting this disaster every miserable step of the way. Well...

At least I was in in it for the fight, that ought to count for something. What more can I fucking do? I can only do what I can do at any given time. Come on, you piece of shit, take off...

"Fly."

I need this shit to kick. I need to pop my big trade cherry. I want all this finding my big trade literary agent nonsense to be over. I'm ready for this little dog and pony show to be over. But first, I still have a bunch of other shit that I still need to say. And "I gotta be me."

The greatest lessons of life are the ones that come with the greatest rewards. What separates some humans from reaping our rewards, from those of us that ain't, is in whoever has the ability to keep going bravely forward against ever-increasing adversity and hardship with an open mind and a peaceful soul.

"We gotta be excellent to each other."

Happy people are open souls. The longer we are able to keep our souls open, the better our lives go for us, and the better off we are. The better off we are, the better everything is, and...

Peaceful humans say what?

And what more could any respectful guy ask for in his life? Besides maybe...

A blowjob every once in a while. And...

Some world peace.

XXXI: December 2005

Friday, December 02, 2005

Our 2005 book industry's Godfather and Godmother got together on the Late Show last night. Oprah travelled to be on Dave's show.
    You go, Dave.
    "See?"
    That's what I totally love about Dave.

Tuesday, December 27, 2005

It's 7:30 p.m.
    We can't diss on a group we ain't a part of.
    We are all good examples of that. (Like me with this.) If you're a member of a group, you're allowed to call things like you see them. (Like I do.) If you aren't a member of the group, we gotta be humble to get along, or you gotta go. (Like they have all been doing what they do to me because of me writing this.) If you ain't part of

the group, your game can't hang with the group, until it does, and unless it can. (Like me with this.)

This has serious hang time.

I'm living proof of that. I got game. My game hangs.

I'm disrespectfully and disgustingly delicious. And...

That's why nobody will ever break all the rules I broke to get us here, and still be alive enough to go double-down in big trade, except me. It's like I said earlier (before I cut that part out in one of my yesteryear's re-edits) I'm nothing but a diamond in the rough. I'm perfect the way I am. I'm perfect with all of my personal imperfections. What would covering up the nakedness of this artwork accomplish? Look at all of this crazy shit. It's all of me, and my nakedness, on display.

Somewhere out there, some big trade literary agent and a big trade publisher is gonna get all this crazy nonsense, and me. My big trade literary agent and big trade publisher is gonna be excited the way I am about the way all of this nonsense was created. I just know they all will. And then when that happens...

The only other thing that needs to happen is lots and lots of people need to read all of my crazy nonsense. And then...

Everything is the way it is on purpose.

Everything in here and out there is intentionally done this and that way.

I reach all the way deep down into your unconscious mind and grabbed ahold of you by your spiritual soul.

Do you feel me? Can you see what I am saying?

The things we are uncomfortable talking about are the things that hold us back and keep us down. The skeletons in our personal closet hold us hostage. Our personal secrets keep us from forming deeper connections with all of the beautiful souls around us. And...

All that stops us from achieving our even more powerful greater stuff.

Woo-woo choo-choo.

Did you know that...

Peploe olny need to raed the fsirt ltteer and the lsat ltteer of ecah wrod to be albe to raed sutff and konw waht soembdoy wrtoe. Wrod up. As lnog as all the mddile letetrs are awlyas trehe swheomree, ppeloe's birans can slitl intsanlty raed wahteevr it is we witre. Deos tihs solw you dwon when you raed?

Woha. Tihs is a tirp.

I learned that from watching Brainiacs on the Channel G4, on my HDTV, one day long, long ago.

"See?"

There's more than the one and only way to become a nobody wannabe big trade authors' author and a completely huge success story.

It's 9:22 p.m. My Baby and I are currently home alone together, and she needs me. More to come... Later...

Now, it's 12:42 a.m. My Baby is fast asleep next to my naked body next to her naked body. And I am spending some more of my time, wasting my sleeping time, being here with you, writing more of my phony bologna nonsense, instead of just going to sleep tonight. And with all of the different shit I wrote about thus far, I can totally see and understand some of your personal/professional risk in believing what I have already said, but...

What do you have to lose, your dignity, the respect and admiration of your peers? It's as easy as this...

And...

Back in April, eight months ago, I had a literary agent who handwrote me a letter that went...

"If you think your attitude, your bad grammar, your foul language, and your surly photo make this project more appealing, you're greatly mistaken."

And to you, sir, I say...
"Hello." And...
"Surprise." And...
"Here I come to save the day!" And...
When I received that big trade literary agent rejection letter, I was spoiling for a heated war of words. I mean, I had no idea people actually lived their entire life protected away from anything beyond our picture movie industry's "G" rating. I booked our trip to New York City the day after his letter came in. And look at me now...

Right now, I can't sleep. I'm too charged up to sleep. So, here I go...

I'm proud to be a United of American States citizen, where I know I'm free to express my oppression, even if nobody cares. And if they started caring about things I care about, all the better. Speaking of...

I'd like to be a peace-loving third-party supporter. But...
Our Democratic Party needs me.
And I just now figured out that I need them too. In fact...
My Dear Fellow 2005 Progressive Democratic voters,
Recently, two of our states held elections, where tons of people voted to end our Marijuana Battle in the war on our drug users. Forty percent of the citizens (who came out to vote) said "yes" they want to make small quantities of marijuana completely legal in their state.

In the past two Presidential Elections, different groups of voters got together and influenced the elections in a way that has the Republicans currently ruling all three Branches of our American government today. Here in 2005, our Executive, Legislative, and Judicial Branches are currently all conservative. And I'm here to say…

All of these humans are getting everything way, way wrong. So…

Let's not try this political trifecta again for a while. Okay?

How are we Democrats gonna keep the Republicans from claiming any kind of a majority from now on? We need some more voters to show up on our side. And it just so happens…

2005 has 40% of America's marijuana voters consistently voting to legalize marijuana in all of our different local elections. And…

That's a boatload of people. And…

That boatload of people ain't being represented by any of our current 2005 government representatives. We got a boatload of people who ain't got no voice. We are a growing number of people. We are growing something good. Humans have cannabinoid receptors in our brains for a reason. Our Creator put them all in there. Then, our Creator sprinkled cannabinoid receptors throughout our entire human bodies. And a growing boatload of people ain't got no say so. So…

I'm gonna be the first to stand up and speak for all of them and loudly say…

"We are our pro-marijuana Americans. Today, we are only 40% of every election turnout. But our numbers are growing and getting boat-load-y-ier every day." And…

All of our citizenry of Democratic voters showing up to vote blue will easily counterbalance our 2005's conservative Republican voters. Take a stance. Vote. And tell our pro-American/pro-marijuana position people that you are standing-up with us.

Come one. Come all. Step right up. Don't be shy. Come out of the closet and vote your way into our way better way in our future America.

Last year, in our 2004, just under one million American marijuana users were handcuffed and hauled away in our American taxpayer-funded War on Drugs. That equals out to one marijuana possession arrest every 32 seconds, around the clock, in every minute, of every day, throughout the entire year, last year. We arrested a lot of people for marijuana in 2004. And the same thing happened the year before that. And the same thing happened the year before that. And the year before that, all the way back, for over three decades, and we are still counting. Pre-today's-2005, tens of millions of American marijuana-using peaceful people have already been arrested and processed into our American Judicial System. How much longer do we need to pour our valuable American resources into this? When will we stop torturing peace-loving people via our legal system? And...

Speaking of peace-loving people...

If we break our Laws, we can go to jail. And...

If we wind up in jail, we can wind up in prison. And...

We all can all lose our rights to be (and the privilege of being) a good solid voting American citizen.

So...

My Dear Fellow American Marijuana occasional Users and Healthy Alternative Substituting,

Why are some of our pharmaceutical products resulting in death? PTSD...

Anyone?

Let's change our Laws. We can do this. All we gotta do is get the Democratic Party on board with us and vote with them. Our 40% of America's voters can't be wrong. Did you know that 40% of our United States of Americans didn't want our America to preemptively strike Iraq in the first place? And...

Look at us now. The latest polls show us flip-flopping away from us starting this war in Iraq, especially after Katrina just came in and caught us with our britches down around our ankles and all of our dicks in our hands. And...

I can't stay awake anymore.

Oh, look at that. The Sun came back up again.

It's 8:30 a.m.

I gotta go to sleep.

Wednesday, December 28, 2005

It's 11:07 p.m. I pulled another all-nighter last night. I wrote and wrote and wrote. I stopped writing this morning at 8:30 a.m. That was when my Baby woke up. I had to ask her if it would be all right if I stayed in bed and took a little nap before we went to work. An hour and a half later, she got me up, and we went to work. It was a very rough morning for me today.

We made it out the door, and down the road, at 11:30 a.m. We pulled back into our garage at 2:30 p.m. It was a killer workday, not really. Most of our regular workdays recently, have been two or three hours longer than today's workday. Business is slow right now. We ain't making very much money right now. But then again, ask any cleaning person you know...

I bet they all will say, "I hope things change sometime soon." And I know because...

We always have to work way too hard to make a dime, and then to squeeze that dime. And I guess this is just a part of what being a tortured, starving artist is all about. And speaking of...

At my first house today, a lot of different shit popped into my head all at once, and it suddenly hit me, and I suddenly realized something. And I didn't even see it coming. Everything came at me from out of no place all at once. Just like that and then there it was. And right now...

I know exactly what I'm supposed to do. All right...

Here we go...

You might want to sit down for the rest of this book.

This is really big.

Is everybody sitting down? Okay...

Let's go...

In lots of our United various States across America, 40% of voters went to their polling places and politically voted, "Yes, I want to legalize and decriminalize small amounts of marijuana please."

Nationwide in 2005, 40% of our last presidential election is a shitload of votes. And that's a lot of voters, who currently ain't got no government representative representing them. And speaking of becoming a rock-solid Democrat...

If we Democrats get on board with the peace-loving peace pipe people, we'd have a hell of a lot more Democrats than we currently have today. And everything would probably work out great, if we Democrats weren't so utterly lost. But...

We Democrats are so utterly lost. We are completely scattering in all different directions in 2005. We are just a great big herd of cats. We ain't got no leader. We ain't got no Captain. The captain's office is currently empty. And...

It's been vacant for a long time. So...

Starting right now, from this day forward, until I decide to resign, I'm gonna become our unspoken spokesman of the unheard people. And...

I'm also gonna become our new Captain.

"I'll be your oober-liberal Captain Democrat."

I am whoever I want to be. And just like that...

I got 40% of America's voters in my front right pocket. And I got all of my fellow Democrats in my back left pocket. And in-between, I got a hairy set of giant balls.

And outside of whatever happens to be in here, back in our

scientific reality, I'm just a guy making tons and tons of money from writing this book, living in my Baby's palatial estate, being naked as often as I can, working on some other stuff, meeting Dave face to face, and living the Captain Democrat lifestyle. You know? It's just...

In here, I have the freedom to expose myself more freely, if you know what I mean. And speaking of...

We ain't got no time for no more goofing around. And...

Connecting the Web of Humanity:

Every time I get to this part, in my head, I always hear Stephanie Miller's shortened version of "The Girl From Ipanema".

I gotta get my political ass back to working my ass off right now. And our new vote blue political policies really can't wait any longer. So...

Here we go...

As your new Captain Democrat, and the voice of a special interest group that has 40% of our voter's votes in 2005, I want all of my people to meet, mingle, and merge. And someday, I hope to throw a big annual party at my palatial estate. And...

Since nobody voted for me, except me, nobody will be able to throw me out of the two offices I just moved all of my shit into, except me. I appointed myself. And I'll remove myself from my joint positions at the appropriate time.

I'll know when it's time for me to pass it on and step away.

It's 11:56 p.m.

"Who's your daddy?"

I've only had 90 minutes of sleep since yesterday morning. I'm worn out. I'm sleep-deprived. We'll talk more about all of this later.

My 2005's broke-ass has to go clean some more homes and houses in the morning. So...

Goodnight.

Thursday, December 29, 2005

It's 5:58 p.m. Today, we made it out the door and down the road at 11:30 a.m. After we cleaned our three houses, we had to go the bank, post office, and grocery store. We pulled back into our garage at 4:15 p.m. Now, it's 6:00 p.m.

Tomorrow and Monday, we don't have to go to work.

We get to have another four-day weekend.

Now, it's 6:46 p.m. Bill Nye, The Science Guy, is doing a thing on DHDTV. And...

Connecting the Web of Humanity:

One of the dudes Bill Nye was talking to just said, "Science is provisional."

I had to look it up. And according to my thirty-three-year-old big-bad-red dictionary, "provisional" science means science provides for the time being, pending permanent arrangements.

"See?"

It's like I was saying earlier. We discover something new, and then everything we know changes all at once, just like that. And we never know, until we know. You know? Take me...

Two days ago, I was going along, minding my own business, doing my own thing, and then all of a sudden, from out of nowhere, I appointed myself as our Captain Democrat, and became America's oppressed marijuana supporters' giant booming big-balled American voice. And...

I'm feeling like I'm way behind. I got tons and tons of brand-new shit to do. I have two brand-new paths to explore. It feels like I'm starting out all over again, like I can't write right now, I gotta go. So...

It's 11:56 p.m. "And I'm your daddy."

Why? Wherever I go, there I am, with you, the same as mine is with me.

We gotta find a way to mend a broken relationship. Do you even know each other anymore? Did you just stop talking to one another? We slowly evolve all the time. Sometimes, our souls just drift apart. And speaking of me...

I look at all of my precious time I've poured into this, losing out on spending our extremely valuable time connecting my soul with my soul's peeps, and them losing out on pouring their time into connecting their valuable spiritually with my soul, because I'm spending way too much of my quality time with you in here connecting my valuable spirituality with you in here, instead of out there with them. And...

267

My family is lost without me.

I am the King of my Castle.

It's late. I'm getting up early tomorrow. We have some chores to do. Plus, we're home alone all-day, all-night, and all-day again tomorrow, before our kids come back home. And...

Then, we are practicing for empty nesting again. I can't wait. And...

Right now, my Baby and me are all alone. And, instead of concentrating all of my everything on her, and just being all by ourselves, with just the two us completely alone, I'm working on more of my nonsense by writing all of this brand-new shit for you personally, and...

"I'm sacrificing what?" And...

I'm still killing myself in my seasonal Gilligan cleaning suit, that quite frankly, I ain't got no time for anymore...

Why? And speaking of a great big giant...

My Captain Democrat job comes with some heavy-duty obligations and responsibilities. Of which, some people in my position would normally take lightly. Let me go. Now you know. Rock and roll is here to stay. "Hey-hey."

My family's health insurance is going up again in March. It just keeps going up every year. Now, we're looking at $13,680.^{00} dollars a year just in health insurance premiums. And that's only if nobody gets sick. And in order for us to have such low monthly premiums, we now also have a brand-new higher deductible. And now, if my Baby (or me) ever has to see the doctor about something, our brand-new higher deductible will just about kill us. Somehow or another, we were able to re-obtain health insurance. But now...

I simply can't afford to go see any of my doctors, even if I wanted to. And...

If we don't pay our new monthly premiums on time, for whatever reason, they will cancel our health insurance. If we ever really needed to use our new health insurance for something big, we'd lose it before we ever knew what happened. If we lost our ability to make our income from week to week, we'd lose our ability to pay our bills. If we can't pay our bills, we lose everything we have.

A lot of people are skating on thin ice financially.

I know I am not alone. I live in the real world. And speaking of the real world...

I think we Americans need us Democrats to build our new national healthcare system that covers everyone, no matter what. And together, we can turn marijuana's red-ink governmental problem Battle of our War on Drugs into a national black-ink solution. And then, we can pour the extra of some black-ink solutions into the serious start of building an education system like no other. We also need to totally rebuild the crumbling infrastructure of our entirely outdated broken nation. And honestly...

When was the last time we Americans went dancing in our streets?

I'm going to try to put all this nonsense down for a little while. It's hard. I'm totally inspired to write right now. But we're home alone together and I'd like to use what's left of our precious time wisely. My Boss says I can type all of this in starting at 7:00 p.m., Saturday. If that holds true, all of this will be in the mail on Monday, January 02, 2006. Where is it going? I don't know. But...

I got a grass-roots national platform now. That means I'm as good as gold. I'm totally in on a sure bet.

Big trade is gonna make me super-rich. Things are gonna change, I can feel it. And it's all thanks to who?

You.

So...

Thank you. It's 1:32 a.m. Goodnight.

Growing means _____. And it's a, if you've read everything in here up to "this," you know what I'm talking about.

Every time we change, we grow. Every time we grow, we change into our new person.

Why do we change? How do we change? And why do we blame people for changing themselves into the new people they became? Since when is changing into a better someone doing someone else something wrong?

Like how are we supposed to stop ourselves from changing into a new person? We are all highly adaptive creatures, so why do some people criticize other people for being too damn adaptive? I don't get it.

Why must a fuck buddy and a fuck buddy, or a husband and a wife, or a partner and a partner, or a cozy little civil-unioned threesome, or the banker, the barber, the baker, and each of their orgasm makers, not want to get along, and go along. Speaking of…

It's 1:55 a.m. Fuck!

Time keeps on slipping into the future. And…

Come and listen to my story about a king in his bed. A poor housecleaner trying to keep his family fed. And then one day he was vacuuming up some food. And some crazy nonsensical shit went off in his head. Black ink, it was.

Black gold. Ink wars. And speaking of…

The night is just wasting away again. My fingers hurt from holding my Rolling Writer way too tight and writing way too hard and way too much all at one time. I need to get drunk. I need to get laid, again. You know? I've got way too much stuff that needs to be done. My Baby and me ain't got much of our alone time together. If you know, you know. You know?

It's 3:18 a.m. Good night for real this time.

It's 5:59 a.m. I can't sleep. I'm too charged. I'm too wired. I'm crazy, like a fox. Every ounce of my shit is a license to print money. Do you hear what I'm saying?

And they say shivery is dead. Ha! Mimicking is the sincerest form of flattery, the sincerest form.

Saturday, December 31, 2005

Happy Anniversary Baby!

Eight years ago, I married the girl of my dreams.

And this is it. I'm done. It's over. I'm gonna flush this whole entire gigantic pile of nonsense for good. I'm done. I'm gonna have to hang up my old clunkity Gateway computer, instead of my Panasonic vacuum. I might have to shoot this thing and finally put it out of its misery.

If this thing doesn't get off the ground here real soon then the world will never know about me and mine. And the world will never get to meet America's new millennium Captain Democrat and I won't get to be the loudest silent voice of 40% of America's voters. And nobody will have ever had the chance to know all of that other shit that you now know about us being human enough to see our own humanity because of human souls. And...

So anyways...

It's starting to look like I'm gonna have to quit this writing shit and do some kind of other shit altogether. I don't want to quit doing this writing my shit, but what more can I do?

I've been looking at warehouse jobs in my local newspaper and on the Interweb. Before we run out of our revenue options, before we run completely out of money and time, we still have a tiny bit longer. I don't know what I am gonna do yet. But no matter what, I have to start making money somewhere. I can't just keep writing shit that ain't ever gonna get to go nowhere.

I'm downright proud of this. I'm downright tickled about all I've already accomplished. Look at how far I've gotten. Look at what page number we are on. I'm downright proud of all the laborious work I had to put in this to get us here. I am carrying both of us all the way to here. This is the biggest project I have ever undertaken in my life, and the two of us are both right here together, and we are both reading all my nonsense together. And...

Now, we are all up inside each other's heads. And...

If my shit ain't worthy of big trade's giant stamp of approval, I just don't know what to say.

So...

XXXII: January 2006

Sunday, January 01, 2006

Happy New Year!

Since December 27, just five days ago, I generated a ton of new material. And the beat goes on. "This" was my 71,401st word. If I can't get it done in this many words, or less, I can't get it done. I've done my part. And that's that. I worked my ass off.

I paid my dues. I earned the right to write all of this nonsense.

I'm standing up in here with nothing but my naked truths. And I've been ejected, dejected, and rejected. In fact...

I've been turned down a hundred different times, a hundred different ways, by over a hundred different literary agents. But who's counting?

Right? And...

Honestly, at the end of a hard-ass long and heavy workday, who gives a shit about anything?

Right? And...

I've had it. This is the end of the line for me. This is as far as I'm willing to go. I'm gonna be done. And...

You're gonna have to be done too. That way...

We can both be done at the exact same time. It's been nothing but fun for me, and...

XXXIII: February 2006

Monday, February 06, 2006

Today, the Time Warner Book Group is our fourth largest big trade institutionally structured big trade business currently still in business in the United States of America. Our whole entire USA only has six big trade publishers to choose from in 2006. And our Time Warner Book Group is currently in fourth place. Not Gold, not Silver, not Bronze, but they still receive the purple big trade ribbon for participation. (Today, in 2023, we only five left.)

And in this today of 2006, Time Warner sold its Book Group to France's Lagardere for (five-hundred-thirty-seven-point-five-million dollars) $537,500,000. And...

That's exactly what I've been talking about all along. Everyone throughout our USA book industry just keeps making some more of their excuses, instead of making themselves some better-looking P&L Statements. And...

Six months ago, Red McCombs (Red) sold our Minnesota

John E Zett III

Vikings to Zigmunt Wilf (Zigi) for (six hundred million dollars) $600,000,000.

No other NFL teams were for sale in 2005.

If any other NFL team were for sale back then, they would have all been more expensive than the Vikings were valued in 2005. Yeah, we sucked so hard, we were the only team scraping the bottom of the anything back when, and our fans have never had a problem booing when our team sucks. And...

Six months ago, Red sold our NFL's suckiest 2005's least most expensive team in all of the 32 teams in 2005's NFL to Zigi for $62,500,000 (sixty-two-point-five-million dollars) more than the total net worth of our 2006's fourth largest big trade publishing company.

"See?"

Everybody in our book industry keeps telling me I'm wrong. And the rest of the world keeps screaming I'm totally right.

"SKOL!"

And...

XXXIV: July 2006

Tuesday, July 18, 2006

If you are paying attention to what is going on around in the world around you right now, you know we live in a scary time. And speaking of scary times...

It's 4:30 a.m. I gotta meet our new sub-contracting cleaning business's window washer in four hours and thirty minutes on a jobsite. Yikes. I need to get my ass some sleep. So, goodnight.

Thursday, July 20, 2006

We had big storms last night. We lost our electricity for seventeen hours. It's a normally hot summer. And all of our groceries thawed. Everything in our refrigerator and freezer had to be thrown out. We have to start all over again.

Our storms also took out my computer, a six-year-old Gateway. It's a good thing I start everything new with pen and paper. Thank goodness I can still "old school" write this. I'm glad we still have pen and paper. And tomorrow, I gotta go find something called a "Power Supply" and hope I can get her running again. What the fuck?

Before the storms came last night, I changed my manuscript's format for the first time. It may not sound like a big deal, but it was for me. I finally relented on my rebellious way of doing this my way.

I also changed my title back to what it was before. My manuscript looks weird to me now. But somehow or another, it was all reading much better than it did.

I guess big trade really does know what it is doing. Who knew? You know?

It's 2:15 a.m. We have an unusually long day of cleaning ahead of us tomorrow. And I got tons of yard work to do while my computer is down. We have lots of large trees. Our storms made a huge mess last night.

Friday, July 21, 2006

It's 1:50 a.m. Here's the thing...

My money is always way too tight. I can't afford to spend my money on a new power supply for my 6-year-old Gateway.

My kids have abandoned their 5-year-old Gateway. They got some big bad scary hand me down from their Aunt and Uncle. If you know, you know. You know? So, anyway...

Can I take the hard drive out of my 6-year-old and put it in my kid's abandoned 5-year-old? If I do, will I be able to access my files, or am I completely fucked? I just made tons of really good changes to this manuscript. And the only place I saved my new changes was on my hard drive. My last backup was too fucking long ago to have to try to reproduce all of this new growth ring shit again. Replicating some of our old shit? Are you crazy? What does that even mean? I was cranking on this as hard as I could until that storm killed my computer. If you know what I mean, you know what I mean. You know? So, anyway...

Can I Frankenstein my two Gateways into one computer? And, if I can...

Will it truly ever work? Or...

Do I have to start all over on where I was on my last saved copy of my re-writing this book? When was my last external save? And which pile is that one in? Where is it hiding around here all over the place up in here? And what if I don't want to start all over again on all of the recent salable changes, I just made to all of this? And...

Ain't no easy feats never. And speaking of ain't no easy feat...

I may or may not be able to rescue all the recent work that happened, and all I can do right now, right here, on this particular night tonight, is lay as still as I possibly can right here next to my Baby, naked skin next to naked skin, (yummy, yummy, yummy) with her sleeping, and me writing some more of new shit down with a pen and a writing pad in the middle of the night and...

Speaking of our ain't no easy feats and ain't no such thing...

Can I plug my 6-year-old hard drive in the Master position in my kid's abandoned 5-year-old Gateway? Is that even possible? If it is, can I plug my 6-year-old hard drive where my 5-year-old hard drive was plugged in and move my 5-year-old hard drive plug in to the Slave position? And then, will I be able to get back to the document I was working on before my 6-year-old Gateway kicked the bucket in the middle of the storm in the middle of some night? And how did some racists assholes get to name our computer components and main bedrooms? Yeah, that all happened, and...

Can all of my recent work be rescued or is it just gone? And if it is gone, what the fuck am I gonna do? I ain't got no clue. So...

Let's just do something and see what happens.

"FUCK ME." And...

Goodnight tonight.

I gotta get some sleep now.

Monday, July 24, 2006

Don't ask me what the fuck I did, because I ain't got no fucking clue. But somehow or another, I was able to hot-wire my two computers together. I didn't know what I was doing, and I don't really know what I did, and I still don't know if it was all even possible, but I was able to rescue all of this important shit. That nonsense worked. And now, I have this whole thing backed up on multiple floppies. Against all odds, I was able to save all of my most recent shit from being totally lost forever. And I did it all by myself. And...

I hope I never have to do that sort of nonsense again. I worked on it for $39^1/_2$ hours straight. I stayed up and worked straight through from early Saturday morning all the way to late night Sunday. Today, when I got home from work, I put everything back together, and cleaned up my mess on my floor. And I am just now writing this down.

So anyway, we're back on the road to getting published. Next stop, big trade.

But right now, I need to go to sleep. I'm sleepy.

I still want to become a big trade author.

I'm still interested in doing the job. Speaking of right now...

My computer is all brand new to me. And my rescued manuscript has a whole new look to it too.

I can't believe I didn't reformat my manuscript sooner. This totally changed the way my manuscript looks. Now I see why they want everybody's manuscripts to look like this. This makes total sense to me now.

Quid pro quo... (Something for something...)

It's 2:26 a.m. I can't sleep.

Here's what I learned about a PC. A PC has three basic parts, a power supply, a motherboard, and a hard drive. Everything else on a PC is either software, tools, or easy to play with toys.

The PC's hard drive stores everything and tells the motherboard how to do what. A motherboard is screwed into the inside wall of a PC. A motherboard is a big green thing with all the weird looking nonsense plugged into it. A motherboard is usually buried deep inside the box of a PC. And the big green thing doesn't like to be touched, except in certain spots.

Our souls are a lot like that, too. In fact...

We are like computers, in that, our conscious cognitive minds are our physical body's hard drives, our souls are our body's motherboards, and being alive supplies our body's human power. When we go to sleep, our brains work like computers and our consciousness can GoTo sleep. And speaking of...

Our souls freely fuck with us when we dream. And...

I gotta try to power-down my cognitive brain enough to get to sleep tonight. So, goodnight.

Thursday, July 27, 2006

It's 12:34 a.m.

My brand-spanking new to me 5-year-old Gateway Windows Frankenstein Millennium Edition is beginning to give me troubles. I think it needs more memory.

"FUCK!"

If it ain't one thing, it's always gonna be some another.

Life is always a fucking uphill battle, every fucking uphill fucking step of our every uphill way.

And...

I'm still peddling as fucking hard and fast as I fucking can.

XXXV: August 2006

Wednesday, August 02, 2006

I just picked up my pen Wednesday night to write this. And now I have to put my pen back down. It's way too early for me to pick up my pen and write on paper tonight.

Now it's 1:37 a.m. Technically, my current right now is Thursday morning. And I've spent the last four of my previous night's reworking all of this nonsense. I'll be glad when I'm done with this book. On second thought...

I need a vacation.

I need to step away from all of "this" for a little while.

XXXVI: December 2008

Saturday, December 20, 2008

Two years later…

My Baby and me are busy finishing up working the evening shift at a "Distribution Center" (warehouse) to help them get their "Products" (50/50 Made in USA/China) out to (you) "The Customer."

I wish I could go into more detail, but they made me sign something that said I couldn't say anything about what I did, or anything about what they do, or anything about how they do what they do, or anything more than what I've probably already said too much about already. But I can say that this year (as bad as our economy seems to be here in 2008) 400 people started working there in the first week of November 2008. And all of us worked straight through this past week. That's a lot of people. Everybody showed up every day and we all worked our 40-hour workweeks.

My Baby and I both went to work there. My Baby worked at one end of the warehouse and I worked on the opposite end. We were able to spend our breaks and lunchtimes together. And we were glad to have our second jobs. So, right in the middle of spending all of our days cleaning houses, and giving away all of our weekday evenings working in a warehouse during these past six weeks...

My Baby's mom passed away.

She was a great lady to get to know and to have known. She will be greatly missed. If you know, you know. You know? If not, all I can say is...

You really missed out on knowing someone great.

XXXVII: February 2009

Saturday, February 21, 2009

Dear Mr. Law Professor,

    I just listened to the entire speech you gave via a free podcast on my Apple App. I'm writing this down because you said our neuroscientists are using neuroscience to discover that the Amygdala (the region of the brain responsible for human emotion) can overpower our Dorsal Lateral Prefrontal Cortex (the region of the brain responsible for our humanistic, rational deliberation.) You also said something like, every attorney who's ever tried to use this neuroscience discovery, as a defense strategy in their courtrooms, have never been successful, and you hoped it always stays this way. That makes me gotta say, I totally 100% agree with you. And...

    I graduated from Itasca High School in 1984. And I worked at my local steel mill for 10+ years. Lived there, worked there, went in a totally different direction, and I've been a self-employed-professional cleaning tortured-starving-artist ever since. I'm a 42-

year-old layman. My motto: I don't get paid to think about anything other than what I'm doing. And "Safety First…"

And I don't mind tooting my own horn about this, but my Dorsal Lateral Prefrontal Cortex is almost as wide as my Amygdala gets deep. And speaking of stepping off into all of this as deep as deep can possibly get us…

Looking at the big picture, we will be a lot farther down the road to a better understanding of our humanity when Science and Religion stops bumping uglies in the middle of humanity's bed and finally gets married.

And that's where I'm trying to step in. And…

I'm writing some stuff about something that no respectable person in any noble profession has come close to dreaming up. And you said that you were always on the lookout for the next big thing. Well…

The next big thing is gonna be, yes…

"We all have our own individual spiritual soul."

Spiritually? Yes, please…

And if you want some big solid answers to the personal questions your Professors/Colleagues cannot answer, I hope for your sake, you are reading this. And for all of their sakes, I hope they are too.

Sincerely,

John E Zett III

PS. Yes, we have no cognitive control over Freud's unconscious/subconscious mind. We are all unable to cognitively control an emotional spiritual/soul. But no matter what, and at all times, we are expected to be able to control ourselves by the way of the cognitive part of our brain.

And honestly, until I first heard it from you yesterday, I didn't even know that our brain had such a thing as an Amygdala. Then, I had to go look that shit up. And my thirty-seven-year-old-big-bad-red dictionary never heard of it. So, I went on-line to look it up, and they told me what it was. But I did already know our brain has an unconscious mind, our spiritual soul, and everyone's emotional side, and that's the thing giving us our imagination. And our modern brain clearly has two elegant sources of intelligence. One part of our intelligence is everything that comes from our thinking brain's cognition. And the better half of our personal intelligence comes from our imaginative subconscious/unconscious minds. And...

My book is our first-ever delicate surgery of re-attaching everything I said up in here to our brain's more important Amygdala and each individual Dorsal Lateral Prefrontal Cortex...

- Our Amygdala (and whatever other imaginative unconscious brain activity we have) gets all of its intelligence from our spiritual soul. Our spirituality is built in.
- Other parts of our brain are handling our five senses and our other mobile physical stuff. And...
- Our Dorsal Lateral Prefrontal Cortex (and whatever other conscious brain activity we have accumulated along the way) gets its intelligence from our scholarly cognitive intellect.

See? It's really simple. And, no muss, no fuss...

I am totally using our human Amygdala and our brain's Dorsal Lateral Prefrontal Cortex to scientifically present my brand-new hypothetical soul theory to you and anyone else aspiring to have a distinguished career in all of my nonsense, by saying...

Our amygdala gives us our religious/spiritual human soul. And all of this spiritual awakening automatically turns all of our different religions, based on our best neuroscience and scientific reasoning, into scientific reality. Go ahead, test me. And...

I know I'm right. Gosh, I hope you read this.

I mean...

Do you ever get any free time or down-time? Jeepers...

You're awfully busy.

XXXVIII: February 2010

Friday, February 05, 2010

I'm back. Did you miss me? It's been another whole year since I have seen any of this nonsense. I saved it, backed it up, and put it away, up on my upper shelf, in the back of my closet. And now...

I'm back. Dusting, and dusting, and dusting, and...

Here I go, starting all of my todays on pen and paper all over again. More ink on another brand-new legal pad says "What?" And...

Yes...

We're still living check to check, week-to-week, and cleaning homes and houses day-after-day. I say we...

I mean, my Baby and me are still together 24/7. And we are still madly in-love with each other every minute of every day. And finally, and more importantly...

We're empty-nesters. And...

We are five-for-five on consecutive high school graduates and in cranking out five splendid, thriving young adults. And speaking of our five...

Here is your little snip-it on how we did...

We have all been very busy. And...

All five of ours have tried to further their high school educations more than I have mine. Three are still in college. One has finally started talking about going back. One of them does not own a car. Three of them have pets. Three of them go to work for a living. And three of them still live in my state. But one more of them is moving out of my state next month. And all of them came home for Christmas. And then...

One of them called me four days ago and told me I am going to become a grandpa.

Can you imagine? Me, a grandpa, at 44-years-old...

I'm so excited...

I can't hardly stand it.

I think I'll make a pretty good grandpa. I think our grandkids are gonna really like us. And I can already tell you how we already feel about all of them yet to follow. And if you know, you know. You know?

Sunday, February 21, 2010

My Baby and I can no longer afford to have health insurance for ourselves. The costs have climbed to a point that makes our personal health insurance policy way too expensive to maintain. But, each and every day, these days - today, tons and tons of people (literally) are losing their healthcare coverage. So yet again, I know that we are not alone.

America desperately needs the Democratic Party to build a medical safety net that catches more of its citizens. It's the only right thing to do. We have a moral obligation to look out for our fellow citizens. It's all about the humanity of America and our own individual compassion toward our citizenry. And right now, there is none.

We are the only industrialized nation in the world without our own nationalized healthcare system. But...

Not just nationalized, our national healthcare system has to be nationalized better than any other country out there has ever fucking done it before. Why???

Because...

This is the United States of America!!! And...

We have the right amount of diversity (from what our forefathers envisioned) to strive for and achieve our currently maintained worldly status. We need to turn Medicare into our new Single Payer healthcare system and call it "AmeriCare."

Fourteen years ago, I set out to write a book about how we all have a human soul secretly hiding deep within our human being and how all of that connects everything to anyone's individual ever after. But instead, I decided to focus my attention on writing about how we are able to use the way sex changes us into helping us find our human souls and our missing spirituality. And after we are able to seek out and find our hidden spiritual souls, then maybe we can start connecting the web from this cold cruel world to our individual personal ever after afterworlds. But...

After only finding failure and rejection, I totally changed my mind about making all this become about any of that. So much so...

Now...

I am writing whatever I want to write. I showed up as just another human having a spiritual soul. I explained how the participation of our soul automatically makes us have better sex. And then...

Connecting the Web of Humanity:

We got lots of stuff going on today. And it's only Sunday, February 21, 2010.

I gotta Carpe Momento. (Seize the moment.)

I took Latin and Spanish in the 8th grade. And I did better in Latin and Spanish than I did in English.

Wanna see?

XLIII: October 2002

Tuesday, October 01, 2002

It's day one. And I am starting all over again. ;)

Okay, I said that. And...

There is no need for any of this to become awkward for either of us, so...

Here I go...

The more humans read, the more humans know. The more we know, the more we humans understand. The more we humans understand, the better our humans become.

Does the majority of our population deserve to be excluded from the betterment of ourselves simply because we don't easily understand all the incomprehensible words every word authors commonly use in books today?

I read today's 2002 newspapers. Newspapers are supposedly written on a low-vocabulary reading-level. And I'll nervously admit, I have a hard time reading the newspaper sometimes. Newspaper journalists have huge vocabularies.

To me, an author's vocabulary should match the vocabulary of our intended audience. Today, more and more of us have a vocabulary that is smaller than the book industry's discount-card-carrying-preferred-club member.

Here in 2002, we have over one-hundred-million households nationwide. And the vast majority of award-winning books, currently sitting at the top of the book industry with just a few million sales, are way too overwritten for the solid-average-American-consumer. The current and past state of our public education system explains why things ain't better than they is. And it also explains why everything ain't going so good for our book industry. The United States of America's education system failed to work for a whole lot of us.

And all of the people working their asses off in our book industry, by doing what they've done before, end up shutting out more people than they let in. But in their defense, when our total existence is all wrapped-up into a tightly controlled environment, we don't really know what it's like on the outside.

I know what it's like. I understand.

The steel mill's office people never heard about all the shit that happened on our floor. They never saw all of the shit we pulled. And all of those shiny-shoed people didn't have our linguistics coach either. They didn't understand what it was like to be us, and we didn't understand what it was like to be them, much like how today's book industry people and average Joe America don't get each other.

Tuesday, October 08, 2002

Desperation breeds inspiration. Big names are big money.

I'm a nobody with no money. In fact, I'm flat-ass broke. I have been riding on the edge of a financial cliff my whole life, just living check to check. And throughout my whole entire life, I always worked my ass off.

I started out writing this badass manuscript. But nobody wanted it. So, I'm slowly spending all of my time reworking that into this. That being said, ready or not...

Here we go...

This shines a big-old spotlight all over our souls. This points to wherever your soul is aiming to go. This educates people about sex, so much so, we will all become better lovers, one by one.

Six years ago, I set out to write about how we are able to use the way sex changes to help us find our soul. And once everybody finds their individual souls, we will connect humanity's web from this cold cruel world to our individual personal ever after afterworlds.

But after only finding failure and rejection, I have totally changed my mind about making this be about me and all that. So much so, that right now,,,

I am writing whatever I want to write about. This book shows you my soul. It also makes science and religion get married. It will explain how the participation of our human soul automatically makes us have better sex with our lovers and quality time with those around us. And then with lots of quality time...

Who knows? You know? We got lots of stuff going on today. And it's only Tuesday, October 08, 2002.

I gotta Carpe Momento. (Seize the moment.)

Saturday, October 12, 2002

Six years ago, I saw a psychic. She was the one who planted the seed for this whole writing gig of mine. Had we never met; I would have never in a million years grown to learn I could earn a few bucks per book by pouring my soul out into our world. Writing all of this shit never entered my mind until then.

Since then, I've been to a million websites, and read tons of contradictory crap about all the different rules a writer has to know, knew, done, did, and do. Today's book industry has lots and lots of rules for every author to follow.

Everybody has to do whatever the book industry says to do and be original at the exact same time.

How does that work? How do we do that? And how is that working out for them, here in 2002? And...

I spent over ten years working in a steel mill. And, like an uninjured soldier being teleported out of a battlefield, and materializing back inside our Pentagon, I had to walk out of the bowels of my Melt Shop, filthy, dirty, stinky, extremely sweaty, and wearing my old steel-toe work-boots, to enter a world of beautiful people, nice carpet, and really clean offices every now and again. And being as honest as I can...

That's the only thing I'm doing with all of this delicate nonsense.

I'm filthy, dirty, stinky, and stepping out wearing my old comfy "Made in America" steel-toe work-boots, and I'm marching deep into the American book industry's nice clean carpeted offices to announce, "When it comes down to enriching and improving more lives, for the love of our fellow humans, and fellow human beings, who doesn't deserve an equal opportunity?"

Everyone should be reading books all the time, in fact...

Book reading should be kicking ass and taking names. It should be America's number one pastime. But, it's not. And...

Down in the bowels of my steel mill's Melt Shop, our fix-it guys used to say, "If it ain't broke, we ain't fixin' it." When things were working, even if things weren't working to their fullest ability, they'd always leave whatever was really broken alone, until everything stopped working. And...

The book industry derailed itself somewhere back along the line when it failed to stop and pick us up from wherever our American school system dropped us off. And it looks to me like the book industry's people are scrambling around in their individual chaotic boxcar offices, doing the same scholarly written highly polished work they did yesterday, last week, last month, and last year.

Clickity-clack.
Clickity-clack.
Clickity-clack.

Monday, October 14, 2002

I'm a high school graduate. I crawled out from under a little Texas schoolhouse and graduated way back in the day, way back in '84. I had my last English class even further back in '83. And I ended my personal English classes lessons in my junior year of high school with an average of 70%. Then...

I did what a lot of us did in 1984, I graduated from high school, and found myself a grown-up job.

And today, I'm here to say, when it comes down to all of today's current bookworms verses me in a caged match...

I can't read for shit. But I'm pretty good at math. So much so...

"I can make timely change."

Let's say we have a Benjamin, and after we roll up all of the federal, state, and local taxes, a half of a decent dime bag cost us ninety-five dollars and eighty cents.

"See?" Just like that, I already know what the change is. Do you? How much change that it? Change is good.

Change is a way for us to keep up with the times.

"Ways to Increase Government Revenue – 101."

Connecting the Web of Humanity:

For our better tomorrows, Nevada recently put the marijuana 2002 legalization out there. And...

The local non-voters let us down again. In all that is peaceful, decent, and civil; Nevada could have been the start of something long overdue. We are the people. We have a say in what's what, but at the end of the day, the ones who count the most on certain issues don't give a damn enough to do their civic duty and show up to vote.

Writing grabbed me by my big hairy balls. And now, it won't let go. All of our nonfiction books are vehicles for information. Hop on. Let's go for a ride. No don't...

I got a problem. My big hairy balls are in this ever-tightening noose. And then, I keep getting slammed into brick wall after brick wall, dead-end after dead-end. It's been one fucking failure after another, every step of the way, for me. But...

I ain't trying to fool nobody.

I ain't no writing expert. I ain't never been no. "And you can quote me on that."

If I was a writing expert, I sure as hell would not keep telling myself that I ain't none. I just keep hoping that someday, somebody will see the method in all of my madness.

The best of the best of our teachers are the ones who connected, challenged, or entertained us, when they were teaching the lessons of our yesterdays. The best of the best teachers engage their student's souls. And some teachers are dry people. Dry people bore us unless we're dry too. If we're dry, we can identify with other dry people, and our human souls connect. And speaking of not connecting to our growing disconnect and entirely missing the boat...

I ain't never been much of a book reader. I keep finding nonfiction books to be as dry and boring as my school's textbooks were. Then again, maybe I have unresolved issues with an English teacher, and I'm just projecting. Maybe I can't diagram my paragraphs or any of these sentences. And what the fuck does any of that shit matter anyway? I've got some totally brand-new shit to write about. And...

All I know is...

Learning some of humanity's new shit should be fun and super easy. People go to nonfiction books for information. When we can't stay awake long enough to turn the page, or we have to constantly stop to look up every other fucking word in our brand-new each year's little pocket dictionary, learning some of our new shit becomes difficult as hell.

And that kind of nonsense makes me feel stupid. But I'm not stupid. In fact, I'm a pretty smart dude. I went to school. I earned my high school degree. My American public education hasn't been worth jack-shit out in the real world yet, but I did the whole cap and gown thing. And I know others who went to my little Texas schoolhouses, and I watched them learn a lot more out of it than me, but in my defense...

I had a plan.

I planned on getting "the fuck" out of high school with a diploma and going to work on rotating shifts at our local steel mill. Back then, our mill had time-and-a-half overtime, all kinds of benefits coming-out-the-ass, and an-extra-four-bucks-an-hour-all-day on Sundays. And my dad worked there. And all I'm saying is, "I know I'm not alone in my insignificant reading ability, or my barely skating by in my English class, and doing whatever else I needed to do."

And then...

The CBS News tells me, "Eighty percent of our human baby's car seats are improperly installed in our motor vehicles." And then they went on, and on, and ended it with, "The installation manuals were written too far above the average American reading level."

Google: 'car seat instructions hard to read'...

"See?" That's what's wrong with our book industry.

Our car seat industry's authors overwrote our installation manuals just like the book industry is only interested in publishing overwritten books. Our under educated is killing us, and,,,

Eighty percent of the American do-it-yourself child safety seat installation technicians can't read well enough to properly install their children's legally required automobile accessory.

"Hey, honey.

Look.

They made us a picture book.

Well, it's about time.

Thank God.

Oh, I can do that."

How easy do we need to make things? How easy can I make things? My-Alluring-Brand-Of-A-Brand-New-Way vs. The-Book-Industry's-Never-Do-Nothing-New-Going-Nowhere-Way...

Live. Be there, by being here. And for being here...

From the bottom of my heart, I thank you.

Just recently, the book industry had enough foresight to put out a whole complete line of "dummy" and "idiot" books. You know? Looking at their current huge success, everyone has to know we're here, and we have a whole lot of us. You know?

Dummy/Idiot books are marketed to people like me and people like a lot of us. And...

They all have cute titles. But honestly, at the end of our endless backbreaking days...

We ain't no dummies or idiots. We are all lots of super-geniuses in our own special ways. We are all Super-Good at doing all kinds of things. We spend our entire lives living the lives we live. We might not be super-geniuses at being able to read award-winning scholarly written literature or make our writing look more bookish than it already does, or properly install our kid's car seat without needing a ding-dang picture book, or make our grammar look like we have more book smarts than we got, but on the whole and for the most part, we seem to be doing an okay job of doing our jobs, living our lives, and holding down our millions and millions of our individual households, without needing to buy a bunch of our book industry's 2002 selection of books.

And...

Keep doing what you are doing, and you'll keep getting what you are getting. Doing the same thing over, and over, and expecting different results is crazy. Ask Einstein. The book industry is ignoring a ton of regular hard-working cash-heavy American consumers just sitting around waiting for something better to throw their disposable income at. And I'm saying...

"Regular hard-working easy reader people can be easily turned into discount card-carrying preferred club member full-fledged bookworm customers too." It's easy. And...

Adding more customers to our big trade reading database is what it's all about. Isn't it? Well then...

Knock, knock big trade...

Regular easy reading people need books that just flow along. Regular easy reader people like a little bit of some of the goofy shit mixed in with their straight-up truth. And speaking of being as truthful as I can be...

I want to show up in the literary world as naked as I was born into our physical world. And,,,

I don't want anybody to try to do their best to try to dress my shit up. What do I need to hide? ...The fact that my academic education sucked more than your ginormous academic education? ...The fact that I can't write worth a shit? ...The fact that I've been secretly disguised as a mild-mannered cleaning professional for the past six years? And, I'm just saying...

Connecting the Web of Humanity:

"Hello?"

Writing ain't brain surgery. And if it were, we would all have to get completely naked for some of all that nonsense too. Before this...

I never wrote anything that got anyone famous, nor have I won any writing awards, and I ain't never wrote anything for the general public, before any of this neither. And yet, with all of that, working as hard as it possibly can against me, here I am.

"Surprise." And...

I want the world to see me for all I got and all I can bring. And I'm not interested in anyone fixing the fucked-up way I write, or trying to change any of this nasty horrible shit I can't help myself to say. I just, have to, say my peace. I got some "serious" shit that needs to be said. And...

"I got some big hairy balls. Don't I?"

Why can't brand-new nobody wannabe big trade authors step out into the whole wide world and write some fucked-up naked shit like this? How can someone get away with all of this complete and total nonsense?

I ain't no author's author. I am a new millennium word artist. And that's what makes this shit pop. Today is a new day. Are we all in for a new way?

"Hey. Hey." Me, too.

The stink on my artistic expression is strong enough to stand up for itself. My filthy dirty nasty Made-in-America steel-toe workboot words are rising-up off your screen.

This shit is like reading a pop-up book. Can you see what I'm saying? My words literally jump off my paper pages, and out of your digital screen, depending on your version. And...

But let's stop there and get very serious for a minute, I'll do anything I have to do to get my big trade book deal, and make this "book big book thing" happen. But...

And then again, and on the other hand, the only thing I want to do is appear on Dave's Late Show.

I love Dave. He started when I was in high school. I had a paper route. I bagged some groceries. I've been a regular viewer for a long time already. I'm a huge fan. Dave is my hero. As people go, Dave has gobs of serious human integrity. I've been a member of the home audience for long enough to know a lot about Dave. And speaking of just knowing about some human things…

I'll do my best to write everything I write nice & easy, good & sweet. How is it going so far? And speaking of how people tend to go…

Any person who had enough foresight to obtain their higher education should not be cock-blocking our better humanity. People with academically degreed educations can't teach the things I've already thrown down.

Scientifically, my brand-new hypothetical soul theory is just another shot in the dark immeasurable void that surrounds "the everything" we physically know. But…

Before we light-up that part of our knowledge's dark void, let me start by saying…

Please do not be a parrot. Do not repeat anything you read in here unless you just can't help yourself. And if you can't help yourself, go "nuts up" crazy. And…

Always question whatever doesn't seem right to you.

We gotta do your own soul-searching in order to seek out and eventually find our personal deep-down answers to our soul-searching DEEP-down personal questions. And then again…

Sometimes, it's really hard to entirely embrace something or someone who won't entirely embrace you. And speaking of…

I am entirely embracing all of Science and each and every different Religion. But…

Nobody driving around in either one of our two dominating

worldviews will be able to give an inch enough to absorb the other side enough to step out enough to endorse whatever chunky little pieces of shit of whatever happens to fall out of my goofy little book.

And I'm right. And I know I'm right because I know I'm right. You know? And speaking of knowing right from wrong, how do you know when you are right about whatever it is you know something about? It's because you're right. Right? When you know you're right, you're right, and you know. You know? And...

Getting back to what is the everything that we don't know, what do we know?

Monday, October 28, 2002

This is my first of many brand-new days and...I'm dating my writing.

I think my wife is jealous of us.

OMG...

AND...

WE might ALL be having some serious PERSONAL trouble.

When I have the need, and the time, I write. I write whatever is coming to my mind in the moment. I'm writing whatever the fuck I want to write about. When I run out of fresh material, I'll quit writing this nonsense. Everything has a way of happening the way it has to happen. And on another note...

I might have ADD or maybe it's ADDHDTV Either way, I ain't gonna go get it tested.

And then again, and beginning everything new, I might end up just being Dyslexic. And...

Either whichever way...

I ain't ever gonna go get that shit tested. And...

Thursday, October 31, 2002

Happy birthday, to my dad! Hang in there. I'm peddling as fast as I can.

I'm a serious night owl. Late any other night before tonight, I caught a television show about Galileo, who lived from 1564 to 1642. He was an inventor, a philosopher, a mathematician, and a famous all-round big thinker. Galileo invented the telescope. He marketed his new invention as a valuable war toy and sold it to his Navy. Then, he went back to work. He worked a ton of nightshifts to use his invention to study our Heavens.

Man, were our ancestors naïve about the world around them or what? Will we ever be perceived as naïve people?

"They say that history always repeats itself."

Way back when, the only acceptable belief was that everything orbited around Earth. Nobody, back in our day, knew what we all now know today. Today, scientific researchers discover something new, and our whole scientific view changes rather suddenly. Then afterward, we start to see everything with fresh eyes. And...

Galileo did lots of good things to advance the realm of science. But 400 years ago, nobody believed him.

For all of the good hard work Galileo did for humanity, none of his hard work did anything good for him. 400 years ago, people thought Galileo was just another idiot living an undeserved decent life off the stupid war toy he invented.

From his 1600s, until our 1800s, our world didn't acknowledge Galileo's contributions. Our current scientific worldview didn't become popular until about 200 years ago. And actually...

Sometime around 100 years before Galileo, sometime in the 1500s, a guy named Copernicus was the one who really started to think the map of our Universe was totally screwed-up.

The thing that didn't make sense to Copernicus was why we

Connecting the Web of Humanity:

would put our personal world all over our center of everything. So...

Copernicus was the first to remix our Solar System. He was the first person to physically shifted our Sun out into the middle of our everything. Copernicus physically inverted our Earth's position and our Sun's position. Then, he physically made our Sun stop circling around our Earth. And he physically made our Earth start circling around our Sun.

The radical idea of our Earth actually moving around its Sun was completely opposite of what everybody believed at that time. The Copernican Theory went against everything that was thought to be right and true. Copernicus, going way out on all of our limbs, did a very radical thing, and opened a door, becoming the start of something new, for the rest of us being/becoming human.

Thinking things should be whichever whatever way we want...

Don't make anyone right about nothing and dazzle them with brilliance or baffle them with giant loads of nonsense. And...

Some things are the way they are with or without any scientific proof of them being any other way than the way they are. Copernicus didn't provide any of his day of his scientific evidence for his new evidence of his brand-new map of our universe. He couldn't. All Copernicus could do was think about all of his shit and try to write some of his shit down. He wasn't able to dream up anything more than whatever he was able to think about. He lived and died, and all of his shit was way too hot for his time.

It all went down like this...

One hundred years after Copernicus physically rearranged our Universe, when Galileo (created) invented the telescope, he used our first telescope to single-handedly bring Copernican's Theory into our scientific physical reality. Galileo proved that Copernicus was one hundred years ahead of his time. Galileo also proved that both he and Copernicus were a couple of big badasses. And after all of that...

It still took 200 years for the world to accept whatever Galileo said about whatever it was he said he saw in his telescope.

Copernicus was a total and complete visionary, who really ended up being 300 years ahead of our time.

I'm glad I'm not that far out on my radical beliefs. And I believe I'm right because I believe in what I know. If you believe in your beliefs, you know. You know? And...

Galileo spent the rest of his life trying to convince people to see his logical truth. And he failed miserably.

It's super-hard for some people to change their ways.

Sometimes, we just want everything to stay as it is. And...

Everybody loves our human predictability. And we'll always do all we can to avoid our uncertainties. We like to be doing today just like we did yesterday—unless yesterday sucked. And...

The leading edge of discovery will always run into huge human opposition. And speaking of discovering new human shit...

I thought we'd never get to this part. Are you ready?

"You can't handle the big bad scary truth."

Today, some of us live with a well thought out scientific view of our physical world, and some of us live with a well thought out spiritual view of our physical world, and somehow or another, some of us live with a view of both existing in harmony.

Today, scientific fact dominates our world's collective mind with its hardcore scientific way. And today...

Some of us are scared shitless (or pissed off) about today's scientific ways. So, our scientific community disregards us. And...

Way back when, way back in the day, our spiritual beliefs and religious ways totally dominated the collective mind of our ancestor's entire world. Back then, I'm sure some of the people were scared shitless (or pissed off) about the way things were. But...

There just wasn't a whole lot that could be done about the way things were back then. Things just were the way they were for them, much like things are the way they are for all of us human beings, being/acting human today. Speaking of today...

Today, if you don't carefully fit yourself into our scientific community, you're either ridiculed for what you don't know, or you are completely ignored by our scientific community. And if you didn't properly believe in the religious calling of way back when, you were either ridiculed for what you think you knew, or you were wholeheartedly "taken out" by the religious community.

Back then, the religious leaders had unlimited power. People weren't allowed to go out and do the things their people weren't supposed to be going out and doing. Their people weren't allowed to go around believing anything they dared to believe. And those people damn sure weren't allowed to disagree or express any alternative thoughts to the people in charge of the way things were back then.

The religious leaders of way back when had a strictly enforced "don't ask, don't tell" policy in place. And it doesn't seem to matter if it's way back then, or if that policy is still in place today...

The people in charge of us have zero tolerance for the nonconformists amongst us. But...

We're all adults here.

And every adult should already know that change happens instantly, rapidly, gradually, slowly, eventually, and sometimes never at all.

Some things change and some things don't. You know?

Way back when, the Inquisition was all about religious people killing tons of people for not having everybody's same shared religious worldview, for being independent thinkers, and for thinking things ain't the way everybody says it is. And...

Do you want to know something else? Well...

One of Galileo's book-smart colleagues, Bruno, had to face his Inquisition. It had something to do with him saying some stuff that went against the Inquisition's religion. Bruno was found guilty of hearsay. So, they tied his ass to a pole and burned him alive. And man, that's some tough shit to have to think about.

As it turns out in the history books, Galileo was hauled in to face his own Inquisition trial. Knowing what they did to Bruno must have scared every ounce of all the living shit out of Galileo. When Galileo got there, and took the stand for himself, he sold himself out to stay alive. He took back everything he ever said about what he said he saw. He disowned everything he ever wrote to us. He told everybody there that he was totally crazy, and that he made all of his nonsensical shit up. In the end, he just wanted to live his life. So...

They didn't kill him. But long before Galileo sold himself out, and backed away from what he believed in, somebody kind of high up in the chain of command kind of liked Galileo from the get-go. And because of that, Galileo was sentenced to spend the rest of his life under house arrest. And...

For 200 years, after Galileo got arrested, all of his personal hard work was either laughed at, or totally ignored, and our Sun kept happily circling around our Earth.

Then sometime around 200 years ago, they said Galileo was right after all, and then all the scientists got together and flip-flopped our entire Solar System over to the way it is now.

When Galileo left the Inquisition, he was a social outcast all the way up to after the day he died. Galileo spent the rest of his live-long days locked away inside his personal crib. And...

I wouldn't mind spending the rest of my days at home. I'd rather just be home anyway. I'm what most of us would call a recluse, a hermit. It would be really easy to keep me under crib arrest. All I need is a big-time hard-to-get literary agent, a big-time hard-to-get publishing house, and a really big hard-to-get audience. And here's the part where you come in. And...

I promise I'll keep writing. But not tonight, it's late. I gotta go to work in the morning. We have three great big giant homes to clean tomorrow. Then, we have to hurry back, pay some bills, and clean our house, quick like bunnies. And then...

Just like that...

It's time to blow my writing candle out.

www.ingramcontent.com/pod-product-compliance
Lightning Source LLC
Chambersburg PA
CBHW052307300426
44110CB00035B/1990